PATTI M ... memoirist and nonfiction writer, whose 2012 book, *The Mind of a Thief*, was longlisted for the Stella Prize and the Nita Kibble Prize, shortlisted for the WA Premier's Prize for Non-Fiction, winner of the NSW Premier's Prize for History and on the syllabus for English for the VCE in Victoria. Her most recent memoir, *Ransacking Paris*, was released in April 2015 to critical acclaim. Her two previous writing books, *Writing Your Life* and *The Memoir Book*, have been continually in print since publication. Patti is a highly successful life-writing teacher and mentor who offers courses at the Faber Academy, as well as many other writing centres around Australia and in Paris.

Praise for Writing True Stories

'An essential companion for anyone considering embarking on a memoir or other form of creative nonfiction, packed with practical advice on ways to set the mind's juices flowing. Miller is an experienced guide who can help navigate all the dangers, mistakes, excuses and forms of self-sabotage that plague both the novice and the seasoned practitioner. She writes with calm clarity, breaking down the daunting task of a book into manageable segments, providing a voice of steady encouragement and purpose. A rich, practical and accessible source of wisdom that celebrates and forensically analyses every aspect of the writer's craft. This is the complete tool kit.' — CAROLINE BAUM

'Patti Miller believes we all have a story to tell and she has a unique ability to coax it out of us. Whether writing for others or for personal record, Patti helps us to ask the right questions, to jog our memories, and to write stories from our lives. The life-writing process, with Patti as gentle guide, is as much about our own self-discovery as sharing our story. Without Patti, I would never have discovered my creative voice beyond writing the news.' — JACINTA TYNAN

Patti Miller

Writing True Stories

The complete guide to writing
autobiography, memoir, personal essay,
biography, travel and creative nonfiction

Routledge
Taylor & Francis Group

LONDON AND NEW YORK

First published 2017 by Allen & Unwin

Published 2020 by Routledge
2 Park Square, Milton Park, Abingdon, Oxon OX14 4RN
605 Third Avenue, New York, NY 10017

Routledge is an imprint of the Taylor & Francis Group, an informa business

Every effort has been made to trace the holders of copyright material. If you have
any information concerning copyright material in this book please contact the
publishers at the address below.

Cataloguing-in-Publication details are available
from the National Library of Australia
www.trove.nla.gov.au

Internal design by Romina Panetta
Index by Garry Cousins
Set in 12.5/16.5 pt Bembo by Post Pre-press Group, Australia

ISBN-13: 9781760293086 (pbk)

Contents

Prologue ix

Part Two: Masterclasses

Write what should not be forgotten.

ISABEL ALLENDE

Prologue

Writing True Stories has grown out of two earlier books, *Writing Your Life* and *The Memoir Book*, both of which were based on writing workshops I first conducted at Varuna, the Writers' House in the Blue Mountains near Sydney, and have since given all over Australia and in Bali, Fiji, Paris and London. The workshops were designed for those who wanted to write the story of their own or a family member's life.

Since then I have found that many people want to explore a wider area of nonfiction based on their own life experience: travel and sojourn writing, memoir and biography, personal essays, true crime, nature writing and the whole vast territory of creative nonfiction. *Writing True Stories* explores all these areas and offers practical advice for anyone wanting to try these genres.

Expressing the nature of being is an ancient impulse. A few years ago, I saw cave paintings in Les Eyzies in France where Cro-Magnon tribesmen had painted images of bison, horses and ibex on the dark walls of their subterranean gallery. They had taken red iron and black magnesium oxides, mixed them with water and blown the mixture through bone pipes to create the drawings. As I gazed at one magnificent bison painted 14,000 years ago, it struck me that the tribesman had, in a way, left a memoir. He had given me his perception of a significant part of his daily life. More than that, he let me see him recalling, selecting, concentrating, creating—being human.

A pen or computer is not so different to a clay pipe, a drawing not so different to words. The Les Eyzies paintings affirmed my belief that it is not an indulgence but a requirement of the human spirit to try to communicate the curious nature of being.

Part One

Starting Out

1

Exploring the territory

Knowing our story will help us to know ourselves, others, the mystery of life, and the universe around us better than we had before.

ROBERT ATKINSON

What is it like for anyone to be in the world? This is the vast and private knowledge that each one of us has—and the great mystery. No one else can really know what it is like for you to be here on this planet. Others could conceivably find out everything that has happened to you, your entire history, but they still could not know how you experience *being* here. For me, this is the starting point for writing true stories: a desire to express how one experiences life—its shape, its texture, its atmosphere—and a consuming curiosity to know how other people experience it.

Whether you want to write autobiography, memoir, travel narratives, personal essays, creative nonfiction, biography or even edge towards the borderlands of fiction, this book will help you write 'true stories'.

You have experienced being here in the world, have known the joys and perhaps heartaches of life, faced challenges, had adventures, fulfilled dreams, witnessed change, made observations—whatever your achievements or trials, your stories are worth writing. You may have worked as farmer or scientist, prime minister or office administrator, high-school teacher or computer-game designer; you may be famous, unemployed, disabled, wealthy; in every case you have lived your own unique life. Experience of living and a desire to write are the starting point of writing your stories.

It does not matter how old you are or whether you have done anything others consider extraordinary or not. Writing is first of all observation, and then putting the observation into words. For good life writing, the quality of your observation is key—*it is how you see life that matters, rather than what you have done.* Truthfully observing your life and the world around you is the starting point of all writing.

The essential truth is always: what is it like to be in the world? To me, that's one of the most interesting questions of all. What childhood dream, or perhaps dread, led you to this point in your life? What roads travelled, or less travelled, have you taken? What do you believe about yourself? Do you have a compass and if so, what is it made of?

Still, the desire to express experiences in writing is, by itself, not enough. Life is made of days but writing is made of words—can one level of reality be transmuted into the other? Post-modernist thought argues that words can never represent life; they can only represent a parallel world of words, a world of signs. Words are not a 'window' through which we can see reality, they are more like permanent contact lens that construct the world we see according to the colour and thickness of the lens. More than that, the 'lens' also shapes our inner world. Feelings themselves are, to some extent, shaped by words. It is almost impossible to imagine how we could experience the world without language, because we use words to imagine too. Still, acknowledging our 'lens', accepting that words will always form our experience, we can try to set down what we see through them, and how.

Defining the territory

What *is* life writing? Is autobiography different from memoir? And what is the difference between memoir and 'memoirs'? And creative nonfiction? Briefly defining the territory could be useful before heading off on the journey.

Life writing is a general term that encompasses the broad territory of nonfiction writing on subjects of actual experience and observation, an umbrella term which includes autobiography, biography, memoir, memoirs, personal essay, travel and sojourn writing.

Autobiography is an account of a whole life—from one's origins to the present. It can include some family history but concentrates on the individual life, exploring childhood experience, personal development, relationships and career.

Biography is an account of someone else's life, although it too can spread out at its edges to include elements of memoir. The biographer can become part of the story.

Memoir is an aspect of a life shaped by any number of limitations including time, place, topic or theme. One can write a memoir of childhood, or of a year in Turkmenistan, or of a relationship with a parent. Travel and sojourn writing are also part of memoir, although they have some particular requirements of their own.

The term 'memoirs' has come to mean the reminiscences

of the famous in relation to their public achievements. A general or a politician might write memoirs, and in them we would expect insight into military campaigns or political machinations rather than insight into their relationship with their mothers or other aspects of their private personalities.

Personal essays explore ideas in a wide variety of areas— politics, psychology, everyday life—using personal history to elaborate and illustrate the idea. They can also include facts, interviews, imagination, lists—whatever the essayist want to use to develop his or her idea.

Creative nonfiction, sometimes called literary nonfiction or narrative nonfiction, describes 'true stories' that use the techniques of fiction—such as scene and evocative detail—and often the narrator's experiences and perspective. It can include true crime, nature and travel writing, some kinds of biography and almost any area of knowledge—history, geography, politics, psychology—as its subjects.

For you, the writer, the definitions and distinctions may not matter until your manuscript reaches the publisher, who will decide how to categorise it.

The reasons why

Asking why you want to tell this story helps you to focus on the task ahead as well as to clarify whether you want to write autobiography or memoir or creative nonfiction.

Lineage and social history

In a culture where social media and television absorb much free time, there is scant opportunity for the older generation to tell family stories. But there is still a fundamental human need to know our lineage, our roots, perhaps because it fills in what would otherwise be an infinite silent blank before our own existence. To place our lineage in context we also need social history, to understand how people worked, what they ate, what games children played. You have probably wished at some time that you knew what your grandparents' or even your parents' lives were really like. This is your chance to speak to the future.

Identity

Who are you in relation to your family, your community, your cultural background? Particularly when you have come from a community that has been oppressed or marginalised, you may be motivated by a desire to explore the identity of your people. Seeing what you are made of—your culture, your family history—can place your own life in a continuum of other lives and thereby create a sense of belonging. It can help both writer and reader find their way.

Healing

The need for healing can come at any time in a life. None of us is immune forever from suffering. It may be death, adoption, abuse, divorce, illness or any other painful experience that jolts or even overturns your life. Because the experience disrupts all of your previous stories, there can be feelings of meaninglessness and disconnection, as well as pain and grief. Writing is a powerful way of weaving all the pieces of your life back together. The act of writing a sentence is an act of making connections and making meaning. The writer Karen Blixen said, 'All sorrows can be borne if you put them in a story.'

Wisdom

Nearly everyone wants to share something of what they have learned from living. You may have sailed around the world on your own, lived in solitude in the bush, looked after your Down syndrome son or fought in a war; you have learned something about yourself and what it is to be a human being and that is always worth sharing.

Creativity

To explore in writing the experiences and themes of one's life is essentially a creative act. You may be interested in using the material of your life to write short stories, personal essays or memoir. Exploring the creative possibilities of writing 'true stories' is a return to the regenerative source of all literature.

There is another motive that needs to be mentioned. Revenge is a motive not often confessed to, but it does at times show through on the page. A writer may feel bitter and want to punish those who have hurt them. Such motivations have an unpleasant way of distorting the writing; as a perceptive student once remarked to me, 'bitterness does not read well'.

These are some of the reasons why 'ordinary' people write, although the more I work with people writing their life story, the more I realise that there is no such category as 'ordinary'. Every life, happy or tragic, famous or unknown, is extraordinary in its own way. I don't even agree with Tolstoy that all happy families are alike. Happiness is more difficult to write about because the processes of growth and renewal are less dramatic than those of destruction, but happiness is as unique as grief.

You may not know why you want to write your story at first. In fact, you may not really know why you are writing until you finish. You may just have a gut feeling that it has to be done, and the reasons emerge as you write. Unexpected discovery is one of the many joys of writing.

But just asking 'why?' is productive. Drop it into your mind and let it lie there uncoiling. It will nudge all sorts of things to the surface to use when you are ready to start. The motive is the coiled spring beneath your writing. It will generate the energy to get you started and it can keep you going when it seems as though the story will never be finished.

Think about why you want to write your life story. Write your motives as clearly as you can on a piece of paper and put the paper above your work table.

Your story changes others

Before the American Civil War, an autobiography was published that changed the life of the nation. *My Bondage and My Freedom* by Frederick Douglass was an account of his life as a slave and then finally as a free man. It was one of a number of 'slave narratives' that changed the way people thought about slavery and African Americans. These autobiographies revealed the humanity of each person, connecting each one of their readers as brothers and sisters and strengthening a political movement that, in time, freed men and women from slavery. Douglass's personal story had an enormous impact on millions of lives: it helped changed history.

In Australia, especially in the last few decades, there have been a number of autobiographies and memoirs by Indigenous writers that have articulated and strengthened their communities' sense of identity and started to change attitudes in the wider community. Sally Morgan's *My Place*, Ruby Langford Ginibi's *Don't Take Your Love to Town*, Anita Heiss's *Am I Black Enough For You?*, Jeanine Leane's *Purple Threads* and Stan Grant's *Talking to My Country* are all personal life stories, but they are also political in its deepest sense, giving strength and purpose to Indigenous action. These life stories create change in the wider community by replacing ignorance and judgement with insight and understanding.

There are many communities that are sidelined by those in power, marginalised and even oppressed because of their cultural and ethnic background, or because they are disabled, or because of their sexuality, or because they have been damaged by poverty and neglect. Writing about your life, claiming your experience, is empowering, not just for you but for your whole community. Writing your own life is personal, but it can also be a passionate act of commitment to community. Writing your life can create connection, compassion and change.

A confession

I should, here at the beginning, confess the true extent of my passion to know what life is like for other people. The question has been with me since I was a teenager: *What is it like for you to be in the world?* I feel the hunger to know when I travel on a train, or sit in a café, or stand in a queue at the supermarket. I want to go up to each person and ask him or her, what is it like for you to be here in this world with only a set of stories to guide you? How do you do it? How do I do it?

Life writing is a way of exploring that question. It is a genre wide and deep enough to explore any of the questions murmuring or shouting under a life, flexible enough to evoke both the beauty and the terror of being here. It is a vessel that changes according to what is put in it, sometimes formal and elegant, sometimes laid-back and laconic. In life writing you are returning to the well of literature, the place where you are trying to make words say what it is like to be here in the mystery of existing at all.

2

How to use this book

There is no description equal in difficulty, or certainly in usefulness, to the description of oneself.

MICHEL DE MONTAIGNE

This book is for anyone who wants to write 'true stories'. It explores the whole spectrum of life writing, from straightforward autobiography, to memoir, to the complex territory of creative nonfiction.

Life writing is like all creative writing in that it requires art and discipline. The craft and art of words will bring your experiences and observations to life on the page. But it is different from any other writing in that the self cannot be avoided. In reports, academic essays and journalism mentioning yourself is discouraged, but in life writing it is necessary to reveal (or is it create?) yourself as the narrator of a story in which you are also a 'character'.

Each person's story is unique. There is much we have in common, but we each experience these events in our own way.

If you are writing memoir, you probably already have most of the material for your book in your memory, although you might not always be fully conscious of it. If you are writing creative nonfiction, you may have research to do. This book is about how to get the material onto the page.

Because you already have the content of your life story, it may seem easy just to write it down. But then you think: where do I begin? What do I put in and what do I leave out? How do I stitch it together? What can I do to make it more than just a list of events?

This book will answer these questions and guide you through writing your story so that it will be exciting to write and absorbing to read. It will extend the possibilities of life writing into memoir, travel writing, personal essay and a variety of creative nonfiction topics such as true crime and nature writing. It will help you get started and, most importantly, keep you going until you are finished. You will soon realise that the journey of writing is just as valuable as the completed manuscript.

A practical guide—The workshop chapters

Writing True Stories has been divided into two parts.

Part one: Starting out presents fundamental skills and issues of life writing.

Part two: Masterclasses extends the basic skills, presents key issues and broadens the genre into creative nonfiction, creative biography, travel memoir and the personal essay. There is also a chapter on publication options for your manuscript when you are finished.

For ease of use, each workshop chapter is divided into the following sections:

- A *general discussion* of the topic, in which ideas are offered for you to think about, argue with, and be inspired by.
- A *reading*, consisting of short extracts from published autobiographies, which illustrate the topics under discussion. Read the extracts to see how published writers handle the issues. They may inspire you to try something new.
- *Writing exercises* of which there are at least four in each chapter, that have all been tested in many workshop groups. You will find that some result in a page or two while others will trigger a whole chapter. Every person responds differently to each exercise. There are a variety in each chapter, and some may be used over and over again, generating a different response each time. Try them one by one and see which work for you.
- *Life story writers* sections in part one illustrate how the exercises work. They are responses to the exercises written by former workshop members. These are short, many of them written in ten minutes. Read them to be inspired by the writing of 'ordinary' people and to gain confidence in writing your own story.

You can work your way through the whole of *Writing True Stories* by starting at the first workshop and working your way to the end. The workshops have been organised developmentally, but if you like, you can also try random workshop chapters as the interest takes you.

Don't worry about how to organise or structure your writing before you start. The important thing is to get started with the exercises, then, after a while, you can think about structure. If you really need a shape in your head before you start, it might be useful to read Workshop six: Structure.

These workshops will point you in the right direction, help you when you are lost, encourage you to keep going, warn of difficulties, point out places of interest you may not have thought of exploring and inspire you to go further than you thought possible. Use each of the workshop chapters as you might use a map. Pore over it for a while, getting an idea of the geography and enjoying the place names that other travellers have written on it. Use the exercises as tickets—try each one and see where it takes you. Then, map in hand, take out your writing implements and commence your travels. Enjoy the journey.

Rewards and difficulties

Writing your life is more challenging and revealing than most other activities. It may seem like a straightforward task, but once you start paying close attention to the writing of your life you will soon discover that there is more to your story than you suspected. Many emotions lie hidden until you start writing; many thoughts are focused through the act of writing.

Rewards

Self-knowledge
Growth in self-knowledge can occur through writing your life. It seems to be a similar process to psychoanalysis; there is more shaping, more art if you will, in writing than in the free flow of analysis, but you can come to much of the same knowledge about yourself. Of course, writing a life does not guarantee an opening of the heart and mind, but it does offer a fertile ground. Writing well about self, or others, demands insight and

truthfulness. Without true awareness, observations will be flat, stereotypical and dull, written experiences will be thin and tedious. The art and discipline of life writing can reward the writer with self-awareness and awareness of others.

Healing

Writing is an act of integration and meaning and can therefore be healing. In some practices of psychology, 'narrative therapy', or the restorying of one's life, is used to help people feel empowered. While I do not treat writing as therapy, it's clear that many people who have written about trauma have found it has helped heal lifelong hurts. Writing your life is not a remedy for all hurts, but the letting go that comes from forgiving others—or yourself—can bring freedom and the energy to begin again.

Remembering happiness

There is also the pleasure of reliving forgotten happy events. You can become so immersed in present concerns that you don't recall for years the childhood day when you daringly rowed across the lake, or the sunny afternoon you spent walking in the mountains with your first love. Rediscovering these memories is like finding a treasured photograph that you had thought long gone.

Sharing

A rare trust and warmth are generated when you offer the story of your life to another. In a sense you are entrusting them with your true self, and I have invariably found the trust rewarded. There is wonder in the difference of our lives and, at the same time, joy in knowing that we are much alike. A glimpse of what made life valuable to you is one of the greatest treasures you can offer others.

Creativity

Translating a life into words is one of the most creative acts you can engage in—an act of magic, transforming bodies, breath, actions, time and space into words on a page. And like all acts of magic, a life transformed into words will have its own independent power.

Difficulties

Others' feelings

It's not feasible to write about yourself without including something about your family and friends, and, quite simply, they may not like it. Sometimes a hard truth has to be told, but even if you filter what you write about others through rose-coloured glasses, some people may still object. They may feel that their privacy has been invaded and can be suspicious of your motives. Or you may find that everyone disputes your account of events and wants you to write the 'correct' version, that is, their version.

Disclosure

The issue of others' feelings becomes more difficult if you decide to make revelations about immoral or illegal activities. For example, you may want to write about abuse you suffered at the hands of your grandfather, but his innocent elderly sisters are still alive and will be hurt and suffer public exposure if you write about him. On the other hand, should the guilty be allowed to continue to inflict suffering because they are not exposed? The truth can be painful, but I believe there is little hope of resolving issues if people continue to hide the reality of their lives or encourage others to live in illusion.

Unreliable memory

Memory is notoriously fickle. It can be difficult to remember which events happened and in what order. It can be hard to know whether we actually remember an event or whether we are remembering what we were told about it. But there are ways of diving into memory and coming up with gold. To find out more about memory and how to release its treasures, see Workshop two: Memory and other sources.

Stirring up old emotions

Many people find that writing about painful episodes is healing, but others may find that the time is not yet right, that they need further help before writing about those emotions. To write effectively about events and emotions you must, to a certain extent, relive them in your imagination. Only you can decide whether you are ready to face the feelings the writing of your truth may arouse.

Ego

Perhaps you are concerned that writing about the self is egotistical. Don't worry, it is! Ego, or a sense of self, is a condition of our lives as human beings. Writing your life story will strengthen your sense of self. Of course, some philosophies hold that we create the illusion of self to convince ourselves that we exist. Still, if you are not yet ready to spend your life meditating on Zen koans (non-stories of Zen Buddhism designed to liberate one from ego) you will find life writing an exhilarating and rewarding process. Even if you are ready for such a discipline, writing may help you develop detachment as you learn to see your life as a story.

But none of this means that life writing is egotistical in a derogatory sense. Writing the narrative of your life, you come to realise the interrelatedness of all lives; reading the stories of others' lives, you come to understand your own. In fact, as we read autobiography we are also, in parallel, reading our own life, comparing, contrasting, grieving, celebrating. As Deena Metzger suggested in *Writing for Your Life*, when we write autobiography we go deeply into ourselves and come up in other people. If autobiography is 'an archaeology of the self', it is also an archaeology of a time and place and community. Far from being a self-absorbed isolating activity, autobiography is an act of connectedness and interrelationship.

Writing your life story is not quite like any other activity or hobby you may take up. It can be confronting; it is challenging and exciting. You are facing yourself as much as if you were sailing solo around the world, so it is a pursuit for the adventurous. Take care, and remember: the rewards make it more than worth the effort.

3

WORKSHOP ONE
Getting started

*One does not discover new lands without consenting to lose
sight of the shore for a very long time.*

ANDRÉ GIDE

Getting started is always the most difficult part of any enterprise. Losing sight of the shore, of what we think we know, is daunting. With life writing, the beginning appears even more difficult. How do you know where to start? And how do you organise everything into some kind of order?

Don't be daunted, and be content to start with doubts. You don't have to be certain of what you want to say or where you want to go in order to begin. If we all waited for certainty, most things would never be undertaken. Starting anywhere is better than not starting at all. Because this is the beginning of your journey, here are some steps you can take to help you head in the right direction.

Remember, you can only take one step at a time. Concentrate on the step in front of you.

Preparation

For any journey, there are levels on which you must prepare: on the inner, imaginative level by talking and reading about the places you are going to visit; and on the outer, practical level by making lists, booking tickets, packing your bags and selecting your point of departure. Beginning the journey of life writing is similar. You need to prepare on the inner and outer levels.

Read

You can write without reading much, but if you want to write well, you must read. Being a reader will not automatically make you a good writer, but it helps. From reading you learn possibilities of style and form and how to deal with technical difficulties, such as how to move about in time or how to deal with several story threads.

Read other life stories—there's a list at the end of this book—but not too many at first, because they can be so fascinating that you could become an armchair traveller on the journey of life writing. Some people may need to stop reading once they start writing because they are too easily influenced by others' writing style, while for others it is encouraging to continue reading. Either way, make sure you take a step along your own path.

Organise space and time

Organise a writing space for yourself. Set up a table where you can leave all your work materials in place without having to clear them away. You know your own best working conditions: create them for yourself so that you have no more excuses.

21

Make time—if you wait for a spare hour you may never get started. *Make a regular time.* It doesn't have to be long—half an hour each evening, or three hours on the weekend will get you a long way. Establish a rhythm of working—it makes sitting down to write much easier.

Collect and arrange

Collect diaries, letters, photographs, records of any kind. It can be useful to have a noticeboard to spread everything out. Again, don't spend too much time collecting material as it is easy to use it as an excuse for not getting started. Dates and missing information can be added later if necessary.

Overcoming 'One day I will do it' syndrome

This endless delaying tactic usually comes from a fear of failing: if you don't start, then it is always a perfect idea, unmarked by messy struggle. 'One day I am going to write a book' is much easier than sitting down and starting. You need a cunning strategy. Instead of having a vague 'One day I'll start', or a terrifying 'Today I will start', give yourself a precise date in the near future, two or three weeks away, to commence. Enter it in your calendar or diary and pick a writing exercise well before. When the day comes, sit down and do the writing exercise. At first, only allow yourself half an hour. The combined strategies of a delayed start and a limited writing time tend to lessen the anxiety and increase the desire. Keep to the timed routine, but after a few weeks give yourself an hour. Once you are well established in the writing, allow yourself as much time as possible.

Knowing where to start

If you don't know where to start, try the patchwork quilter's method: start making small pieces. Don't decide whether you are writing the beginning or not, simply start writing memories. These short pieces can be three hundred words or three thousand words. It doesn't matter. Doing short pieces will help you gain confidence and you will have made a start without having to leap over the biggest hurdle at the beginning.

You don't have to plan

You don't have to work out the whole book before you start. You can simply start on the exercises and see what develops as you go. Select a particular time or event to begin with and the structure will emerge as you write. If you think you really need to make an outline or plan your structure before you begin, see Workshop six: Structure.

Commitment and courage

Writing a life takes time as well as creative and emotional effort. If you can commit yourself to the task ahead and to being as courageous and honest as you can be, then you will be better prepared on an inner level. Be ready with an open mind and heart for whatever you may discover about your life. Writing memories will inevitably change the way you see your life to some degree. Set out as an explorer, prepared, open-minded and expecting adventure.

Composting

Your stories may take time to emerge. It is important to learn to trust the gestation process that goes on underneath the conscious mind. It doesn't mean that you sit watching television and eating chocolate every evening and the story will grow perfectly formed inside you! But neither does it mean you allow the lack of clear direction or shape to prevent you from starting. You can help the gestation process in a number of ways.

You can clarify your topic by doing some 'pre-writing'— that is, start writing the thoughts floating around in your head. You are not writing the memoir, you are writing *about* it. This pre-writing is a ramble in which you explore the general territory.

'Composting' your material is useful. Often experience feels monolithic and can take time to break down into usable writing elements. Writing too soon can be emotionally overwhelming and the writing can be 'lumpy' and raw, much like the original materials of a compost heap. Time is partly the solution. Write immediate impressions certainly, straight after a birth or death or divorce, but do not expect that this will necessarily be the final or truest word on the matter.

Experience needs to be filtered through the weathers of the self until it finds its richest form. You can help this process along by 'digging' over the memory, that is, writing different aspects of it, experimenting with starting in different places. I saw a documentary about the creation of 'Imagine' by John Lennon, and it was reassuring to see such an accomplished artist try, and discard, all sorts of possible arrangements until he came up with the song that is an anthem of hope even today. *The process of creation is not a straight line but an experimental process with lots of trial and error. Feel free to make mistakes!*

Some writers advise jotting down ideas as they come to you, but I've found if I write something down, it usually just stays in the notebook, not going anywhere. I find it better to have a session of jotting things down so that the thoughts are all on one page and are still in relation to one another, still composting. However, everyone's method is different, so if the 'Jotting things down when they occur' method works for you, keep it up.

It's important in the beginning to 'follow the heat', to begin with the idea or event that you feel most passionate about rather than working out the logical place to start your writing. If you spend too much time working out the rational place to start, you can lose the impetus to begin at all. Start with the idea that excites your interest and arouses your emotions, positive or negative. It doesn't mean you cannot change things around later.

You don't have to do it all today

To paraphrase a well-known piece of advice: you can only write one page at a time. You don't have to write your whole life at once. If you wrote just a page a day, at the end of the year you would have 365 pages! Even half a page every evening would give you a good-sized manuscript. So make sure you have enough light, sit down—and *start writing*.

Ways to begin

Fact

Start with a fact about yourself. This is a deceptively simple suggestion, for once you start considering the facts they multiply in all directions. If you are writing autobiography, a logical stepping-off point is the date, place and conditions of your birth—although, of course, you don't have to be logical! Clive James begins his *Unreliable Memoirs* with: 'I was born in 1939.' He follows this with: 'The other big event of that year was the outbreak of the Second World War, but for the moment that did not affect me.' Suddenly, the bald fact has become a revelation of James's conscious self-centredness and his comic style of juxtaposing unlikely events.

James has used the facts to reveal truths about himself. If you reveal some truth in your opening, something of fundamental importance in your life, it will be more effective than an isolated fact. For example, try to see what there is in the date, place or conditions of your birth that may have influenced your life. Was the year you were born significant in a way that influenced your whole life? Were you born during a war? Were you born in another country? It could be the fact of your ethnic background that has influenced your life, or the fact of being disabled, or the fact of being adopted. There are endless other facts about yourself that would be effective as an opening.

Use the fact if there is a link between it and something of importance in your life. By doing this you are heading the reader off in the right direction; you are beginning the process of shaping your story.

Anecdote

An anecdote is an engaging way to begin. It can be from any time of your life—childhood or just a couple of years ago—but it needs to be one that reveals something significant about your life. W.G. Sebald opens *The Rings of Saturn* with the sentence, 'In August 1992, when the dog days were drawing to an end, I set off to walk the county of Suffolk, in the hope of dispelling the emptiness that takes hold of me whenever I have completed a long stint of work.' The reader is immediately engaged with the emotions, perhaps having experienced them him or herself. Sebald goes on to tell the reader briefly about the depression which came over him before he leads into the walk and the superb exploration of ideas for which he is so rightly acclaimed.

A story from later in life can also work very effectively. Robert Dessaix begins *A Mother's Disgrace*: 'One warm April evening in 1984, in a pleasant suburb of Cairo called Zamalek, three exquisite young men tried to kill me.' In using this scene Dessaix grabs our attention, but at the same time he is beginning a story that makes a link between the throat-cutting incident and one of the themes of the book: finding a voice. He has begun the shaping process.

A symbolic image

Often there are images from memory that seem to be significant. It could be something we've seen once—the moon over a desert—or something we have kept for a lifetime, an ornament we treasure. *Poppy*, by Drusilla Modjeska, begins with the image of an umbilical cord being cut. Each and every life has experienced this cutting of the cord, but for Modjeska it has a particular significance. We immediately feel the separation between mother and child and, as we read on, we discover that this is one of the main themes of the book. The cutting of the cord has become a symbol of separation and alienation. Symbols are the language of the subconscious, of dreams, memory and poetry, and so have a powerful impact on our writing.

Think about your life and see if there is some image you often recall: an unfinished jigsaw puzzle, a broken toy, a path in the bush. Opening with a symbolic image can be a tantalising way to start. It creates a sense of mystery and the possibility of discovery.

A thought or observation

A detached observation or an abstract idea or image can be a provocative opening. Robert Macfarlane opens *The Old Ways* with: 'Two days short of the winter solstice; the turn of the year's tide. All that cold day, the city and countryside felt halted, paused.' The countryside is foregrounded by this opening and the reader knows this will be a memoir about landscape. Christa Wolf opens her autobiographical novel, *A Model Childhood*, with the comment: 'What is past is not dead; it is not even past. We cut ourselves off from it; we pretend to be strangers.' She engages our minds with this meditation on the relationship between present and past. It begins an intellectual discussion, via her own life, of the relationship between Germany's Nazi past and her own generation.

A theoretical discussion as an opening carries the danger of being too weighty and also being overly abstract. Most readers require a sensual and emotional world on the page to engage their attention and may stop reading if the opening is too dense with ideas. On the other hand, some readers are drawn to intellectual challenge and will happily keep reading. If your life is one in which an intellectual frame of mind has been central, it may be most appropriate to open by drawing your reader into the life of the mind.

Seduction and curiosity

When a reader begins your story, they do not know you (unless you are already famous in some field) and so need a reason to get to know you. In reading an autobiography, the reader is submitting to your sense of self, to your consciousness, and most people won't submit unless they have been seduced first. Perhaps seduced is too suggestive a word—charmed might suit better. In any case, a reason to get to know you, to keep reading about you, needs to be offered. By far the most common reason for a reader to be held by a beginning is *emotional engagement*. Most people will keep reading if they *care* what happens to you. For that reason, any beginning that draws the reader in emotionally is most often effective.

Still, each reader is different. Readers can be seduced by different elements: for some it might be personal identification with your situation, for others an intellectual interest in the context, for others it might be the beauty of the language itself. Readers can also be seduced in different ways—some are happy with a slow and gentle introduction, others like the story to begin with drama and excitement. Some readers will be engaged by a quiet evocation of landscape as in the opening pages of *The Old Ways*, some will prefer the exotic danger at the beginning of *A Mother's Disgrace*. There's no one opening that will work for everyone, which is why I suggest that you notice how you like to be seduced when you read—what draws you in—and try a beginning that would engage you.

The other reason most people will keep reading is *curiosity*. Humans are naturally curious—it's one of our most fundamental characteristics, it's how we learn, how we survive. If the beginning of an autobiography contains unanswered questions, most people will feel compelled to keep reading. It doesn't mean you write the question, it just means that questions about what caused this situation and what will happen next need to start forming in the reader's mind. This means you can start anywhere, so long as you create the desire to find if not answers then at least more about what happens to you.

Of course, curiosity depends on interest, on what we care about. For some readers, their curiosity will be aroused by emotional or psychological conflict, for others it could be intellectual or philosophical ideas, and for others it could be a political or scientific question. Again, look to what arouses curiosity in you—what makes you keep reading. Read the beginnings of a variety of autobiographies or literary nonfiction and notice what draws you in. To me, the only unbreakable rule of writing is *write what you would enjoy reading yourself.*

Remember, you don't have to get it right first time. In fact, we often don't really know our opening until we have written our ending. You can always decide later to change the beginning. Don't spend too much time worrying about where to begin. Again, it is better to start in any place than not to start at all. Jump in!

Reading

Boy, Lost   Kristina Olsson

Cairns railway station, far north Queensland, summer, 1950. A girl with fugitive eyes and an infant on her hip. She is thin, gaunt even, but still it is easy to see these two are a pair, dark-haired and dark-eyed. She hurries down the platform towards the second-class cars, slowed by the weight of her son and her cardboard suitcase. It holds everything they own, everything she dared to take.

She finds a seat in one of the last cars—perhaps it feels safe, perhaps she is already getting as far from this place as she can—and settles herself. She has some food wrapped in paper, a dry sandwich, arrowroot biscuits—there was nothing else in the flat. Peter—that is the boy's name—is tired, fractious, out of routine. Somewhere in her weary brain she knows he is echoing her own fear, her own curdled mix of terror and sorrow and the adrenalin it has taken to get her here. She talks to him quietly, she hopes he won't cry. She doesn't want anyone to hear him.

This is the scene as I see it, sixty years later. It is sepia-toned, like the photograph I have of her then. Nineteen years old with a face people compared to the young Elizabeth Taylor, and fine-boned limbs. But the fineness apparent through her thin shift that day had nothing to do with her natural build. She was malnourished, starving. Later, when she stumbles off the train in Brisbane she will be taken away to hospital. No one will know until then—no one could tell—that the new pregnancy she'd protected and kept secret was now well advanced.

But that is days later. Whole days and a lifetime from the minutes she waited on the train, willing it to move, to take them to safety. A lifetime surely because that is how long the journey seemed, how long she'll have, later, to recall over and over, a single moment. The man appears at the door of the carriage, walks towards her—a twisted smile—and roughly pulls Peter from her arms. Later in memory and dream and conversation, she will wonder what else he said to her, apart from those few chilling words. *Don't move*—the Greek accent was heavy and cruel; the baby whimpered, reached for his mother, a biscuit in his fist—*Don't move, you bitch. Stay on the train or you're dead. Him too.* She knew from the brutality of the past months that he meant it.

He waited then, his bulk blocking the doorway, until a whistle blew and the train shuddered. Did she plead with him in those minutes, beg, tell him she'd stay? Did she try to strike a bargain, some pathetic deal? I doubt it. In the parlance of the poker games he was addicted to, she had nothing to bargain with, no cards to play. She had only herself, her own bruised and flimsy body, her poor bullied heart. He didn't want *her*.

In this opening, Kristina Olsson begins to tell the story of her mother and her baby brother in a scene of drama and tension. It is the scene that impacted on the rest of everyone's life, including Kristina's, who was the first child of her mother's subsequent marriage; it means the reader is immediately led into the centre of the story, which will play out over many decades. Read this book not just for its moving story but for its powerful writing and for the way Olsson is able to tell everyone's story, mother, brother and her own, with equal insight.

Writing exercises

1 Childhood story

Write an experience from your early childhood—it could be one you have told a number of times, or one you have never told anyone. It could be dramatic or quiet, but what is important is that you have remembered it, even if only in a fragmentary fashion. Consider whether this could be a shaping story, that is, one that has had an influence on your life. (Fifteen minutes)

2 First fact

What is the first thing you want known about yourself? Your date of birth? A character trait? Your appearance? Your ancestry?

A strongly held belief? Your moment of glory? Write it down and see where it leads you. Let it expand—see what floats up from your mind next. (Ten minutes)

3 Parents

Write an early memory of yourself in relation to one of your parents. It might include what they looked like, what work they did or your early memories of them, but the important thing is to follow the memory rather than trying consciously to include this information. Try the exercise again, writing about the other parent, or any significant person in your life. (Fifteen minutes)

4 Ramble

This is useful if you are unclear about your subject matter. Start with an uncertain phrase, that is, expressing how unsure you feel. For example, you might begin: *I might want to explore that year I spent in London—I don't really know why. It's just that the image of that bare little room with the slatted bed keeps coming to mind. There was one picture on the wall though, a poster of a mountain in Italy. Maybe that's why I went to Italy the following year.* And then you keep on rambling! This exercise is meant to be discursive—a way of loosening the order of the organising brain. Follow any train of thought that arises as you wander. It is like sifting through the contents of a drawer, alert to treasures that may be uncovered. (Twenty minutes)

5 Symbols

Start with an image that has become symbolic for you. It could be an image from nature—a tree, river, mountain—or an object from ordinary life—a piece of jewellery, a passport. Explore the image, unfolding its significance for you. Try not to theorise, that is, keep the writing grounded in your actual life. (Ten minutes)

Life story writers

Anni Webster has completed exercise five to explore the reality and the symbolic importance of a river in her life.

Homecoming   Anni Webster

A child takes an artist's long brush and holds it close to the flat strip of hairs at its base. She thrusts the brush into a slurry of water and earth and sky, plunging so deep that the thick colour coats her hand as well. Squatting close to the earth, she draws a wide lazy scribble that mesmerises her as it goes on and on. The brush wobbles, so the slurry is all over the place. Dollops of colour fall from her hand as she works, the splashes merging into her scrawled line. Standing back, looking at how far she's come, she's satisfied with the shape. But she stumbles on the container of colour and it empties into a wide swathe of blues and greens and browns so that the long river (let's call it that) ends in a wide-mouthed bay.

The view when flying in to Brisbane looks like such a scrawl. The river runs through a shallow scoop of earth from the spine of the western mountains towards the eastern bay. The green lagoon colour of the bay is kept separate from the wider blue ocean by a sentinel line of sand-duned islands. Brisbane spreads out either side of the river, but there is no neat division into north and south, left or right banks. Like a childish squiggle, the river meanders at will, playfully looping back on itself, sometimes almost touching where it was before, shaping a narrow isthmus of land between the banks. When you travel on land, you come across the river everywhere you turn. It's as if it creeps up behind from where you last met it, then wriggles past to be in front again.

Brisbane feels like home to me, although I didn't spend my childhood here. It's a wild and unpredictable place, a little like my life has felt. It's impossible to take one's bearings from the river here. Orientation comes from the sky. Cool sea breezes blow from the east, slate-laden storms from the west; the sun dries the humidity from the northern side of trees, fosters lichen and fungal growth on the southern. Yet the river sets the city's pace, languid and unhurried in its slow slide towards the bay. Brisbane is shocked into action when the river floods from time to time, upending trees and walls, boats and houses in a wild rush that sweeps aside all in its path.

Despite this occasional chaos, Brisbane sits securely, protected by its western mountains, washed by its broad river, held in suspension between land and sky by nature's grip. It can never pretend to be a European city. Brisbane's original custodians, the Turrbal and Jagera, understood its fertile abundance and respected its moods. In extreme weather, the mass of water flowing into the river from a large catchment area can't escape quickly to the bay. The river's sinuous shape slows its passage, so water claims low-lying land. This river needs space. I know how it feels.

Turn to the next workshop for information on other sources you can draw on as you continue with your life story.

4

WORKSHOP TWO

Memory and other sources

*Our memory is a more perfect world than the universe: it gives
back life to those who no longer exist.*

GUY DE MAUPASSANT

Memory, that curiously imaginative recorder, is the main source
for life writers. Memory ensures that things don't just happen
and then disappear without trace—it make a 'record', however
unreliable, of what has happened to us, of our experience of
being in the world—and so provides us with the raw material
of creativity.

In Greek mythology, Mnemosyne, or memory, is the
mother of the Muses, the creative spirits of humankind. In
other words, memory is the mother of creativity. It is also the
mother of thought and of learning; Aristotle said we could
not think without being able to recollect our experiences,
and certainly, without reflection on what has happened there
could be no development of ideas.

36

A sense of self is largely made up of memory. Without memory of events, relationships or knowledge, it seems impossible to construct a sense of self and certainly impossible to write more than a few disjointed words. It's also perhaps our only chance at immortality, to live in other peoples' minds. Understanding the nature and function of memory goes to the heart of who we are as human beings.

The science and poetry of memory

How does memory work? The first, easily lost imprint of memory is recorded by the cells' bioelectrical action. Storing, the changeover to long-term memory, is probably a chemical operation. Our memories thus become part of our biological make-up. We are, literally, made of our memories. Still, retrieving those stored memories can be difficult.

Working with writing students has led me to observe that all memories, whatever their nature, are stored with some kind of sense memory. Recent research on the nature of memory has shown that there is indeed a strong link between the senses and memory. Whenever there is sensory input, the amygdala, the part of the brain that determines the appropriate emotional response, lights up, which means the connection between senses and emotions is hardwired into the brain. As well, sensory memory appears to be spread across the brain, distinct sense memories of the same experience being stored in different places—the smell of the sea in one place, the sounds of waves in another. You only need one sensory aspect of the memory to be activated for all the rest to come flooding back. It is the key to the memory-based approach to life writing rather than the topic-based approach.

A topic-based approach starts with headings like Parents, Schooldays, Jobs. It gets the job done, but the writing has a flatness. This flattening happens because the logical part of the mind, the left brain, is accessed rather than the imaginative, poetic right side of memory. Topics are the result of logical organisation; they come from and are stored in the organising areas of the brain. If you start writing from a topic then you are going into the rational, ordering network of the brain. It is a reasonable network, very useful for building bridges, organising an office and writing academic essays, but not so useful for writing memoir.

Memories are not aroused and connected to one another by orderly logical progression under topic headings, but nor are they stuffed in like so much rubbish. Instead, memories communicate with us and connect to each other via imagery, symbol and metaphor—all poetic associations, which is why I believe *everyone's memory is a poet*. The smell of nutmeg will connect you not to other spices, as the logical side of the brain would have it, but to your father and the Golden Key café in a small country town where, for the first time, you tasted a malted milk with nutmeg sprinkled on top.

Your memory has stored experiences in imaginative patterns. Go into writing via this door of memory and you are entering into the imaginative, creative part of your mind. From there you are much more likely to write with vividness and clarity. There, each memory can trigger another—especially if you write it down. Even people who are sure they have no recollection of a particular period or person are astonished and delighted to find memories flooding back.

How to remember

So how do you open this 'door' of memory? The answer lies in the fact that all memories are stored with a sense component.

- Listen to the music of the era you want to recall and let it 'take you away'.
- Gaze intently at photographs, taking in all the details; try photographs of places as well as people from your past.
- Prepare and eat the food you ate as a child or from the period or place you want to recall.
- Smell, perfumes, flowers, spices, fabrics—any smells that you associate with particular times in your life. Smell is our most evocative sense.
- Touch old dresses or favourite ornaments—it's amazing what our fingertips and indeed all our senses can remember.
- Draw pictures or 'maps' of the places you want to remember, even a room. The act of drawing activates different pathways in memory.
- Use objects—ornaments, jewellery, mementos, furniture—as springboards for memory.
- Re-read books or watch television programs or films from the past. Books from childhood are especially powerful in their associations.

Writing via a particular memory will yield vividness of detail, originality, richness of flow, and even a structure. It means the details will be original and specific to you, to your individual experience of being. The network of association between memories means that pulling out one memory and writing it down will inevitably pull out a whole connected chain of memories. Rather than being stuck on what to write next, you will find a rich flow of memories demanding to be written! Most intriguing of all, if you follow the seemingly chaotic patterns of memory you will find a structure emerging. The poetic nature of memory connections means patterns form without your conscious direction.

Memory is tricky

Even though it is central to our sense of self, to creativity and to thinking, memory has a number of tricks up its sleeve.

- *It can be unreliable.* We are sometimes sure we remember events that can be proved not to have happened. American writer Mary McCarthy told the story of how one of her children believed Mussolini had been thrown off a bus in Connecticut! When she was older and realised it couldn't have happened she questioned her mother about the incident. It turned out that she had been waiting at a bus stop with her mother when a bus pulled up and a man got out. At the same time, the bus driver leaned over and called, 'Mussolini has been thrown out.'
- *It can be contested.* In most families there are contradictory versions of the same event, and everyone is sure their version is the correct one. Few family memories can be verified or disproved, but check your facts as much as you are able. Talk to others who may have been there at the time. Try to line the memory up with other events to check the date. If you are still sure of a memory with which no one else agrees, hold on to it. It is your memory, it is the way you experienced the event, and so it is your truth.
- *It can make things up.* Sometimes it can be difficult to discern what one remembers and what one has been told

or has seen in a photograph or even a dream. The mind is remarkably good at organising information, but it does not always register different orders of reality, especially in early childhood, and it has a capacity to confabulate—to make up—things that have all the appearance of memory.

- *It can be sentimental.* Memory is the storehouse of our lives, crowded and often dark. Parts of it hardly ever see the light, and parts are perhaps best left forgotten. There are other parts, however, that we visit often, gazing at the individual memories stored there and handling them with tenderness so that they become softer and sweeter with each caress. But the polish of nostalgia adds a shine that may not be entirely truthful.

- *It is selective.* In fact, the unreliable and contradictory nature of memory is largely due to this mysterious selection process. It isn't always obvious why we remember some things and not others, but a strong memory of a particular thing makes it very likely that it has some deeper significance for us. Often the memory may seem random, but memory, like dream, often speaks to us in symbols.

- *It can be painful.* There are some memories that you would rather not retrieve. They may be too painful for you or too hurtful to others. If you want to let memories lie undisturbed, that is always your decision. Still, it is true that facing memories again can lessen their power. You alone will know if you are ready to face the emotions they may stir up.

Other sources

One day when you have finished writing, others will read and be moved by your life. Because of the intrinsic magic of words, they will feel some of your delight, sorrow and wonder in existence. Your emotions and experiences will live again in their imaginations. This sharing of another's existence is, I believe, the main reason we read life stories, but a life story is also a source of information.

It doesn't matter whether you have been the prime minister or the owner of the corner shop, your story will provide information about the past. You may want to expand your own sources to give a wider and richer picture of your life and times. You can start on the internet or at the library, gathering information. If you prefer to gather all your material first, a word of warning: not only can research become an unending addiction in itself but facing a large body of disconnected information can be a daunting way to begin! *I suggest you start writing first, gather your facts as you go, and weave in information where it is needed.*

Every piece of writing is like a cloth woven of threads from other cloths. The sources of the threads we weave are various, including research and interviews and original documents. Here are some possibilities for other sources.

- *On-the-ground research.* Take a trip back to where you used to live, your native country, your old school. Look at the physical details with care because they will jog memories of how you felt. In writing *The Last One Who Remembers* I made many trips to my childhood farm and school, and in doing so realised it was the sights and sounds and smells that brought back many memories.
- *Family history research.* While you do not have to include family history, it can be interesting to make links between past events and your life. For most people, internet resources such as databases of births, deaths and marriages, or convict

records, or ship arrivals are the first step, but genealogical organisations can give advice on how to do family history research. Most towns and suburbs also have historical societies with information, books and encouragement for amateur historians. State libraries and local libraries too have facilities for family and local history research.

- *Internet and library research for context.* Lives happen in contexts—historical, cultural, geographic, political—and so it can be enriching to include some of these contexts in your life writing. It doesn't mean including everything, just what interests you and relates to your life. For example, if you are a biologist, perhaps a biological history of a human life would add intriguing details to your story; if you are a fashion designer, then cultural information about fashion would add texture. For more information about how to weave this research into your story, see Workshop eleven: Research.

- *Newspapers.* You can find answers to all kinds of questions in local newspapers. Try libraries, newspaper offices or your state library. Articles and even advertisements from newspapers of earlier periods in your life can be valuable reminders of the social climate of the time.

- *Public records:* These are useful for checking the 'facts' your memory supplies. They are the community's record of your life and their emotionless formality can stand in striking contrast to the actual rich texture of your living. You can check memories against the records held by registries of births, deaths and marriages, the church, the armed services, community organisations, public and private institutions, and schools.

- *Adoption and Stolen Generation agencies and organisations.* You will soon realise, as you research your own life, that you are not alone. All over Australia there are organisations for people who have been adopted or fostered and want to find out about their backgrounds. If you have been adopted or gave a child up for adoption and you want more information, the first step is to approach the government department in your state responsible for community services. They can also put you in touch with a number of other agencies that give information as well as counselling. The taking of Indigenous children from their families to be made wards of the state or adopted has caused traumatic disruption of countless lives. Many people find it especially important to write their stories because not only their personal history but also their cultural history has been torn apart. An agency called Link-Up can help you reconnect to your past if you were taken from your family by government departments.

- *Family interviews.* Family members will often know more about a person or incident than you do, or at least another version of the story. It is useful to prepare some questions first, both for factual information—'What was your grandmother's maiden name?' for example—but also questions for stories, such as, 'What did you do each afternoon when you got home from school when you were a child?'

While researching the facts is important, it is only a part of writing your life story. Life story is not family history, nor is it a litany of well-researched facts or a straightforward historical account—it is a personal journey of exploration, exciting and sometimes confronting. Even if you never find out all the facts, the journey itself will be rewarding.

Writing exercises

Memory

1 First memory

Write your earliest memory. Rather than looking at the experience from the outside, immerse yourself in it. Write down everything you remember: what you can see, feel, smell, hear. Let this memory flow on to other people who may have been there, the surroundings as you recall them. Remember, your memory is a poet, let it have its say. (Ten minutes)

2 House plan

Draw a floor plan of the house you lived in as a child. Spend a few minutes making it as accurate as you can then mentally wander through it. Go from room to room. As soon as you see something that catches your interest for any reason, stop. And start writing. Write about what you see, or what happened there, or who you've bumped into. If the writing stops, go back into the house and have another wander.

This exercise can be used over and over. Vary it by drawing a map of your bedroom, or a map of your schoolyard, or backyard. (Ten minutes)

3 Take an object

Take an object that comes from the time in your life you want to write about. A childhood toy, a schoolbook, a kitchen table. Look at it carefully, let your mind wander over the associations this object has for you. If nothing comes freely to mind, start by describing its physical appearance, when you first acquired it, or its history. Soon you will find that other things are jostling to be written. (Ten minutes)

Other sources

4 Records

Take a document of your life: birth certificate, adoption papers, a school report, marriage certificate. Write the stories connected to it. What has come about because of this document? What went on before it was issued? Who else does it involve? Such innocent-looking items often conceal a world of stories. (Fifteen minutes)

5 Newspapers

Search in a library for a newspaper account of a public event you remember from childhood. It could be a lost child, the war, a crime everyone was talking about. Compare your memory of the event with the newspaper account. Write about it, starting with your recollection. This exercise is a way in to writing about the impact of the outside world on your childhood. (Ten minutes)

6 Interview

Interview family members or friends on any topic related to your life. Ask them to talk about a time that you shared, or a person you both knew. Weave their account into your own. (One hour)

Life story writers

In this chapter, instead of a published extract there are two pieces from workshop participants. The following piece by Bob Pearson is an extract from his memoir, *A Penny on a Friday*, developed from exercise one.

Entry and Exit

Bob Pearson

Our two small heads looked up into the inky blackness. The darkness was broken by the light streaming from the door of the room as Dad's head appeared.

'Don't make any more noise—shh—you've got a baby brother!' The head disappeared then quickly reappeared. 'He's called Harold,' he said in a loud whisper, then it was dark again.

The next few days were spent in a whirl of people and events. I still had not been able to see Harold or Mother. Even though I asked many questions, there never seemed to be any satisfying answers. Now that I had a baby brother, I was happy, but Mary, my sister, did not seemed to be pleased at all. Twice I caught her crying. She had been sent around to Auntie Mary's to stay. Relatives came and went and most of them were in tears too. I asked about Harold, as I had not heard him crying, only to be told that he also had gone to Auntie Mary's, just for the time being.

The following day I came into the house to find Dad leaning on the mantelpiece with his head on his arms. 'I wish I was dead. I wish I was dead,' he kept saying. He must have realised suddenly that I was there and turned around to face me. I noticed that his eyes were red. I asked if I could see Mother, but he just mumbled something and quickly left the room.

It was all rather confusing—and there had been other strange things happening of late. For one thing, I had come in from play to find some men taking something up the stairs; I was not sure what it was as it was covered by a sheet, but it looked awfully like a box. When I asked them about it I was ushered out to play. What I did notice was that the door of Mother's bedroom had been sealed all around with white paper. Why did all those people keep looking at me and mumbling, particularly

Mrs Francis from across the road; she had given me a penny for no apparent reason, and I thought she was still cross with me since I had broken her window with a ball a few days ago.

One morning I was taken to stay with Auntie Hannah, a few doors away. I was given some sweets and a comic and told to stay indoors. It was so bewildering. On a nice day like this they usually told me to go outside and play in no uncertain terms, especially when Mother wanted to get on with her work. Also, why were Auntie Hannah's front blinds drawn? Come to think of it, so were the blinds of some of the other houses in the street.

After lunch, Dad called for me and took me home. We entered to find quite a number of people in the front room, mostly neighbours, but one or two strangers were there. Some of the ladies had handkerchiefs to their faces and did not look very happy. I ran over to Dad and stood by his side. It was then I saw the long yellow box on a stand over by the fireplace. One of those horrible coffins I used to go with Mother to see. In front were bunches of flowers, very pretty, but I hated them because they smelled sort of sickly. People began to walk by the box and as they passed Dad they shook his hand and muttered something. Quite a few neighbours mumbled some words to me but I couldn't understand what they said, whilst one or two pressed coins into my hand. This was great, I thought, as I looked down at the coins. There was even a small silver one, too. I was not taking too much notice of the proceedings as I was more concerned about what I could buy. Sweets, choco-lates—oh yes, a 'Lucky Bag' for Mary, there were all sorts in those. Dad liked 'England's Own', the chocolate caramels. What about Harold? Well, maybe a lollypop for him to lick would do. Yes, and Mother, what about her? I looked up at Dad and said, 'Where's Mother?'

There was a hush as all the mumbling stopped and everyone looked at me, then turned their gaze to Dad. There was a few seconds' silence, and then Dad picked me up and walked over to the fireplace where the box was.

I looked down and there was Mother in a white dress, looking very pale. I leaned towards her and said, 'Mother— what—' Dad cut me short.

'Shh—Bobby—Mother's dead. She's gone to heaven.'

Dad put me down. There was a silence. Dead? I felt like I wanted to cry but didn't. Mother had told me about those people in coffins. They were only shells and the real people had gone to heaven and were happy. I remembered that boy on Whalley Road who had gone to heaven. He was in one of those boxes and he had a sore on his lip.

'When will she come back from heaven, Dad?'

Dad looked at me and said, 'In a while. Now why don't you go out and play.' Outside in the sunlight I thought about Mother being in heaven and wondered when I would see her again. I didn't feel too sad as my mind was really on the sweets. My problem was deciding what to buy from the corner shop; Mrs Hickson had such a good selection—toffee potatoes and peas, liquorice allsorts, Pomfret Cakes, Fry's chocolate bars, sugared almonds, dolly mixtures, liquorice pipes, tiger nuts . . . so many things to choose from.

In bed that night I thought again about Mother. I knew I would see her again, but it was hard to decide how long it might be. One week, two weeks, or would it be before Christmas, because that was such a long way off. Then I remembered something else.

'Dad! Dad!' I called downstairs.

Dad came running up the stairs. 'What is it, son?'

I reached down for my trousers at the foot of the bed and

dug into one of the pockets. I brought out what was now a tangle of sticky sweets.

'Here's Mother's sweets, I forgot.'

The next piece, by Mahima Price, was written as a response to exercise four. One point that may not be clear: the 'mother' she refers to is her adoptive mother.

Adoption Papers   Mahima Price

I remember it as blue, this paper, this clue. Actually, it is a dirty brown colour. It was probably beige back then. Now it has the creases, the yellowing of age. Like me. I smile to myself. Well, it is almost my age. *Order of Adoption in the matter of (strange name, a stranger's name)*, followed in brackets by *to be known as Ann. And in the matter of the Child Welfare Act, 1939, Part XIX*, blah, blah, blah.

There follow six columns headed *Particulars of the child proposed to be adopted*. Only one column is filled in. The stranger's name *to be known as Ann, born 19th April, 1951, at Crown Street Women's Hospital, Father's name: Blank, Mother's maiden name: ...... Mother's Christian name: ....*

There she is!

It is that kind of official paper, with watermarks I can't read. *In the Supreme Court of N.S.W. in Equity No. 734* (pencilled in red) *of 1951.*

As I recount this in 1992 I have an abiding image of a lone figure, myself, walking through a cemetery. There are all these gravestones claiming that here, where there is no sign of life, there was life. These stones, however, bear only names, no details. No details of the life, just that it had existed. Yet somehow, it is as though I, the onlooker, am the ghost.

There is so much death in this paper, dealt with quickly, efficiently, by the Machine, administered by strangers.

I remember the day I first held this paper in my hand. I was twelve. I was captivated by my mother's carved wooden box, the mysterious one she kept in the bottom drawer of her dressing table. So, seizing some opportunity afforded by her absence, I invaded. I wish I could say investigated, but it was pure, unadulterated snooping. I almost said 'invasion of privacy'. How can retrieving information about oneself be an invasion of another's privacy? When you are adopted, any such retrieval is deemed an invasion of privacy, which is guarded zealously by the Law. The fact is that I should never have seen this paper, let alone possessed it. My possession of it I owe to the insight, love and (still) illegal action of my mother. She gave it into my possession when I was in my mid–thirties. Then and now I have no legal right to it.

I digress. I was twelve. Deeply religious, deeply distressed, often depressed. The good Catholic girl blossoming into womanhood. Sin lurked everywhere: in our bodies; in our minds; in what we committed and omitted; and, as women, in our very beings. The impure thoughts of men were our doing, their impure actions our fault. My consolation, my salvation, lay in my absolute devotion, the spiritual nurturance of the Church.

I found the paper. Guilt! I should not see this. I unfold it. I should not do this. My eyes scan to *Mother's maiden name:* ...... *Mother's Christian name:* ...... I drink it in.

My eyes are riveted by the Blank next to *Father's name.* A puzzle of a thousand pieces rushes together in my mind. The princess dies of shame. 'Mortal sin, girls, is the absence of God.' Sister Concepta stared at us, each one of us. Her eyes drilled into me, unleashing the white-hot, searing pain. 'When a person commits a mortal sin, they knowingly banish

God from their lives. Girls, don't let yourselves be lured into mortal sin by the promise of mere bodily pleasure . . . blah, blah, blah.' Her voice recedes as the pain forces me out of my body. Somehow, I watch myself from somewhere near the ceiling, the thousand-pieced picture flooding my mind with the answers to a thousand questions. I am not supposed to be here! God did not plan me! I was conceived in God's absence. There is no plan for me. In a microsecond, my dis-ease, my loneliness, my aloneness were explained.

5

WORKSHOP THREE
Bringing it to life—Detail

*Slow down now, touch what is around you, and out of care
and compassion for each moment and detail, put pen to paper
and begin to write.*

NATALIE GOLDBERG

On a morning like any other morning, I walked into the backyard and saw sunlight glowing on an old bench. My tousle-haired son sat there eating his breakfast in the morning light. His arms looked soft on the old wood, which had stood in the rain and sun for years before he was born.

Later I walked down the hill to the ferry on my way to university. The path led down through a tangle of tree ferns, gum trees and lantana. Underfoot I could feel the damp ground and all around pennies of light shifted on the mosaic of brown and yellow leaves on the steps. In the dim green I saw a red lily. It was still and passionate, the leaves folded away from the flower like broad spears.

The path reached the bottom of the hill and wound along the shoreline until it reached the ferry wharf. I saw an old man with a white beard in a dinghy, bobbing up and down on the sparkling water as he rowed towards shore. The headland behind him was golden sandstone, weathered by wind and sea.

This was a morning many years ago. I have remembered it because, for no known reason, I was paying attention. Most days I got up, had breakfast and went to class as a matter of habit. This day, the veil of habit was torn and I saw the fine detail of the world around me. It was as if the world had been made that morning.

A Russian literary critic of the 1920s, Viktor Shklovsky, remarked that 'Habit devours work, clothes, furniture, one's wife, and the fear of war.' In other words, habit stops us from actually seeing the objects around us, the people close to us, and even our own emotions. Do you find in your own life that you don't actually 'see' the pictures on the wall of your home, or the books on the bookshelf, because they are so familiar?

Such habit causes 'life to be reckoned as nothing', Shklovsky said, but he went on to argue that the purpose of art (writing, in our case) was to tear the veil of habit, to defamiliarise, or to 'make strange'. He didn't mean to make odd, necessarily, but to remake experience so that we feel and see it as if for the first time, with the veil of habit removed. He also said the function of art was to 'restore the sensation of life; to make one feel things'.

'Restoring the sensation of life' is one of the purposes of writing a life. When people read your story you will want them to feel something of what it has been like to be you in the world. To remove the veil of habit and restore life, it is necessary to look at the world with fresh awareness.

This kind of awareness is the natural gift of childhood. A child is seeing the world for the first time. Sand underfoot is hot, the smell of crushed gumleaves is pungent, the earth under the geraniums by the back step is damp. The world is new and the child absorbs every detail. Almost everyone writes well about their childhood because, as they return to it in memory, they write what they see with their child's awareness, absorbed in the world around them. Such fine attention translates into vivid detail.

The question is, how can you bring those childhood eyes into later periods of your life and into the present? Doing this doesn't mean you should look innocently at the world—that is impossible; nor should you look naively—that would be foolish. It does mean 'mindfulness', as Buddhist teaching puts it, in your way of seeing the world. Put habit aside and be awake to your life and to the world around you. Become attentive to the experience or person you are writing about.

We each have our own specific knowledge as well, details from our area of work or our passion. As the American educator Laurence J. Peter said, 'The seaman tells stories of winds, the ploughman of bulls; the soldier details his wounds, the shepherd his sheep.' It can be fascinating to layer in those details that you know so well, that give the flavour of your world.

When you write about any period, try to remember your individual details. Most people go to school, have jobs, have relationships, but the details of your school, work and friendships are unique. What posters did you have on the wall of your bedroom when you were a teenager? What did your best friend look like? What went through your mind the first time you saw your baby's face? Write your unique details.

Which details?

How do you know which details to include? Random or excessive detail can become tedious. You have probably listened to someone tell you all about their trip to Europe, and despite it being an interesting topic, you become bored. The fact is, the mind cannot absorb too many details: it turns off at a certain point and you stop listening.

It is important, then, to be selective with the details you choose. Use 'telling detail', detail that conveys something significant. If the fact that your mother always wore lipstick, even around the house, means something to you, include that detail. You don't have to also include the shape of her face or the way she ate if these are not significant.

Include memorable details, even if they seem unusual or out of place. These mark the uniqueness of your experience. I remember, for example, that when I heard of a dear friend's fatal brain haemorrhage, I first thought, 'Now she won't be able to finish my curtains.' It seems heartless that I should have thought such a trivial thing. But this is a real detail of real life, not a sweetened Hollywood version, and including such a detail helps to convey the jerky state of mind that sudden tragedy can cause.

Go back in your mind to the events you want to write about. Spend some time moving about the scene, looking at things and people. Then you will be ready to start writing with well-observed detail.

Write the names

Part of including precise details is giving each thing its individual name. Instead of writing 'trees', write banksia, snow gum, weeping willow, dogwood; instead of writing 'birds', write magpie, crimson rosella, blue wren; instead of writing 'songs', write 'Moondance', '(I Can't Get No) Satisfaction', 'Space Oddity'. It will help bring the specific tree or bird or song to readers' minds if you can name it. Giving places or events their particular names makes them more memorable. Even if your readers have not seen or heard of it themselves, it still makes the writing more colourful, more interesting. I have never seen the Souk El Attarine in Tunis, for example, but when I read those words a more vivid picture forms in my mind than the words 'market in Tunis'.

As you try to write the details, use concrete words, which appeal to the senses and imagination, rather than abstract words, which appeal to the analytical mind. For example, the concrete words 'moonlight on black water' evoke the sensory experience, while the abstract word 'beauty' describes the interpretation of this experience. Your writing will be more powerful if you name the original experience and let your readers see the beauty for themselves.

This doesn't mean you should load your writing down with description. Too much description, too many adverbs and adjectives, can clutter the writing, make it feel heavy-handed.

Despite what we share, despite the apparent ordinariness of all that we have in common, each life is unique. You are the only one who has lived your life. Your details are unique. Writing them will reveal the wonder in the ordinariness of life.

For more on the significance of details, and especially sensory details, see Workshop ten: Madeleines and unicorns— Sensory detail.

Reading

Purple Threads   Jeanine Leane

The country baked hard in January. Sweat dripped like much-needed rain from the red necks and burnt noses of the pig farmers as they slaved in the hot sun to dig wallows for their suffering sows. Giant white sows, heavily pregnant, sweltered the long days away in the thick grey mud.

The women in town sat in their cotton print dresses on cool verandahs of blue-grey river stone and fanned themselves with imitation oriental fans as they drank weak tea from fine bone china cups. From time to time they pulled crisp white, embroidered handkerchiefs from their handbags and wiped away the sweat that fell in big greasy sheaths of foundation and scented powder from their faded faces. Their mascara ran like black tears. The sun glinted a spectrum of coloured rays from their tinted hair.

The stones that sat in the dry creek beds braced their bleached faces against the midday sun and stared back at the thirsty land. At the edge of the crops on the plain, brown snakes rattled the hollow wheat and the ears clicked eerily in the hot wind. A spark could ignite a huge firestorm of dry grasses and grains that would burn like a furnace. The women at home always worried about bushfires and snakes.

Babies born between November and January might not see rain till August. The sound of it teeming against the tin roofs would see them screaming hysterically at their mothers' breasts. If it did rain in summer the smell was so strong and so sweet against the dry that I'd think nothing of flinging myself face down in the dust just to breathe it all in. When big drops pounded on my back I'd emerge, mud-faced and ecstatic, to dance in the rain with my sister.

The farmers, their wives and the townspeople were always amazed and dismayed at the changing of the seasons. Aunty Boo said they were gammon because the country always turns. The seasons turned and turned again as the river swelled and shrank, dictating the course of all lives surrounding it.

In the August rains the Murrumbidgee would swell. Sometimes it would devour the trees on the flood plain. As the waters shrank the river gums were adorned for months afterwards with the slender skeletons of the cattle and sheep swept away in flash floods. As the bog brown waters receded further through September, the land was bountiful with ducks, fish, goanna, kookaburra, platypus, frogs, snakes, grass and flowers.

Through October the green faded from the tall grass. The river subsided to a flow. Grass lilies of red, flame, umber, yellow, blue, pink, purple, mauve, cream and white carpeted the hills. November saw the river flow slow and ebb as the grasses turned from olive to russet. The lilies wilted as the sun burned, drawing the last reserves of water from the earth. The musky, stagnant smell of drying water was pungent. In December the grasses were bone and the lilies became brown boles that shook in the hot winds. Moths, butterflies and beetles made their way to the hills for some reprieve from the swelter to come.

The January dryness sapped the life and moisture from the grass and leaves. The earth faded from red to brown to beige. Country baked. Creeks became waterholes and the river struggled. Stranded frogs fled stalking snakes, February frazzled. The earth on the hills baked white and the quartz crystal caught in the sun's rays projected amethyst rose and blue through the long days.

Through March and April the days eased and the evenings began to bite. Night fires were lit. Grasses and reeds sprouted along the river. In May, cool winds blew in from the south, heralding the winter. June as dry, crisp ice that coated the hills and clung to the naked boughs like beads. Ankle-deep emerald grass was sugar-coated with frost. Intricate dew-clad spider webs spanned bare branches. By July blankets of fog engulfed the river and roads. Then the rain set in. August saw big swells and deep water engorge the river again. Country turned and turned again, resilient.

Jeanine Leane appeals to the senses to re-create her experience of the landscape in relation to the seasons and to convey the eternal nature of change. The reader can see and smell and hear the land where she grew up. Especially strong is the use of colour to convey her relationship to place. Read *Purple Threads* for an evocative account of growing up as an Indigenous Australian in the outback.

Writing exercises

1 Ordinary life

Write about an ordinary experience, that is, one that many other people have probably also experienced. It could be a wedding, a birth, an accident, your arrival in a new country. Focus on the particular details of what happened that day rather than the general outline of the event. Make it your own wedding, not just anyone's wedding. Although it is a common experience, you are the only one who has lived it from your perspective. Write it with your unique details. (Fifteen minutes)

2 Uncommon experience

Write about an unusual experience. Perhaps you have ridden camels in Rajasthan, or canoed up the Amazon, or seen someone killed in battle. Try to convey the unique flavour of the experience by concentrating on the particular details. There can be a temptation to overwrite when evoking an unusual experience—keep bringing yourself back to the actual events and detail them with quiet attention. (Fifteen minutes)

3 Appeal to the senses

Write about a place that has been important to you—a house, a café, a foreign city or village, a little beach. You need not have stayed long in the place, but it must be somewhere that has stayed in your memory as a sensory experience. Try to evoke the sensory detail of the place—the sound and sight and smell and feel of it. (Ten minutes)

4 Mementos

Take a memento of a holiday from any period in your life, perhaps seashells, a photograph or a souvenir. Holidays by their nature involve different places and people, and are therefore often more memorable than everyday life. Evoke the place, the people, the events and the mood. (Ten minutes)

Life story writers

Judith Bunn has used exercise three as a starting point to evoke an ordinary morning in Melbourne. Note how she gives emotional weight to the memory in her subtle references to love lost.

A Wet Melbourne Morning — Judith Bunn

I run across Collins Street on a wet slate-like Melbourne morning. Around me the cars are sending up fans of water and tram drivers are robotically dinging their bells as warning but Melbourne people dodge cars and trams with the bravado and disdain of urban matadors. In the dim of early morning the coloured lights reflected on the grey bitumen canvas make everything blurred and indistinct. I hit the mosaic tiles of the arcade, brought into sharp relief by the water, their colours ripening with every wet footstep. I make my way down the tiny cobbled lane, my steps ricocheting like a demented tap dancer's against the shopfronts. The rain is pinging off awnings. There is a flare of a lighter followed by the pungent smell of nicotine as a hardy smoker lights up at an outdoor table. I step inside my favourite café and am enveloped by warmth. The chirrup and murmur of gentle conversation is interlaced by the crack of staccato laughter. The waitress sits me under the radiator and I settle like a snowman under a tropical sun, the heat dribbling down my body, worming its way slowly to my toes. I order my breakfast and tea. As I wait, I look around at the usual push. I don't know anyone but I have names for the regulars. There's Mr No Neck, there are the Baby Lovers, a young couple so obviously in love it makes my heart sink, and there's Che Guevara, the cool dude all in black with the beret, reading something worthy, no doubt. I watch people talking. I can't make out what they are saying by their words but interpret via the pantomime of their hands: palms up/palms down, hands sweeping, fingers like pincers indicating size, a fist for anger.

The never-ending surge and pull back of conversation lulls me, until the whoosh and spurt of the coffee machine jolts me out of reverie. I watch the cloud of steam rise and the aroma of crushed beans steals around the café. My Earl arrives. I wrap my gloved hands around the little white ceramic teapot. After it has brewed enough I stir and listen to the spoon hit the china with a reassuring tinkle. I take the first sip and taste its weediness and feel it burn and course its way from lips to belly. An involuntary sigh of pleasure leaks from my mouth. I watch people pass in the laneway, their brightly coloured umbrellas involved in some synchronised butterfly maypole dance as they bend and weave to avoid hitting each other in the confined space. I listen to Norah Jones singing quietly in the background, something about lost love and broken hearts, or some such nonsense, and I am momentarily crippled by longing for him but my breakfast arrives and diverts me off that road to hell. Fluffy yellow clouds of scrambled eggs, woody strips of crunchy bacon, fleshy bread and strawberry jam, and I am content . . . for now.

6

WORKSHOP FOUR

Bringing it to life—Scenes

You will have a moonlit night if you write that on the mill dam a piece of glass from a broken bottle glittered like a bright little star . . .

ANTON CHEKOV

'Bring it to life' is a mysterious piece of advice often given to writers. It assumes that writers have the power of the gods to give life. People even remark that a writer they admire 'breathes life into his characters'. And, in a sense, writers do give life to characters and to their surroundings. A fiction writer creates imaginary characters, gives them traits and actions and speech; writers of true stories do not create characters but they bestow life by giving the people they know actions and speech on the page. They make events come alive by creating a three-dimensional world on the page.

The well-known injunction 'Show don't tell' sums up this idea of bringing scenes to life—it simply means rather than recounting everything as if you are telling the story over a cup of tea, show us at least some of what happened as if you were acting out the events on a small stage, dramatising the events and people in your story. Showing and telling are sometimes also called 'scene' and 'summary', which indicates the difference between the two approaches. Both are necessary in life writing.

Perhaps the easiest way to see the difference between showing and telling is to compare two accounts of the same event.

Passage A—Telling (summary)

While I was in India I stayed at an ashram in a huge shed with hundreds of other Foreign Ladies. I felt lonely and alienated and it made me judge everyone around me in a harsh and nasty way. I read books while the others were out of the shed and pretended to meditate when they were around so they wouldn't question me in broken English. I remember when I went out one morning I was unpleasant to a perfectly innocent American girl because her naive manner and flowery sari irritated me.

Passage B—Showing (scene)

The chanting stopped suddenly and I knew the others would return to the shed in a few minutes. I closed my book, *A Passage to India*—I was always appropriate with my novels—and sat up and crossed my legs in an approximate lotus position. No one would speak to me if I looked as if I were meditating.

Opening my eyes a little, I saw the German woman on the next mattress slip out of her sari and begin her yoga in

T-shirt and underpants. She looked supple, her limbs at ease even as they stretched. My body felt thick, as if the blood had congealed in my veins. I wanted to cry out, to wail and frighten all the Foreign Ladies. Instead I went to the bathroom, put on bright red lipstick and went out into the morning, blinking as I stepped into the brightness.

The grounds were crowded with dusty buses parked in every available space and, between them, women untied bundles and children chased each other. The smell of coriander and turmeric drifted from the open-air kitchen. I bumped into a blonde American woman I'd seen in the meal queue.

'What's going on?' The words sounded pinched, as if my throat were closing over.

'A festival of *saddhus*. Isn't it wonderful!' Her scrubbed face beamed. Her just-washed blonde hair was plaited severely down her back and she wore a pale floral sari. I felt pleased with my vicious red mouth.

'Where are the *saddhus*?'

'They are with Swami. They have come from all over India. They wander across the country and their only destination is Truth.'

'So I've heard.' Her unquestioning eyes and ecstatic twanging grated. And her floral sari. At least Indian women wore defiant crimson and emerald and sapphire blue. Westerners, I decided instantly, shouldn't be allowed to wear saris—they always look so prim.

'And do you think you would like to be a *saddhu*?'

'I'd be anything Swami wanted me to be. I believe he wants me to teach in Hawaii. That's where I'm from. That's where I can do most good for Swami.'

'I suppose so. And the beaches are nice too.' The American's eyes clouded uncertainly and she tugged her sari around her shoulders. I tried to smile but it didn't work so I walked away abruptly.

In Passage A, the author is telling you how she felt. There is no evidence of this, however, no actions or dialogue, and you may not be convinced or even interested. It is told or summarised from the outside and there is no room for you to make up your own mind about what was happening. At any rate, the account would probably not arouse any emotional or moral response in you because there is nothing in it to remember, nothing to appeal to your senses. The experience has been interpreted and the interpretation, rather than the experience itself, has been written.

In Passage B you can see and hear the alienation turning to sour criticism. You don't have to be told how the author feels, you can see and feel it for yourself. 'Showing' mimics life, in that all we get in lived experience is what people do and say—there is no analysis or interpretation running alongside the situation. We 'read' the situation and interpret it ourselves. Similarly, you read this passage and interpret it yourself from your own knowledge and experience. The writer is not controlling your response, there is space for you to react. Your senses respond to the sights and the sounds and you make up your own mind.

Of course, you are not really seeing or hearing anything. It is the illusion of writing, which makes you feel you have seen and heard and smelled an event, which has existed for you only as words on a page. This is the magic of words, that they have the capacity to create not only events but people to whom we respond as if we knew them ourselves. How do you create this sense of a three-dimensional world?

Appeal to the senses

The writer gives us the feeling of knowing people we've never met and being at events we've never experienced by 'tricking' the mind into believing it is receiving information from the senses. The 'trick' in writing is to evoke your world, your life, so that the mind receives the information as coming from the senses. That is, write the sound, smell, feel, taste and look of your life. Then the reader's body reacts—her heart beats faster, or his mouth waters—and now the reader is living your life!

Instead of just telling us about your beloved grandfather or your teasing uncle, create a scene that shows us. Instead of telling us about what happened that day in the schoolyard, let us see and hear what went on. Write the bell ringing in the background, write the buzz of the flies around a sweaty face, the meat pie with tomato sauce left on the bench.

Dialogue

When you first start writing conversation you may find that it sounds formal and stiff. This is because writing is structured differently from speech. Hardly anyone speaks in perfect grammar. Speech is looser in structure and contains more fragments, more repetitions, and more 'filling-in' words. In speech, people rarely say anything precisely and they do not recount what they are doing. That is why speech in soapies often sounds false—characters say exactly what they mean and recount large chunks of their activities to move the story along.

To write a conversation effectively, you need to break a lot of the rules of written grammar. Listen to real conversation for a while. Then try to write the way people talk. You will find that it is probably too repetitious and perhaps almost incoherent when you try to read it on the page. Cut it back for the effect of 'natural' speech. For instance, you don't necessarily have to write all the 'hellos' and all the 'umms' for conversation to sound natural.

Make sure everyone doesn't sound the same. Each person has a different rhythm of speech and uses different words. Vary the lengths of each individual's speeches and use their characteristic words and phrases. This might include swearing, which some people feel uncertain about using. If you are aiming for authenticity then it may be necessary to convey character, age or attitudes.

You may find that you remember an incident but cannot remember exactly what everyone said. It doesn't matter. Hardly anyone remembers exactly what anyone said. But you can remember the gist of it. That is enough to create the dialogue you need to bring it to life. Approximate what people said, use their characteristic words and phrases. Let them speak.

You may feel uncomfortable putting words into the mouths of your family and friends, knowing that this may not be what they actually said. You may feel it is a kind of lie to make up someone else's words. The truth is, writing *is* a kind of lie. It pretends to be life, to be flesh and blood and breath; it is an astounding, bald-faced pretence. But sometimes, most times, the truth needs the help of 'Let's pretend' to be conveyed with any power. Write what is likely, create the living, breathing feel of your family and your times. It will be more truthful, more real, than a flat, factual retelling of events.

Action

Dialogue does not exist in a vacuum and there is much in life that is unspoken. Writing the action, the movement of life, is a vivid part of showing. Watch the movements of people as they are talking, or when they are performing any kind of action, and you will see that we 'read' a great deal about what people are feeling, about their personality and even their character, from what they do rather than what they say.

Include the gestures of people as they speak if they are relevant. Include what people do, how they go about things, how they walk. For instance, describe your father in action—cleaning a camera, dressing for a party, eating dinner—rather than writing a static portrait. Vivid writing is more a movie or play than a photograph.

Setting

Place, time, weather, dress—all these elements and more are part of showing. Where things happen—in a paddock, around a dining table, in a bazaar—whether it is early in the morning or mid-afternoon, during a snowstorm or a sweltering summer evening, all 'show' the reader more about your life. You might think it is 'padding', but setting is not just background, not just the context of a life: it affects the life. Look at how filmmakers use details of a room—colour, light, furniture, ornaments—to give information about class, character and ambitions, as well as to create mood. Use the senses to help create the 'space' in which your life has happened. Make sure the words are precise: instead of saying a 'lovely' room, evoke the oval shape, the wood panelling, the long windows looking down over the rose gardens.

Show everything?

'Show, don't tell' is an absolute piece of advice that you are not meant to follow absolutely. Your life story would be much too long if you dramatised every event in it. Besides, lots of events do not bear dramatising; it would give them a significance they never had in real life.

Showing is like a close-up in a film, emphasising or drawing attention to that particular material. It pulls the reader closer emotionally, makes them feel it's all happening right in front of their eyes. It creates character and develops narrative in a vivid and engaging way.

Telling is more like a long-shot, giving an overview of the situation in general and creating a sense of distance or emotional space. It can be descriptive and can create a rich impression of a period or person. It's useful for creating a strong narrative thread, establishing a narrating voice, recounting important background and exploring ideas.

Too much telling and the reader can lose interest. It is like a conversation where only one person speaks and everyone else has to listen. The listeners long to hear a different voice, to see some action, to have the chance to respond. It can also become too abstract and analytical and make the reader feel emotionally disengaged from the characters.

On the other hand, too much showing can make the reader feel it's all at the same intense level, with no room for a breather. Too much emotional closeness can be just as much a problem for the reader as too much distance. It can also bog the story down in its moment-by-moment reconstruction of events.

As you can see, showing and telling also affect pacing—how slow or fast the story moves. There is more on this idea in Workshop fourteen: The magic spell—More narrative.

Both showing and telling are necessary. Show your readers some of the lived experience of your life so they will be engaged and involved in the story you are recounting. Tell your reader of events and ideas when you want to cover time more quickly or when you want to explore your thoughts. Some writers can get away with using just one or the other—Frank McCourt's *Angela's Ashes* is almost all 'showing', Vladimir Nabokov's *Speak, Memory* is almost all 'telling'. For most writers, a rhythmic to-and-fro between the two is probably the most effective way of exploring and revealing their experience.

Reading

In My Mother's Hands   Biff Ward

I know it was one of the first times I felt the sense of doom which later became familiar. It's a knowledge children have which has no words but is made up of angles of light through a window, the quality of an absence, the rush of feelings with nowhere to go, a miniscule tightening of skin and lips.

She's not here, I said.

I want an apple, said Mark.

Get one.

He walked through to the dining table and reached to the blue crystal bowl which had been a wedding present. He stood munching while I climbed up the shelves of the kitchen cupboard so I could reach the Lactogen tin at the top.

Here's the sultanas, I said, swinging down with one hand while the other clutched the navy-and-gold tin. We can eat them while we wait.

We played in the garden, slow motion play with stones and sieves in the dirt, our ears pricked for the sound of someone, anyone, coming up the side path. The sun was nearly behind the plane tree in Mrs Courtney's yard when we heard steps. We ran to the corner that looked down the narrow strip of black between our house and Dorothy's picket fence.

Dad. Dad. We ran to him.

She's not here. Mum's not here.

He bent over and squeezed us each to him, then put us down, straightened his shoulders and went inside. We followed him, our beacon. We followed him as he made a tour of the house, coming back to the dining-room sideboard where she kept her handbag. He sat heavily on one of the cream chairs with its leather seat of mottled green and black. He opened his arms so Mark sat on a knee and I leaned against his leg.

I have to go and find her, he said in a heavy voice. He looked from me to Mark. Will you go into Dorothy's and wait for me there?

We nodded.

Dorothy had curly black hair and she smiled a lot. She was bathing her son, Little Mark, who was two. I could help with that.

It was dark when Dad came back. I heard him say 'police station' to Dorothy while we were trying to show Little Mark how to eat his bread and butter with his mouth closed. I saw Dad kiss Dorothy on her neck near her ear as we left.

Where was she? I asked as we went up Dorothy's yard to the hole in the fence.

It's okay, she's back now. Don't worry, he said.

When I was in bed, nearly asleep, their voices rose.

I had to do it! she shouted. I had to go there!

Giving yourself up to the police is mad. He was trying to control his voice, trying not to yell.

I should be in gaol, she said.

Oh, God, he groaned.

How had he known where to find her? What took him to the police station on Military Road with its bricks the colour of dried blood? Maybe she'd done it before.

And what of Mark and me? What effect was her strangeness having on us?

On clear nights when one of them went to draw the curtains, I would say, No, leave them open.

When they left the room and I was in darkness in my narrow bed, I twisted my head to look out the window and up into the sky. The beam of my eye rose over the fence, the backyards, out beyond Mosman, beyond Sydney even, to a larger place where anything was possible and there I could search until I found the star that was mine. I stared at it until I had to blink. Trying to believe that it was possible that somewhere there was a planet just like ours with a girl just like me, lying in her bed which had the same sheets and bedcover as mine, staring at my world, yearning to find me in return.

Ward delicately presents the unspoken fears of a child where the adult world is observed but not comprehended. She begins by telling the reader of her 'sense of doom', then moves to showing a series of small scenes that let the reader see the source of the anxiety. This allows the reader to feel the emotional distress of the child, from the child's perspective. Read *In My Mother's Hands* for a sensitive portrayal of a family in which the mother is mentally ill, and the father, while accomplished in his field, is unable to help or save his wife.

Writing exercises

1 Five words

In one minute, write five words naming character traits of a family member or someone else important in your life. Use abstract words like generous or suspicious, not concrete words like tall or fat or blonde. Then select one of the words and a write a scene from memory 'showing' that trait. Do not include the word or any of its synonyms anywhere in the piece. The reader should be able to see the trait in the actions, dialogue, setting and mood of the scene you write. You can, of course, do this for every word in the list. You will come up with some good pieces to include in your life story. (Twenty minutes)

2 Tell and show

There are two parts to this exercise. First, recall a friendship or love affair. Tell the story of how you first met and got to know each other in no more than half a page. (Ten minutes)

Second, write the same story, this time *showing* how you first met and how your friendship developed, using specific incidents, dialogue and description. Leave a day or so between doing the two parts of this exercise so you can take a fresh approach in the second part. This is likely to be pages longer than the first, even though it deals with the same material. (Thirty minutes)

3 An argument

Write the dialogue of a significant argument. It may be with a friend, lover, parent, son or daughter, business associate or opponent. Try to be as fair as you can in representing each person's point of view. Remember that dialogue happens in specific places, so include the location and whatever else may have been affecting the conflict, for example, an extremely hot day, or a sharp wind, or loud techno music. (Thirty minutes)

4 Vague memories

Select an incident you have always remembered even though you can't recall the details. Bring it to life by writing possible details, for example, the colour and style of the dress you may have worn, and the conversations you may have held. Think about the location, the weather, what other people were wearing. I don't mean you should write details that are completely imaginary but to use memories from other times to create a convincing picture. If your husband usually wore his sleeves rolled up, write that his sleeves were rolled up, even if you can't remember noticing his sleeves on that particular day. Write the words of conversations that you know happened, even though you cannot actually remember a single phrase. This is a good freeing-up exercise for people who feel they cannot put words into other people's mouths. (Thirty minutes)

Life story writers

In an extension of exercise one, Susan Wilson has written six short scenes from her father's life to 'show' his character without comment or judgement.

Six Scenes from a Life
Susan Wilson

1

He sits in the lounge room next to the table where the box of God's promises is kept.

'Daddy, Daddy.' I clamber onto his knee.

'What does this word say?' and I hold up my book to point to the word.

He grasps each arm and lifts me down.

'Work it out yourself,' he says.

2

My mother stands outside the bedroom door.

'Stan, talk to me. Nothing is solved if you don't tell me what is wrong.'

I watch from the corner of the hall.

'Please,' she begs.

It is three days before he speaks again.

3

He sat opposite me in the middle of the three-seater lounge. Without preamble he said, 'Your mother is worried about you.'

I was pre-anorexic and could hang my handbag on my hipbones.

'What about you, Dad? Are you worried about me too?'

He crossed his arms, narrowed his eyes to slits and said nothing in a very loud voice.

4

Dad sat beside Mum's hospital bed. No longer conscious, her lungs filled with fluid so every breath was a scream for oxygen. The staff indicated they could make her more comfortable with morphine.

'No,' said Dad. He sat upright in his chair, hand palm out in a stop signal.
'Only God takes life.'

5

When my father moved to a retirement village, I helped him clear the basement workshop. He had every tool known to man.
'These are good as new, Dad.' I added another to the pile.
He shrugged.
'I bought one every time I was angry with your mother.'

6

Dear Dad, wherever you are, do you remember your last words to me?
'I think I may have missed out,' you said, in a little boy voice.
Have you seen what you missed out on, Dad, through that hair-line crack in your carefully constructed fortress?

7

WORKSHOP FIVE
Finding your voice

If only one could write as one talks . . .

HENRY MILLER

All writers have a distinctive voice, which conveys a sense of their individual being on the page. Voice is how the writer 'sounds' as the narrator, the person telling the story. It is constructed by personality and experiences and is unique to each writer.

Your writing voice will reveal more about the kind of person you are than anything you write about because it contains your characteristic approach to yourself, others and the world. If your approach is laconic then, probably, your voice on the page will be laconic; if your approach is playful then your voice will be as well. Your voice on the page will be most at ease when it echoes your speaking voice.

But which speaking voice? We all use different voices for different people and different situations. When we speak to our mothers, we will no doubt use a different voice from the one we use for a lover, different again for our employees, or boss, our children, sisters, or the shop assistant at the department store. We each modify our voice according to the relationship, showing different aspects of ourselves each time, so much so that when we have to speak at the same time to two different people with whom we have widely different relationships it can be very awkward! So how do we know which voice to use when we are writing for an unknown audience?

And then there are all the inner pressures on voice. All the books you have read can get in the way and influence you to write in the voice of writers you admire; if you try to write in a 'literary' voice, you may end up sounding as if the books you've read are stuck in your throat. Or you might be worried about what people will think of you and your voice will become stiff and 'proper'; or hiding something and your voice becomes jerky and evasive; or trying to please everyone and your voice becomes bland and over-sweet; or feeling angry and sorry for yourself and your voice becomes accusing or manipulative; or feeling superior or righteous and your voice becomes distorted with pride.

But you do have an authentic voice, the one you use when you feel accepted, when all the aspects of yourself come together, the voice you use when talking to someone whom you trust and with whom you feel 'at home'.

Some tips for finding an authentic voice

- Imagine that your only reader is a trusted friend. Someone who accepts you as you are, someone with whom you can talk about anything without self-consciousness. You don't have to try to impress them, but neither are you self-indulgent as you may be in a diary or journal.

- Try not to imagine what other people will think of you when they read your story. Everyone will think something different—we can't control that in life, let alone on the page. Every time you think *Oh, what will my mother, or sister, or the woman at the yoga class think?* firmly put it aside and keep writing!

- Try not to manipulate the reader. That is, try not to get them to feel sorry for you, or angry for you, or impressed and amazed by you. Let your stories speak for themselves. Most readers react strongly against a voice that is pushing them to feel in a certain way.

- Read your writing out aloud to someone else or onto a recording device every now and then, to check the voice. See if the rhythms and expressions sound like you. Or ask someone else to read it aloud to you to see how it 'sounds'.

- Try the 'secret writing' in the exercises section of this chapter. It will allow you to practise your voice without anyone hearing—or judging—for a while.

Aspects of voice

Tone

Your tone of voice when you speak varies according to the situation and it is the same for writing. The underlying voice is the same, we know it is the same person writing, but the tone changes according to writer's attitude to the event. The tone may be philosophical, ironic, serious, lighthearted, mocking, detached, tentative—or any other possible attitude. Tone can be very flexible, but overall it needs to be reasonably consistent—one very sarcastic section in an otherwise serious account might be jarring, for example.

Point of view

Point of view, or perspective, describes where you are 'looking from' as you write. For autobiographical writing it sounds as if it ought to be simple: you are writing from your own point of view, from the 'first person' (I), so that's all there is to it. But even within yourself there are different perspectives. Writing about a traumatic event from the perspective of the following day will be different in both detail and interpretation from a perspective ten years later; writing from the point of view of a child will be different to that of an adult.

You may find yourself falling into a child's point of view when you write about childhood incidents. It can give a fresh childlike quality to your writing. On the other hand, writing from a child's perspective can be limiting, or it can become overly 'cute', or claustrophobic.

Your point of view of incidents will not necessarily be the same as that of others who were there at the same time. Who is to say whose view is correct? You are the only person looking at your life from your vantage point, and you are free to say what you can see from there.

While autobiographical writing is almost always in the first person, you can vary it by writing about yourself in the third person (he, she). This can be an effective antidote if you feel you are becoming self-indulgent and is also useful if you find an incident too painful to write.

Tense

Tense (whether you write about events as if they have happened in the past, are happening in the present, or will happen in the future) can affect the voice because it reveals point of view.

Most autobiographical writing is in the past tense from an adult perspective. A change in tense means there has been a change in perspective, and therefore a change in voice and level of language occurs. For example, 'I am Daddy's special little girl' (present tense, child's perspective) has a completely different voice from 'I was my father's favourite child' (past tense, adult perspective). Generally, a piece of writing is more coherent if it doesn't change tense too often. You will probably find it easiest to write in the past tense, but every now and then something may seem so immediate that you will want to write it in the present tense. Go ahead, break the general rule. Writing in the present tense can make events more vivid and can also make the voice more intense, more urgent. Try not to slip back and forth in tense to no purpose as it becomes confusing to the reader.

Remember, voice is cultivated by everything we experience and read but it is also an individual characteristic. Write what you think and feel and your voice will become apparent. Being unsure at first you may wobble, becoming too flowery at times, or stiff, or unconfident. Keep writing. Later, as your voice develops, you can go back and edit.

For more on narrating voice, perspective, distance and narrating position, see Workshop twelve: The storyteller's seat—Narrating position.

Reading

The Long Way Home Kate Shayler

Little girl. Standing in a cold room. Alone. Sobbing.

A voice from the other side of the door.

'You're not coming out until you stop that crying.'

Thinking at the voice. Shut up you nothing. You big fat

skinny stick nothing. You're not in my life. Don't say things to me. You're not in it. You're a nothing.

'. . . very naughty girl . . .'

Shouting, 'I want Daddy. Oh Daddy, Daddy.'

Knowing he's in my life. He's mine.

Why did he say we have to live here now? Not with him. I don't want to. I told him I don't want to. I shouted at him. To make him know. Shouted at his back. I don't want to stay here. I want to go home with you. He kept walking. Away. The louder I screamed, the further away he went. Couldn't he hear me? Couldn't you Daddy?

'Daddy. Oh Daddy, Daddy. Please don't leave me here. Please.'

They held onto me, those stick hard hands. They wouldn't let me run after his sad old back. Leaving. The skinny stick things took me and Kenny. Kenny didn't cry. He just made his face all hard and he wouldn't talk. He didn't get shut in the room where cry babies have to stay.

Why doesn't Mummy come? She could make things right. She could cuddle me. Rock me. Make this not be happening. Safe and warm. Big and soft. Daddy said Mummy's dead, said she can't come back. Course she can. I want her. She's got to.

And Kerry. I want baby Kerry. She's ours. I want her. Where is she? Daddy hasn't got her. Is she with Mummy? Well, why can't I go too?

Noises on the other side of the door. Bad noises. Not our noises. I want Mummy.

I had been a perfect child. Not the perfection of the Aeroplane jelly girl on the swing or the angelic toddlers in the Pears soap ads and certainly not the perfection of never being naughty.

No, mine was the perfection of being totally lovable. I was so secure in my mother's love that I felt my perfection at the very centre of my being. Memories of that time are few but I want, I need to take the journey back to them. I need to go back to my family.

My father was a plumber then, in his early sixties. He worked in a factory that has long since been pulled down. My mother, who gave birth to us in her forties, cared for us three kids, her three K's, in our little house at the top of a hill in Marrickville. The pram that took us into the world beyond our house now pushed my memories back into that world where I was perfect . . .

For a long time the only memory I had of my early years was a little girl who might be me, standing alone in that huge, cold room, sobbing.

Then I heard a more gentle voice say, 'You can come out now. Look, here's Kenny. He's not a cry baby. No more of that now or you'll have to go back in there by yourself.'

The child who came out of the room was not me. Not the whole and perfect child. She died in there or perhaps she was lost. The child who came out was broken, frightened, secretive. Alienated from the world that gave her life and self.

Getting lost took moments and years. Finding the child I was is the longest journey I have ever taken. This story and the writing of it are the journey home.

In *The Long Way Home*, Kate Shayler uses the point of view and voice of a child to convey the terror and loss she experienced when she was placed in a home. The intensity of the child's experience is conveyed with short sentences and childish language. When she shifts to an adult perspective, the rhythms of sentences, the level of language and the insights are those of an adult. The voice has changed to a more reflective one, the perspective is outside the situation rather than right inside it. Read this book for the way Shayler moves between the child and adult perspectives as she explores her journey back to the child who was loved and perfect.

Writing exercises

1 Secrets

Select a topic where you are most likely to be wary of other people's opinions, then tell yourself that no one will see it, you will not include it in the final manuscript. Begin with the sentence: *I am the only person who will ever see the following, so I am going to write down exactly what I think and feel.* Continue with the complete freedom of knowing there will be no judgement of what you have written. When you finish, you can even destroy the pages. But before you do, read back over them and see whether the voice has become more honest, whether it has more energy and authenticity. This is a good exercise for writers who feel they cannot openly say what they think and feel. (Thirty minutes)

2 Child/adult

Write about a childhood experience from the point of view of a child. Write in the present tense and with the feelings and thoughts of the child. (Fifteen minutes)

The next day, without re-reading it, write about the same incident, but this time from the position of being an adult. Write it in the past tense, adding in any adult attitudes or insights that you wish. (Fifteen minutes)

3 Friends and others

Imagine that someone in your family is going to read what you are about to write—perhaps a son, or mother, or sister. Then select an event that is difficult for you to be completely open about—for example, your first love, or what you did on your first overseas trip. As you write, keep that particular reader in mind. (Ten minutes)

The next day, try the exercise again, but this time, imagine your reader is a friend with whom you are always open and honest. (Ten minutes)

Compare the voice in the two pieces to see if there is a change in both voice and content.

4 Another view

Write an incident from any time of your life in the first person but from the point of view of someone else who was there at the time. In effect you will be writing about yourself from someone else's point of view. Try this from any number of other people's points of view—a parent, a brother, a teacher, a friend, an enemy. See if your writing voice changes when you are writing from someone else's viewpoint. You may not use the results of this exercise in your life story, but it is a great way to see how point of view can influence voice. (Fifteen minutes)

Life story writers

Samantha Selinger-Morris has a distinctive humorous voice in this story about her college years in Canada.

Borrowing Jeans	Samantha Selinger-Morris

My belly was tight as I pulled open the heavy, curlicue-etched wooden door of Paige's armoire. I ran my eyes up and down her military-neat piles of clothing—categories: flat, flatter, flattest—and then cocked one ear slightly towards the ceiling. Listening for the jagged *c-l-i-c-k-s* of the key entering the front door lock. My synapses were exploding like Pop Rocks.

Paige and my other roommate, Marnie, were close friends. They'd go to parties thrown by the most popular fraternity on the McGill University campus, while I'd sit in bed and read Toni Morrison's *Jazz*, pretending that this was what I'd rather be doing. My tiny room smelled of stale potpourri. Their large white rooms smelled clean, like freshly snapped flower stems.

The three of us were united by one thing, though. We were all dumped at the tail end of last year, our first at the university, by the girls we had originally planned to live with.

Marnie, about five feet tall, had a bob, and brown hair so curly it appeared to grow out from her head horizontally, like the top of a mushroom.

Her father owned junkyards, but she carried herself as if he owned Tiffany's. When she walked, she'd thrust her hips forward and hold her shoulders back, as though every step was being taken poolside, towards a maid holding a silver tray, upon which her martini rested.

Paige was richer. She was four feet eleven and had a clipped, nasal voice. Like a Jewish Lucille Ball, minus the laughter. She liked announcing that her father could do you a favour.

'My dad's guys could help you,' she said to me one day, standing in the middle of the kitchen, one hand on her hip. She lowered her eyelids mid-sentence, and kept them shut for a couple of beats. This is how I imagined the Queen of England must look like when she tells members of her family to stop sucking people's toes.

I was the working-class member of the trio, the tallest, and highly strung, like a schnauzer. If my voice were a bark, it'd have been a snappy yap. I had a talent for feeling hard done by, and complaining to one friend that another must be ignoring me. People just loved this. It's a testament to just how endearing this was that when my friend Lauren dumped me as a room-mate the previous year, it was for Caroline, who was a known kleptomaniac.

I scanned Paige's pile of jeans, looking for her Big Stars. At $150 a pop, these were jeans for throwing back shots with boys named Jordan. (I imagined.) *Ink, seagull grey, TV-static black.* No. No. No. There! The dusk blue ones.

I ripped off my own jeans—frayed Levi's—and wiggled into Paige's. They were four inches too short at the bottom. But, hey, would you look at that? They still fit at the waist. I turned side-ways, sucked in my stomach and looked in the mirror. I smiled, satisfied.

8

WORKSHOP SIX

Structure

*I built a temple in my head . . . Its hallways were as lofty as
a cathedral, and the arch of each window as supple as a bow.
Its corridors were the passages of my own brain.*

LISA ST AUBIN DE TERÁN

Like a bowerbird with his kingfisher feathers and cicada shells,
you have gathered your memories together. They lie tumbled in
a heap, a treasure house of your life with a light now shining on
it, catching some memories and making them glow. Some you
have written down and some are still waiting to be written. By
now you may be wondering, how do I put it all together? How
do I know what to put in and what to leave out?

You could just leave it as a random collection of bits and
pieces. But it seems there is an impulse in humans, as well as
in bowerbirds, that makes us want to order our experience
according to some kind of underlying principle.

But that doesn't mean structure needs to be worked out

before you start. In fact, structure created before the fact of writing is often artificial and limiting. Real structure comes from within the material itself, is not separate from it, which is why I like to leave a discussion of structure until plenty of writing has been done.

Writing is a journey and if you plan every detail of your journey before you start it leaves no room for discovery. Of course, you need a general plan of where you are heading, and you can use this chapter at first to make a rough map of the area, and later, to shape more specifically the material you discover.

What is structure anyway?

Structure is what gives *unity* or wholeness to your writing, the feeling that what is included is meant to be there, contributing to the story as a whole. Without it, memories would be a random collection, difficult to read with sustained interest.

It also creates *cohesion*; helps your writing 'hang together'. Without some kind of structure holding it together, writing may become fragmented and give the impression that it is falling apart.

Structure gives *shape*. As a building's design gives it a distinctive shape, structure gives a sense of form to what we read, pleasing our aesthetic sense.

Most importantly, structure creates *direction* and a sense of there being a *destination*. Without it, a reader will say 'this writing doesn't seem to be going anywhere' which implies that *we expect writing to take us somewhere* as if it were a path—that is, have a direction and a destination. In other words, we expect a memoir, or in fact, any writing, to be 'about' something, to have *meaning*.

Some believe there is no inherent meaning in life, that structure is created by us so that meaning may be created; others believe that structure and meaning are inherent in life. Either way, we depend on structure to make meaning of the written stories of our lives.

Watch children playing with a jigsaw puzzle; the pleasure of each piece joining; the irritation when a piece will not fit. We humans appear to take an innate delight in one part fitting with, connecting to, another and thereby revealing something meaningful. This delight is the basis of structure, the underlying principle of form.

It doesn't mean that everything ought to fit snugly or predictably together—you might be making a collage with overlapping pieces rather than a jigsaw, or the spaces between things might be significant. But it does mean there will be a sense of each thing belonging (unity), in that sequence (coherence), and holding together (cohesion).

Of course, you could have all these elements—unity, coherence and cohesion—and simply end up with a nice orderly arrangement. You could admire it for a bit, but then it would become uninteresting. There's obviously more to it.

Approaches to structure

The practical processes of structure are: the *selection* of events, the *order* that you place them in, and the *emphasis* you give each event. Each of these structural steps contributes to create a sense of what your life has been about, to its meaning. What memories you select, where you place them in relation to other memories, and what emphasis you give them according to space and amount of detail will each affect the meaning. In fact, it would be possible to use the same selected events of a life and change the meaning entirely by changing the emphasis. For example, writing three chapters about the impact of a divorce will create a different meaning than writing one paragraph—the shift in emphasis creates the shift in meaning. In creating or altering the structure of your autobiography or memoir, you are creating or altering its meaning.

The bowerbird instinctively structures his material according to the theme of the colour blue. It is not quite so easy for us; it could take quite a while before we discern what is patterning our writing. It may help to have a few possibilities in mind.

Chronology

This is the most usual way of ordering a life story. It means arranging your material in a time sequence, starting at your birth and continuing stage by stage until the present. Chronology on its own does not create structure—time sequence becomes a structure when there is also an unfolding of stories, themes, ideas or images.

When you arrange the events of your life chronologically, you could use chronological divisions or 'markers' taken from your own interests to help create structure rather than just a time sequence. For example, if you are interested in politics and history and have felt they have been shaping in your life, you could align historical events with your own life; if you are interested in music or literature, you could align songs or books with your life; if you are interested in nature and natural cycles, you could use a 'seasonal' patterning—the spring, summer, autumn and winter of your life.

The chronological divisions you use will depend on your own life. Memory has its own associations, patterns, connections.

It has already developed its own divisions as it has silently gone about its business of storing information. Try to discern your memories' chronological divisions and use them to order your material.

In life, events rarely happen one after the other. Many things happen at once and it is often difficult to tell when events begin and end. A strict chronology just doesn't apply, but chronology need not be a stiff, artificial order. It can be made to ebb and flow, to race forward to the end of an episode and then back to the start of an event running parallel to it. It can be flexible as well as straightforward and easy to use.

Topics

If you are not interested in arranging your experiences in time, try a series of selected topics. Write only about the aspects of your life that come under the topic headings without being concerned whether any event happened before or after any other event. The structure works like a patchwork quilt, or a collage, where pieces are placed according to relationships of colour and texture and patterns, rather than time sequence.

The topics you choose depend completely on what you discern as important in your life: you may choose to write about your relationships, your beliefs, interesting individuals, travels.

A 'framework' may be necessary with a topic structure to hold it together, to give it unity and coherence. The framework could be made of connecting pieces from a particular time or place, for example, you could bring your readers back to your present–time room or garden between each of the topic pieces. You could also use a symbolic image to hold the topics together, such as a jigsaw that the topics fill in, or an album where you write 'snapshots' of your life, or a map with the journey of your life marked on it. In his memoir, *Toast*, English chef Nigel Slater uses the image of food in each of hundreds of small pieces to unify his account of childhood. Eric Rolls uses the five senses to shape *Celebration of the Senses*, in which he explores the physical and emotional experience of the senses. Such frames are appealing as they are shapes we recognise already and offer both variety and cohesion.

Themes

Themes, the underlying issues or ideas in writing, are revealed in patterns of action and in images. In fact, in all the arts, the repetition of an element such as a colour or dance step or musical note or architectural form is used to create a sense of relatedness and meaning. It is drawn from the human response to rhythmic repetition in nature—our delight in the ripple of a mackerel sky, or pleasure in the beat of waves hitting the shore. Such patterned recurrence creates a sense of events happening not at random, but with purpose and meaning. So it is that the repetition of ideas, events and images throughout a life story creates a sense of meaning.

A particular experience might provide the theme. Life-changing events such as a severe illness, a divorce, leaving your homeland, the birth of a child or a 'road to Damascus' illumination can all provide a specific theme. Nothing happens in a vacuum; the lead-up to the episode, the experience itself and its repercussions set natural limits, which at least give you the basic shape of your story as you explore the themes.

When you look at your life you may notice that a particular experience keeps recurring. Perhaps you kept falling in love with the 'wrong' person; you may see that as the theme of your life. Maybe reaching for the stars is your theme, or never giving up, or the search for identity, or being an outsider. Perhaps your theme is a difference which you experience as defining, such as coming from another culture, being disabled, being homosexual. Use your theme to decide what to put in and what to leave out. Instead of including everything you can think of, include only those experiences that relate to the theme. Bring to the fore experiences that reveal your theme, that is, write about them in more detail, open a chapter with them, refer to them in other contexts.

Themes can be underlying, not directly mentioned, or overt, openly addressed. I structured *The Last One Who Remembers* around the overt theme of how stories influence our lives. I wrote stories from my life and fictionalised tales from my great aunts' lives and gradually grouped them into sets of stories such as 'landscape myths' and 'romance and sex fictions'. But there were also underlying themes, for example, the 'butterfly effect' of apparently insignificant lives like the great aunts', the way their quiet actions reverberate in countless lives.

Again, images can be used to strengthen and highlight your themes. In *Ransacking Paris*, the image of the bee, an ancient symbol of communication and creativity, became a unifying image as the fragmentary stories of a year in Paris unfolded. Look at your life for an image that is symbolic of your themes.

Ideas

For some life writers, the main motivation is the exploration of an idea. The events of their life, their memories, are included to illustrate the ideas. The unfolding of an idea is a strong structure as you will only select those experiences that help with the unfolding of the idea. Writing shaped by the desire to explore an idea tends to be more intellectual and the language more abstract—it tends towards the personal essay. Alain de Botton's books are all shaped by ideas—knowing the self, travel, status, work—and only include aspects of his life to illustrate the idea. For more on writing about ideas, see Workshop twenty: Random provocations—Personal essay.

Narrative

Narrative, or story, is the single most powerful way of structuring life writing. Narrative is strong because it arouses the irresistible desire to know 'what happens next'. Because it is so important, the whole of the next workshop explores its possibilities.

The different ways of structuring are not necessarily used separately: chronology must have themes to be more than an orderly list; chronology will also have various narratives and perhaps an overall narrative as well; topics will have sets of stories and a variety of themes. Experiment with the possibilities.

Length

Finding the right length for memoir or life writing is part of finding the form. Memoirs can be any length, but published books of memoir are usually somewhere between 50,000 and 100,000 words. There is no advantage in padding out experience that only requires a short piece. In some cases you will find that an article or essay-length piece will serve your purpose, rather than a book-length memoir. Sometimes a set of stories or essays will be more effective.

Structural steps

Here are some practical steps to starting the structuring process.

First, write a 'ramble' exploring the territory you think you want to write about. This is a means of thinking on the page, a way of mapping out and clarifying what you think you want to do.

Next, brainstorm, that is, write down every topic, person, event and idea that you think you want to write about. It can be a list, or all over the page, but it must be a 'storm', not an already organised arrangement.

Now you can do some rough arranging, grouping stories in a way that, to your organising brain, go together. (Always remembering that there may be other links that only your 'creative' brain will see and which will emerge later on.)

Then, pick one of the elements from your brainstorm and start writing. Pick a piece which seems significant to you, that is, one that has shaped you in some way, perhaps a turning point. There, you are on your way!

Reading

The Old Ways   Robert Macfarlane

At four o'clock the next morning the skylark alarm clocks woke me. A slow mist had filled the valleys. The sky was white above but blue at the horizon line, as though it were a dome and the blueness had run down to its brink. Looking from my long-barrow observatory I understood Thomas's comparison of the high grounds of Southern England to 'several chains . . . of islands or atolls . . . looming dimly through the snowy still mists of morning'. I was on one of the most easterly islands of this archipelago: away to the west, though I could not see them, rose dozens more of the chalk summits.

Those early-day miles were magical, up and down hills, through beech and coppice hazel woods, with a marine light in the beech woods that gave the feeling of walking in cool water. Among the trees, a taste of moss in the mouth; green silence.

Here and there people had used chunks of chalk to write on the grey bark of the trees: initials, stars, or squiggles like the looping signature Corporal Trim's walking stick leaves on the otherwise blank page in Laurence Sterne's *Tristram Shandy*. Chalk is a substance that marks and is easily marked— that writes and is written on. Areas of the Western Front, where Thomas would fight and die, were chalk landscapes, and one of the most affecting cultural outputs of the trench war was the land art that both German and British soldiers made there. These were men who knew their lives were likely to end soon, and the instinct to leave a trace was strong in them. Soldiers chipped out flat lumps of chalk and carved them into hand-sized plaques bearing memorial messages for dead comrades: 'Thiepval 1915, In Memory of Your Wilhelm'. British gunners used chalk nuggets to jot joke messages on the casing of the big shells: 'May It Be A Happy Ending', or 'To Fritz With Compliments'. Sappers on both sides created miles of tunnels through the chalk. Down in that troglodyte world they scored, in idle moments, hundreds of doodles, graffiti and messages into the walls. Many of these are now lost, but near Soissons there remain the outlines of fantastical female figures: summoned from erotic dreams, there in the terrible dark.

By eight o'clock I was on a hilltop by a Bronze Age round barrow, looking onto Luton. I shambled through the town's outskirts, down Gooseberry Hill—a smart little street with neatly trimmed borders and bright bedding plants—past lime trees and health clinics. A postman rang a doorbell, nodded a greeting to me. Cars on the commuter cut-through raced past. Everyone else was starting their day, but I'd already walked ten miles and was tired. I envied them their eagerness. I left Luton's western outskirts along an alleyway between a cemetery and a row of houses.

Then the ground began to lift and I was soon on the summit ridge of Dunstable Downs, where scores of people were having fun. I sat and rested in a cooling wind and watched children flying kites. My legs preserved a ghost sense of stride, a muscle memory of repeated action, and twitched forward even as I rested. My feet felt oddly dented in their soles, like a mark knuckled into soft clay. How had Flann O'Brien put it in *The Third Policeman*? When you walk, 'the continual cracking of your feet on the road makes a certain quantity of road come up into you'.

That day's walking was as hard and bright as the first. I passed through fewer built-up areas, and felt at times as if I were moving covertly from spinney to copse by means of hedgerows and green lanes. One of the woods through which I tramped was white with wild garlic, the air heady with its stink. I followed the perimeter of Whipsnade Zoo and saw five wallabies lolling in the shade of a hawthorn bush.

Thomas's many foot-miles on old chalk paths made him a connoisseur of their particularities. In summer, he walked overgrown lanes of hazel laced with white bryony, whose flowers were boiling with bees. He followed 'dark beech alley[s], paved with the gold and green of moss and walled by crumbling chalk'. He liked discovering neglected paths on the point of disappearance, 'buried under nettle and burdock and barricaded by thorns and traveller's joy and bryony bines'. He loved the border crossings that path-following enabled: the holloways that issue into hot fields of wheat, or the transition from tree-shade to the glint of meadow grass. But I doubt he ever saw a wallaby.

Here Robert Macfarlane, an English 'nature writer', structures his story around the narrative of a walking journey interlinked with the work and life of an English poet, Edward Thomas, who died in the First World War and was also a solitary walker. He moves easily from personal details about his walking and his observations of nature to the life and poetry of Thomas. Read *The Old Ways* for its engaging structure around walking and poetry, its shaping of ideas through the narrative of walking, and its exploration of English and other landscapes.

Writing exercises

1 Chronology

Write a strict chronology of the major events of your life as a list. Start with whatever you think of first and continue with whatever you think of next. The only rule is that it should all be in chronological order. Look at what you have included. If you are lucky you will have drawn up the outline of your autobiography structure with a minimum of fuss. On the other hand, you may have written only about the public events of your life, and not what was really important to you. If so, try one of the other exercises. (Ten minutes)

2 Photographs or songs

Choose a set of photographs or songs from throughout your life—arrange them either chronologically or according to topics or themes—then use each one as a springboard for writing about people, events, relationships, yourself. (Ten minutes each)

3 I have always liked

Begin with the phrase 'I have always liked/loved ...' and then continue on with some specific object, event or experience, for example, the sea, forests, autumn, carnivals, unpicking things, climbing trees, embroidery. Then explore it—tell stories about it, discuss it, tease it out. In this way you may find a connecting theme or image for your life story. (Twenty minutes)

4 I have/have not

This exercise is based on a discussion in which the English poet Robert Graves lists what he has and has not done. He details an odd assortment of facts about his life, from having walked near Mt Etna when it was erupting to being questioned for a murder he did not commit. The exercise is to write continuously, everything you think of that you have and have not done in your life, and don't cross anything out. The odd things that come into your head when you haven't got time to prepare can be indicators of underlying themes. They can point the way to the most important stories. When you look at your list you may see a recurring pattern, a theme. (Five minutes)

An extension of this exercise is to take items from your list and expand on them.

5 The only record

First, you have to imagine that in one hour the ability to write will be taken away from you forever. In that hour you have the chance to write whatever you wish to be recorded about your life. It will be the only written record of your existence in the world. Begin. It's a chance to perhaps see the bones of the story you want to write. (One hour)

Life story writers

Lucienne Fontannaz has used exercise three to create a structural link between her cultural heritage in Switzerland and her current life in Australia.

Rock Pool Ritual   Lucienne Fontannaz

I have always loved to swim in natural pools. Mountain lakes, set high up amongst majestic peaks, were my favourite places as a child. Time stood still as I would float in their dark shadowy reflections, or follow with tentative strokes a sunbeam that managed to pierce the surface of the water from between the rock faces.

Legends of the Swiss Alps tell of a winged female dragon, the 'Vuivre', who from time to time also enjoyed a bath in the high lakes. Before entering the water, she carefully placed on the shore her precious single eye, as luminous as a diamond. Devoid of sight, and now vulnerable, she would nevertheless abandon herself to an escapade of water frolics.

Although very far away from these alpine sites, I still follow the same ritual, early each morning, as I swim in a small area of surf surrounded by a circle of rocks called the Bogey Hole, at Sydney's Bronte Beach. I leave my glasses on the sand, and as everything slides out of focus, I feel slightly unguarded. The sea invites me to a timeless space and I sense the water's tranquil or restless touch rippling through so many layers of self, offering alternatively serenity and disquiet. When the Bogey is calm and shallow, it reveals and frames the bronzed bodies standing amongst the small fish and seaweeds, a vision caressed by the low sun. We convert into a silent community of worshippers and the sea pool resembles the Ganges, bathed in its spiritual light.

But when the high waves and powerful turbulences turn into moving walls of water, when I catch sight of surfers sliding down these steep hill waves, I see and dream of mountains. My wet and blurry eyesight catches the pale wintery light, the froth turns into snow and the swell rises into overpowering peaks. The cloud formations occasionally glimpsed along the horizon become a distant mountain range. I revel for a moment in the completeness of this improbable image.

Then I squint the water from my eyes and see in the distance the arms of the surf club clock reaching far too low down. Returning to the now gritty shore, I recover my diamond eye, complete with its shiny acrylic frames, and walk towards my new day's work. Everything is in sharp focus again.

9

WORKSHOP SEVEN

Inventing the story—Narrative

We owe it to each other to tell stories.

NEIL GAIMAN

Story, or narrative, is probably the oldest structure in the human world. Even as the first people developed speech they must have begun telling stories. Imagine our forebears crouched in the firelight, forgetting the dangerous night as they listened to the stories of their world. Perhaps they heard the wisest of them tell how the moon came to be in the sky and why the seasons changed in a rhythmic way. They must have spoken to each other softly, persistently, keeping the unknown night from invading their souls with fear.

Stories are conveyed in the visual arts, music, dance and drama, as well as through words. People in all cultures have always used story to make sense of their lives. Experiencing life is not enough, is somehow unfinished without telling the story of it. It is the story that reassures us that it has really happened and that gives it meaning.

People say 'I've lost the plot' when they feel confused or their life feels meaningless, suggesting that we all need a 'plot' to continue on with life. In his book *The Man Who Mistook His Wife for a Hat*, Dr Oliver Sacks writes, 'We have, each of us, a life story, an inner narrative—whose continuity, whose sense, *is* our lives. It might be said that each of us constructs and lives a "narrative" and that this is our identity.' This is another way of saying our stories create our sense of self—without our stories we cannot exist.

This inner story tries to make sense of what happens to us and, in some instances, can even create what happens to us. We depend on the continuity of the inner story for meaning and direction in life. The Buddhist monk Chögyam Trungpa, in *The Myth of Freedom*, says this continuity is an illusion that the ego generates to avoid facing impermanence. He calls the inner story 'internal gossip'. He could be right, but still, I am not yet ready to give up my internal gossip.

If you, like me, are not yet prepared to live entirely in the moment without an inner story, you can use that story to help you structure the writing of your life. Your inner story can provide the central storyline around which events unfold, shaping the narrative.

Narrative

What exactly is a narrative or story? We all know when we are in the presence of a story, but for the sake of clarity, here's a definition: a story connects events so that cause and effect are revealed, and so that each revelation creates the curiosity or desire to find out more until the desire is satisfied.

The traditional narrative, a classic narrative arc, is often drawn as a geometric shape, demonstrating the way the elements of a story develop.

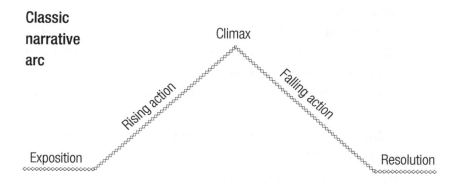

Classic narrative arc

The classic narrative arc follows the principle that a story should have a beginning, a middle and an end. It's one way of telling a story: *exposition* (explaining or setting up the situation first, for example, a family on a large farm); *rising action*, or *inciting incidents* (introducing an element or series of elements that complicate the situation, for example, the father has a road accident, the son blames the mother who has left after an argument, there is a drought, the bank threatens to call in its loan); *climax* (the father faces death, the mother comes to his side through the first rains which flood the creeks, risking her own life); *falling action* (the father has pulled through, the family saves the farm); *resolution,* often called *denouement* (old conflicts are resolved, the crops wave in the breeze, the future beckons). You could try arranging the elements of your story in this traditional pattern.

Plot

These elements, however, can be plotted in any number of different ways. If story makes links between events, plot is the order and emphasis of those events, which means the same story can be plotted differently. As mentioned in the previous chapter, the practical processes of structure are: the *selection* of events, the *order* that you place them in, and the *emphasis* you give each event. Which memories you select, where you place them and what importance you give them will each affect the narrative.

In thinking about plotting, ask yourself: what is the heart of the story that you want to tell? Is it about the resolution of your relationship to your mother? Is it about your struggle with your adopted daughter? Is it about the search for your own identity and role in life? These questions will reveal *le fils rouge* (the red thread) as the French call it, the thread that will lead the reader through your story.

If you see your story from the beginning you will be able to arrange the elements of your life with a particular order and emphasis, which can then be refined in rewriting. But you may not know the answers to these questions until later—which is why I suggest that you start writing first and ask yourself these questions as you go. As the story becomes clearer, you can select and emphasise memories that contribute to it, and cut or drop back memories that don't.

You don't have to include everything—*just because something happened is not necessarily a justification for including it*. When the American columnist Russell Baker was writing his life story, *Growing Up*, he realised he had made a mess of his first attempt because he had included all sorts of experiences without knowing what the real story was. When he realised it was about the relationship between a strong woman (his mother) and a weak man (himself), he began again, saying, 'I am now going upstairs to invent the story of my life.' He didn't mean he was going to make it up but that finding the story helped him to shape his material, to know what to concentrate on in detail and what to leave out as irrelevant.

Plot suggestions

- Start with a lead-up to the climax, then cut back to the beginning and show how events led to this situation, then write the climax and the aftermath.
- Start with a mystery or puzzle, which is then unfolded by cutting back and forward in time.
- Start with a turning point, or hinge, then move back to what happened before that, then what resulted afterwards.
- 'Plait' three or four different stories in and out of each other by telling part of one and then another and so on, coming back to each story in turn.
- Use 'flashbacks' to explore the roots of the particular episode you are writing about.
- Place all events in chronological order, letting the time sequence pull the reader forward.

Narrative pull

Narrative pull or tension is what draws us through a story— we are curious to find out 'what happens next', we want to turn the page. It is based on a pattern of withholding and giving information in an enticing fashion—like drawing a bird along a path with pieces of bread. If you want the reader to follow you in a certain direction then the 'bread' needs to be spaced out, but not so far apart that the reader flies off. It also has to be in an unfolding order, not a jumbled pile, and has to appear to be going somewhere, preferably not around in circles.

You can create narrative 'hooks' by dropping hints about information you are going to reveal later. I don't mean obvious remarks like: 'Little was I to know that this man would later be my undoing.' That kind of hook sounds corny and manipulative. But you can create curiosity by suggesting later developments or by writing the character or situation vividly to create a mood of anticipation.

Practical narrative steps

- Brainstorm all the story elements you think you want to include.
- Write each element on a card and then arrange them in chronological order.
- Now arrange them in one, or all, of the plotting structures I've suggested above. Which one works best? Is it back to chronology? Start writing each of the story elements, beginning with whichever card you have placed first.
- As you read back over what you have done, be ready to rearrange the order. Once it is written, you may now see connections which mean a different order might work better. More emerges in the process of writing than you can see beforehand.

Whatever stories you write, it is best not to force a plot on a loose collection of events; it may lead to distortion and awkwardness in your writing. If a story shape suggests itself and seems to suit your writing, then try it. Perhaps the whole idea of life having a plot is a fiction anyway. Seeing our life as a story may be a human way of managing the unknown, the darkness at both ends of our lives. For more on narrative, see Workshop fourteen: The magic spell—More narrative.

Where to end

Oh yes, that difficult last chapter! You could write a new last page for your life story every day, but assuming you want to finish it, here are a few suggestions that apply more particularly to straightforward autobiography rather than memoir or other types of life writing.

How to end can depend on the structure. If your structure is chronological, you could end with yourself sitting down to begin writing your life story; or, if you are writing it as a journey of discovery, you could end with the most important discoveries of your life. Look to your structure and you will find the note to end on.

Endings can depend on beginnings. Re-read your opening chapter and see if you could connect the ending to the beginning. For example, if you began with a humorous anecdote, you may be able to finish with one; if you opened with an image from nature, you may end with a similar image.

The recurring themes of your story can reveal the ending. You can use the ending to sum up the important issues of your life. If you have ever wanted to state your case without interruption and have the final word, here's your chance.

You could finish with a glance towards the future. You have been exploring your past for a long time; a look forward can make a satisfying ending.

It can be interesting to finish by comparing the world at the beginning of your life to the world now—the changes you have seen. This is effective if you have been writing about your life as a social history.

Reading

The Mind of a Thief
Patti Miller

'D'ya have any blackfulla in ya?' The skinny woman across the room looked directly at me.

I was at a gathering of Wiradjuri women Elders in Wellington, the country town on the central western plains of New South Wales where I grew up. It was a while ago now, because my mother still lived in her own house a few streets away. The other women, standing around the table with their cups of tea and biscuits, stopped chatting and listened. It was their regular meeting at the Aboriginal Health Centre and they had been discussing the usual problems: drug and alcohol addiction, violence, sexual abuse, heart disease. It seemed every woman there had one family member, or more, struggling with at least one or more of the problems, but they laughed and swapped stories as they attended to business. I was a ring-in from the city; I'd offered to help them write their stories and so the Elders had suggested I come up to talk to them first. They had been amiable and listened politely as I outlined how it might work; now business had finished and they were waiting. The woman's question felt like a trap of some kind but not too dangerous.

'No,' I said. 'Not as far as I know.'

I was aware of my accent falling into the flatter, broader sounds of my childhood. It was an automatic adjustment towards whomever I was talking to; it slipped either way, posh or broad. It bothered me. I couldn't even hold onto my own accent.

The skinny woman grinned and everyone who was listening chuckled. Cups were put down on saucers and arms were folded. It was clear they all knew what she was getting at and they were preparing to have a bit of fun with me. Despite my family's long history here, I was an outsider. I'd been away too long. And even though I had grown up in this district on a farm only twenty kilometres away, none of the women looked familiar to me. I suppose people change after twenty-five years.

They were still waiting. It was still my turn.

'Why? Do you know something I don't?'

The woman grinned again, her eyes sparkling with the mischievous look of someone who likes to stir. She was in her forties, about the same age as I was, dark-haired and dark-skinned.

'Don't ask me,' she said. 'Ask Joyce Williams, Bill Riley's sister.'

She pointed to an older woman with grey curly hair, small and neat, the only one I'd thought looked interested when I spoke during the meeting. I had met her brother several years ago. Bill had come to see me at my mother's house when he heard I was looking for someone to tell me local Aboriginal stories. I was researching childhood stories and was looking for the ones I hadn't heard, the Aboriginal tales of how the hills and rivers and rocky outcrops were brought into being. Bill was a great storyteller.

I had found Bill in a roundabout way through my youngest brother, Terry, who used to have an Aboriginal girlfriend and played in the Aboriginal cricket team. Terry was accepted as one of them, I'm not sure why. Perhaps it's because he has always had a 'watching from the edge' air about him, aware of but not really part of the busy world. One of the Aboriginal men I talked to had said, 'Terry's just like an Aborigine, worse sometimes.' And then he laughed.

The women watched me as I circled around the narrow crowded room towards Joyce. The Health Centre was in an old corner shop, a nest of different-sized rooms freshly painted and fitted out, but still poky. I had to push past several chairs, which made a scraping noise as they slid on the floor. It was mid morning and already hot in the closed-in room. I felt sweat trickling down under my black top.

'The others reckon I should ask you if I have any Aboriginal in me.'

Joyce looked at me shrewdly. 'The whitefullas and the black-fullas have two different stories about who's related to who in this town.'

The other women burst out laughing. I stood there feeling like an unwilling clown. I hate not knowing what everyone else knows.

'Ya dad's Don Miller.'

It was more a statement than a question so I just nodded. There were dozens of Millers in Wellington, not all of us related. It didn't even occur to me until later to be surprised that Joyce, a woman I'd never met before, knew who I was, who my father was, who I was related to.

'Ya heard of ya dad's grandma, Rosina May?'

Of course I'd heard of her. My father used to tell us about visiting her smoky, dirt-floored hut when he was a boy. He always said she was 'a blackfella', but we didn't really believe him because he always grinned when he said it.

'Well, my grandfather was John May, Rosina's brother. Ya dad's grandma and my grandad are brother an' sister. So me an' you, we're cousins.'

Now it was my turn to grin. I'm as red-haired and freckle-faced as they come. There's no way I would have imagined I had Aboriginal ancestors. I could hear my heart beating.

This story in *The Mind of a Thief* begins the narrative of a native title claim and the story of my own connection to Wiradjuri country, the land where I was born and grew up. The hidden nature of the connections, the discomfits and complications, are introduced in this scene. Read this narrative nonfiction for the unfolding of a complex narrative as well as for the way it combines memoir, research and interview.

Writing exercises

1 Turning points

Write a list of what seem to you to be turning points in your life. Select one of them and write about it. You can keep doing this exercise until you have written about all the turning points. In fact, you could organise your whole life story around turning points. (Fifteen minutes each)

2 Plotting forwards—and backwards

Select an event that has unfolded in your life where you can see a beginning, a middle and an end. Write it in three paragraphs, one for each section. Then try beginning at the end and telling it backwards. This does not mean reshuffling the paragraphs but writing them again, so that the story works told backwards. A number of films have used this technique, starting at the end of a relationship and then showing scenes progressively back in time to the beginning. Does forwards or backwards works best? (Fifteen minutes each)

3 An object lesson

Select a series of objects from the specific era or place you are writing about, perhaps jewellery, books, a passport. You don't have to physically have the things anymore—it could be a list of objects. Use each object as a springboard for writing a story. Explore using the objects as a way of structuring the memoir by creating a 'frame'—perhaps you are taking them from a backpack, or a drawer, or a removalist's box? (Fifteen minutes each)

4 Seasons and elements

Select a sequence that appeals to you such as the seasons (spring, summer, autumn, winter) or elements (earth, air, fire, water) or colours, or whatever appeals. Then write a piece about each item in the sequence using stories from your life and your thoughts and feelings about them. Combine events from a variety of times if you like. (Ten minutes each)

Life story writers

Steve Castely has written about a turning point in his life. He shows great narrative discipline in the way the real significance of the memory is not revealed until the end.

Watching Mummy   Steve Castely

One by one Mum removed the photos from the lounge room wall, wrapped them in newspaper and shoved them into a cardboard box: Lynda, my four-year-old sister dressed in a white frilly dress, Mum and Dad on their wedding day, our grandparents at Christmas dinner, me in a sailor suit just perfect for a two-year-old, and of course more sepia photos of her favourite toy cocker spaniels. All removed until the walls were bare. Bare like the rest of the house—memories deleted.

This morning we'd kissed Dad goodbye and stood on the porch as he left for work in his new FE Holden sedan. The scent of his Poppy hair oil lingered as we watched his car purr down our suburban Ashgrove street and disappear around the corner. Seconds later a moving van chugged to a halt in front of our driveway.

'Truck, big truck,' I yelled.

'Come in,' Mum called to the removalists.

'Get in the playpen,' she said to us.

'Take everything and I'll pack the boxes.'

The men wearing overalls started hauling everything out to the big black truck. The lounge suite, beds, cupboards, table, chairs, refrigerator, rolled up carpets, and dozens of hastily packed boxes disappeared as Lynda and I watched in wonder from our cage.

I started to cry.

'Shhh,' Mum said, passing me a bottle of tepid milk. I raised my arms hoping to be picked up, cuddled and kissed, but she was too busy. I sucked in her lavender scent, so much better than the smell I was sitting on.

'Here's an apple for you, Lynda. Eat it, don't move and look after your brother.' She returned to packing boxes.

'Don't forget the washing machine,' she yelled. 'The Simpson's in the laundry. Grab the pegs off the line too. Leave nothing.'

Full to empty in just four hours.

A car horn tooted out the front.

'Grab the playpen. My sister wants it,' Mum instructed the movers.

She bent down and picked up the spaniels, putting a ball of fluff under each arm and walked out the door.

'What about the kids?' a packer asked.

'He wanted them, he can have them. Shut the door on your way out,' she called, walking down the steps and into a new life.

The door closed. Lynda and I listened to the car drive away and then the truck after it. We were left with only silence and emptiness. Alone on the bare floor we reached for each other and cried, not daring to wonder if Dad would return from work.

10

WORKSHOP EIGHT
Style matters and editing

Well-ordered words are as a honeycomb;
Sweet to the soul, and health to the bones.

PROVERBS 16:24

Style is a stretchy word. It can refer to a correct or acceptable use of language, well-chosen words and well-formed sentences, but it also refers to a writer's characteristic approach to the use of words. When we say we like a writer's style, we usually mean their individual way of putting words together. The choice and flow of words, the style, affects the reader as much as the content. Style as a characteristic approach *is* individual. It is formed by your particular personality, by your reading habits, and by your sensitivity to the impact of words—the subtleties of meaning, sounds and rhythms.

The discussions in this chapter are not aimed at changing your style—your style is your own and no one can give it to you—but at developing the clarity, power and beauty of your style.

Of course, these are value-laden terms and you could argue we all have a different idea of what they mean, but I believe that well-chosen words and well-made sentences are just as recognisable as a well-made table or car or ceramic pot. There is a quality in the materials and workmanship and function of good tables, cars, pots—and literature. In any field, it takes time and experience to develop sensitivity to quality. In literature, wide and deep reading is the best way to develop your awareness of the qualities of style.

Still, there are fashions in writing style as in everything else. Television and film have influenced writers to 'show' rather than 'tell', as writers realise that their readers know how to 'read' the world on the page without long explanations. Earlier in the twentieth century, Modernism, which valued economy, over-turned the wordy style of the nineteenth century, but we still recognise the quality of nineteenth-century writing just as we appreciate the quality of an ornate vase, even though it may not be to our taste.

These are a few of the particular style issues that often require the editor's pencil.

Understate

It is as true in writing as in conversation that what is *not* said can be as revealing as what *is* said. Writing is often more powerful when it is understated rather than over-explained. Don't always give in to the impulse to spell everything out—a few well-chosen words can be more effective than an outpouring. Overwriting is most often a problem when the subject is strong emotion—trust that those reading your story will have experienced some of the same emotions and let them connect to your experience in the silence around your words. Holding back a little will give what you do write more power. As Strunk and White put it in *The Elements of Style*, 'It is seldom advisable to tell all.'

Economise

You might think writing is one place you can be free of the need to be economical, but spending adverbs and adjectives too freely can result in clutter. Rely more on exact nouns and verbs. As Strunk and White note, 'it is nouns and verbs, not their assistants, that give good writing its toughness and colour'.

If the verb is exact, you often don't need the adverb, for example, 'cicadas droned sonorously'—the verb *droned* does the job well, it doesn't need *sonorously*. Instead of 'he walked slowly', you could say 'he strolled' or 'he dawdled'.

If the noun is precise, it doesn't always need a string of adjectives, for example, 'round pregnant belly' doesn't need the extra adjective *round* as pregnant bellies are always rounded.

Too many adverbs and adjectives can be like pouring a tin of house paint over a figurine, obliterating rather than revealing. On the other hand, you could argue the rhythm and sound pattern of your sentence needed *sonorously* or *round*, or that your overall style was meant to suggest abundance. You can see that I am treading delicately in this disputed territory! You don't have to give up adverbs and adjectives—I certainly have not—but it's a matter of being more selective.

Sentences—Lost and found

Sentences make pathways through your writing. If they are too long and convoluted, your readers can become lost; if they are too short, often readers can feel unexpectedly jerked to a stop. On the other hand, long sentences can be useful for creating a languid, easygoing, expansive feel, for expanding an idea, for unfolding a narrative in a continuous thread. Short sentences create punchy action and force attention. Jump now.

The length and structure of sentences is central to creating the rhythm of your writing, the beat of the words, which underlies the meaning. Rhythm is often just as important as the content; it needs to work with the material, not against it. Reading your sentences aloud can help you hear the rhythm.

Try reading this aloud:

It is hot. The sun is high overhead. I am on a beach. I close my eyes. I stretch back. The deckchair sags beneath me. A voice cries out my name. I don't open my eyes. I feel relaxed.

Now read this:

The sun is hot, high above the beach. I close my eyes and stretch back on the deckchair, which sags a little beneath me. I hear a voice calling out my name but I am so relaxed I don't open my eyes.

The first set of sentences is too abrupt and jerky for a story about sitting on a deckchair on a beach. It also seems 'mannered', that is, too self-consciously trying for dramatic effect.

Some specific sentence structure problems:

- A confusion of tenses. If the tenses keep changing the reader can become confused about what is happening when. For example, *I sit at the table. My boyfriend leaned across and stroked my cheek.* The two different times, present, then past, is disorientating.

- Starting with a participle—as I just have. It often leads to confused meaning: *Sitting in the truck, he caught my eye.* It is unclear who is sitting in the truck.

- A qualifying phrase or clause too far from its noun—*I started down the track in my father's truck, overgrown with thistles and paddy-melon vines.* It sounds as if the thistles and vines are on the truck, rather than the track.

- A mixture of metaphors: *He took a trebuchet to her defences and when her knees folded he held her up. Then he unbuttoned her body and like a bird she flew through the glowing light of love.* Medieval machines, buttons, birds and lights create unintentionally humorous clichés rather than clarity.

- Too many ideas in the sentence. A sentence is built to carry one idea or event. If it is overloaded it starts to sag in the middle and can lose its load (meaning). Many sentence problems can be solved by breaking the sentence in two and making two new sentences.

Paragraphs—Finding a way through

Paragraphs are an expansion of one idea, each sentence following from the previous one. Clear paragraphs often have the central idea in the first sentence, the *topic sentence*, which is then unfolded, examined, expanded or illustrated. However, when we are expanding an idea in the first draft, our creative mind often jumps around, finding different ways of approaching the idea. It can result in a paragraph where the sentences are out of order and thus difficult to follow. When you edit your work, check whether each sentence follows from the one before.

Style and big issues

Birth, death, love, beauty, truth, fear, passion, grief, joy: these are powerful experiences, but it is often difficult to evoke deep feeling. The words themselves—truth, joy, grief—create a smokescreen between the powerful reality of the experience and its communication to others. Perhaps that is the function of the words: not to express the experiences but to protect us from being overwhelmed by them. The words are abstract and generic, like labels on boxes whose contents are hidden. The labels make the boxes easy to identify, but the contents are not engaging until the boxes are opened and each individual piece is taken out.

The following suggestions are for those who want to tackle large issues as they write their life story, but they apply equally to all writing.

Write the particulars. When the feeling or idea that you are writing about is overwhelming, you may look at what you have written and see a string of clichés. Your experience is valuable and does not deserve to be trivialised by trite language. Instead of trying to describe the feelings, write down the details of what you saw and did and said. The sense details will trigger emotions in the reader—it's the way our brains work. Write about the brooch your wife wore when you first fell in love; write of the metal bed frame you stared at as you battled cancer; write about the crooked teeth of the policeman who announced the accident early one morning. These details convey the lived reality of your experience.

Look behind the word. When you tackle a huge issue head-on, the intellectual mind will try to grasp it with abstract words, which can result in detached, even bloodless, writing. Try sidling up to the issue; have a look behind it and see that it is actually

124

made up of lots of moments. Try writing about these moments without using the abstract words that label the experience. At a workshop a few years ago, I set students an exercise of writing about a strong emotion without using the word itself. One student wrote about his wife's last weeks, describing how she had sat at a table in their backyard and given her jewellery to their daughters before she died. He quietly detailed the jewellery box, her hands, the opal ring, the shadow of the sunshade across the table. As he read his story to the class we all felt the love, grief and loss, even though he had not used any of these words.

Of course you will need to use abstract words at times as they can communicate ideas quickly, but if your writing lacks warmth then perhaps it's the overuse of abstraction.

Move from detail to 'big picture'

You may want to write about your life in relation to the larger world, the political and social environment or a wider philosophical and moral context.

Instead of having separate sections on politics and social conditions, or on your philosophy, weave these into your personal story. Start with a personal detail and use it as a springboard for writing about a connected issue in the wider world. For example, you could write about your brother being called up for National Service in the army and being sent to Vietnam, and use that as a way in to expressing your thoughts on the morality of war.

This idea of moving from personal detail to wider context applies to writing about beliefs, philosophy and values. Too much abstract philosophical discussion becomes dry and can begin to seem airy and insubstantial, even when it is your lifeblood. Most of us need a good solid table of actual events that we can see and lean on as we discuss philosophy. Give us the table and we will happily listen to your thoughts.

Humour

A humorous style is often very winning. It is easy when you are involved in writing your story to become too earnest. Don't forget the absurdity of daily life, the funny events, the entertaining people. I don't mean you should force humour in serious moments, but don't forget that there has been laughter as well. Some techniques for humorous writing are:

- Observe unusual events with a straight face, for example, calmly describing your elderly aunt in bikie gear as if it were an everyday event.
- Use ironic comments, where you mean the opposite of what you actually write; for example, in a humorous article for *HQ* in 1991, 'Bathing with Sarah', I wrote, 'In this calm and balanced way I make all my life decisions,' meaning, of course, that I was panicking and irrational.
- Overstate; for example, from the same article: 'I, preferring to die of a drug overdose than appear uncool . . .'
- Understate; for example, describe your boat sinking under you in the Bay of Naples as 'a minor hiccup' in your travels.
- Incongruity; for example, using unlikely combinations as Clive James does in the beginning of his *Unreliable Memoirs*, when he puts the Second World War and his own birth on equal footing in terms of importance.
- Tell the truth unexpectedly. It is shocking and funny when people unexpectedly tell the truth; for example,

forgoing politeness and saying what you really think of someone.

- Use a different level of language unexpectedly or contrast language with the material, that is, use very formal and correct language in a rough-and-ready situation, or rough language in a polite situation.

Free style

At times, because of either fear of what others may think or lack of confidence, writing style can become stiff and overly 'correct' and too impersonal. Perhaps it's a hangover from school or university, when we had to use an objective style and formal voice. It's worth giving yourself permission to say whatever you like, however you like, at least for a while, to find out if there is a more relaxed or more energetic style lurking beneath the correct surface. Let that streak of cheekiness or quirkiness have a voice. You can rage, ramble, rebel, rant. Your style might be found in breaking all the rules—at least for a while.

Style and editing

Don't worry about getting each line perfect in the beginning. Very few writers produce the finished manuscript in one go. Think in terms of drafts, that is, rewriting and editing your work. It is part of the writing process to write a first draft, which may be rough, and then to work on it, refining the style and structure. It is not unusual to write three or four or more drafts. First you pour out, then you edit.

If you can accept a little imperfection at first you will find your writing will flow more easily. If you worry about making every word and sentence perfect first time, it can block your writing or your style can become too self-conscious. The creative writing mind works better if it is not constantly worrying about making mistakes. At the same time, the act of concentrating on language itself does focus the mind and new insights can emerge, so as with most advice, do not take this as an absolute. Try to steer a course between allowing your thoughts to flow onto the page and being aware of the power of language to diminish or enhance experience. The first draft can have gaps, confusions, patchy bits, excesses—that's all right, so long as you are following an image or an experience, or a line of thought on the page. In the next draft you can exercise more discrimination and judgement as you expand, clarify and cut.

Think in terms of two 'read throughs'—once for structure to see if it is working overall, the second time concentrating more on style. Before you start rewriting, read this chapter again—and consult a style manual such as Strunk and White's *Elements of Style*. Then you can be ruthless about what needs to stay in your manuscript and what can be cut away to reveal your story with more clarity, energy and beauty.

Reading

The Feel-Good Hit of the Year   Liam Pieper

Dad was feeding the cat when they arrested him. Ulysses was a sweet, stupid animal and all he wanted from life was to eat. From the second he got up to the moment he fell asleep, he would stand in the kitchen mewing with the polite, steady rhythm of a gondolier's cry. My dad, a light sleeper, was usually the first up, and he was shaking out the contents of a Whiskas box into a tray when he looked up to see a detective holding a weapon on him.

Ulysses dashed away as the plainclothes officer tackled and cuffed Dad, returning a moment later to dine after surmising that the Armoured Regional Response Team swarming through the house was not interested in his breakfast.

When it comes to raids, there are two kinds of cop: the old and sensibly jaded, and the young and dangerous. Every raiding unit has a few surly youths who find it just as unbelievable as I did that someone has armed them, and they charge into the situation like extras from a crime drama, all fired up on the adrenaline of kicking down a door.

These cops were the excitable kind, running on the intelligence they'd extracted from Francois that painted my folks as drug lords. So as the response team dashed through the house, they were dismayed to find it full of children. They stomped about for a while, crunching Lego underfoot and tripping over stuffed toys in their search for contraband, until they realised they weren't going to find a secret meth lab on the premises.

You could tell they weren't sure how to interact with us kids. We were too young to push around and our tiny wrists couldn't hold bracelets. After a while they just ignored us and went about their business, turning the house upside down while we howled for Weet-Bix and someone to turn on the cartoons.

In the end, a kindly older cop took us outside and let us ride in his patrol car while my parents were being rounded up.

'Can I play with the siren?' I asked.

'You're not supposed to sound the siren unless there's an emergency.'

'Isn't this an emergency?'

'Oh, go on then.'

Weeeeeeeeee!

What fun! It was like being inside the *Ghostbusters* car, and I imagine doing the same thing today would be as wicked fun as it was then.

My uncle was summoned to look after us while Mum and Dad went down to the station for processing. The cops were decent enough about it. The only brutality my parents endured was from one disappointed senior sergeant who clucked his tongue, shook his head and gently berated them: 'Come on, guys! You're too old for this shit.'

Pieper uses a humorous style—irony and exaggeration and incongruity—to write about a police raid on his home when he was a child. It was probably a frightening experience, but he tells the story as entertainment. Read *The Feel-Good Hit of the Year*—its title already conveys his tongue-in-cheek style—for its humour and insight, and for the way Pieper is able to modify his style when he writes about later tragedies, in particular, the death of his brother at the age of twenty-one.

Writing exercises

1 Minimal journeys

Write about an important person in your life or a significant event. Now cross out every adverb and adjective. Read through what you have written and notice how the style has changed. Does it still work? Could you find more precise nouns and verbs? Read through again and decide which adjectives and adverbs you really need. You don't have to drop adverbs and adjectives forever, but this exercise can make your writing clearer and sharper. (Fifteen minutes)

2 Breaking out

Make a list of topics you would not usually write about. It might include such things as: my body, things I have lost or broken, things I hate admitting to, places I have slept, my friends' faces, people I have only met once. Select one of them and write whatever comes to mind. Write with the thought that no one is going to read it—write what you want, however you want. (Fifteen minutes)

3 Music

Try writing to music. Select different kinds of music, from rock'n'roll to classical, and see whether it affects your writing style. (Fifteen minutes)

4 Seriously

Select a serious episode in your life, but one you can see the funny side of as well. Write the episode seriously, then the next day try writing it humorously. Which one is most effective? (Fifteen minutes each)

Life story writers

There's not a word wasted in Tanya Lake's economical piece about driving in the desert. Using mainly dialogue, the style is pared back, giving it energy and impact.

The Warlpiri Mob   Tanya Lake

There's no speed limit in the desert. I'm squashed in the middle
of a car packed full of Nakamurras. We're driving halfway
through the heart of Australia, from Darwin to their home in
the desert. There's Janet Long Nakamurra, her daughter Bayu
Nakamurra and Grandma Molly Nakamurra. Behind the wheel
is a white fella, Peter—Janet's 'husband'. He's sucking back beer
like a baby at the bottle. Each time he finishes one he throws
the can behind his head. Our feet crumple the empty yellow
XXXX beer cans.

Midnight passes and I wonder how long this trip will take.

I wake to see Peter pissing in the middle of the highway.
We can hear him fumbling with his zip, the jangling of metal
and his cursing. I unclick my belt, swing my feet over to the
front and launch into the driver's seat. As he turns towards the
car I pull the door shut and lock it. Janet's eyes flash from velvet
skin that merges with the blackness. Peter zigzags back towards
us. He lifts an arm to the door handle and grapples. His head
lurches to window level, the lines of capillaries on his nose like
a map of the moon.

'Hey! HEY! Get outta my seat.'

'Shuddup, Peter! Get in the back! You can shuddup!' It's
Janet, and it's the first time I've heard her so animated.

'It's cool, you have a rest. I'll drive from here, I'm wide
awake,' I say.

'It's my car,' says Peter. 'Geddout.'

'No, it's not. I hired it.'

'Yeah, Tanya, you tell 'im! You tell 'im. Peter! Geddin' the
back. It's 'er car. An' shuddup or I'll 'ave your DNA on my
nulla-nulla.'

'Don't growl me. Quit your humbug, woman.'

'Don' 'umbug me. I'll 'umbug you.'

He heaves into the back middle seat, where he's forced to sit forward. He whacks my head.

'Turn ya high beams on.'

'They're on.'

Whack. 'Nah they're fuckin' not.'

A road train appears in the rear vision. Whack. 'Turn 'em off.'

'They are off.'

Whack.

'Don't hit me.'

Whack.

I pull the car over and we stop.

Whack.

'What are ya doin'?'

Our car sways into the vortex of the road train's passage as it roars on and on, giving us a moment.

'I'm not driving until you stop whacking me . . .' I pull out my lunch pack. 'Now. Who wants some avocado?'

'Dat look good,' says Grandma Nakamurra.

I spread some on a cracker and pass it to her.

'Seems to be some kind of nut.' She holds the avocado half to the console light then takes a small bite. 'Tastes good!'

Peter finally resorts to silence and then snores as we rumble onwards.

Part Two

MASTERCLASSES

11

WORKSHOP NINE
Midway blues—Continuing on

'What else was I in, Jo?'

ALAN MARSHALL

Once, when I had finished writing a book, I wrote to a fellow writer, thanking her for keeping me going. She didn't know she had kept me going, she had not said anything to me, had not given me any advice—it was her approach to her writing that had inspired me. When I read her books, I could see that she always worked, step by step, towards a clear, simple expression of what it was she could see. She had kept me on track.

You have been writing for a while now. Perhaps it has been sailing along, or perhaps it has been a struggle at times. Or you might have come to a full stop and need to start again. Or you have too much to do and you don't write often enough, or you simply keep procrastinating. There are so many ways to not keep writing.

This series of extension classes is designed to help you keep going by dismantling some of the obstacles and by strengthening and extending your writing practice. It will take you 'back to the well' to renew the fundamentals of clear, vital writing, extend your skills, and encourage you to keep taking the next step.

Whether you are beginning—again—or halfway through, it's worth reminding yourself of the value of telling your story. Children love to hear stories of their own escapades even before they can properly tell them themselves. In Alan Marshall's short story 'Tell Us About the Turkey, Jo', a little boy listens to tales about his life told by his older brother: 'He looked at his brother expectantly and, as the brother spoke, the little boy's eyes shone, his lips parted, as one who listens to a thrilling story.' The brother then tells a number of stories about the boy narrowly avoiding disaster, such as when he was kicked by a cow and when a ladder fell on him. When he runs out of stories, 'The little boy stood in front of his brother, entreating him with his eyes. "What else was I in, Jo?" he pleaded.'

Why do we all have such a desire to recount our lives, to be in a story? Stories tell us what kind of people we are, how we *imagine* ourselves. If we cannot imagine ourselves, we cannot exist. Of course we exist as a being, but I mean as a self-aware personality. Stories are the warp and weft of a sense of personal self. *Our stories create us.*

Our stories validate who we are; they are our personal myths. Myths convey the truths and values of a culture; personal stories are repeated to convey truths and values about ourselves and so are mythical in their purpose. Like myths in ancient and traditional societies, our life stories connect us more deeply to each other and to the world around us. If a people's myths are destroyed, their culture is also destroyed. We only need to look at the impact of colonial powers on indigenous peoples to see the damage inflicted when a people's stories are undermined or negated.

The work of mythmakers or storytellers helps maintain a community's sense of meaning. The absence, in the West, of communally accepted myths about the meaning of life makes personal storytelling all the more necessary.

The need, and the ability, to make meaning is the unique characteristic of humans, the foundation of self and of society. It is the source of art and culture and religion, and at the same time the source of much of man's inhumanity to man—a war could not be started without a good story. Without meaning, it is very difficult, if not impossible, to continue doing any task for very long. Life writing is fundamentally a way of finding or constructing meaning and is, it seems to me, an intrinsically valuable expression of our unique humanity.

The stories of our lives cover the earth and connect us to each other in the deepest way. The fundamental condition of being here in the world is, I think, our essential separateness, our sense of being within our own skin. Except through art, we cannot know what it is like to be someone else. Even love does not allow us that privilege. The separateness of another is a difference to be respected and honoured. The greatest gift is when another human being can let us know, through the writing of their story, what it is like for them to be experiencing the common mystery of being here set down in the world.

But that doesn't mean it is always easy to write your story. Getting started is one thing—it takes a leap of faith and courage—but keeping going can also be difficult. There are many ways to stray from the path or to feel blocked. Let's have a look at some of the midway hurdles and ways of getting around them.

Leaping the hurdles

- *Does anyone want to read about my mad mother/trip to India/life on an olive farm? Is it worth it?* These questions can discourage you from writing anything. My solution is to change the question from 'Does anyone want to read it?' to 'Do I want to write it?' Is it important enough to me that it is written? Once I'm sure it's necessary for me to write it, then the hurdle of whether other people will want to read it falls to the ground.

- On the other hand, practically speaking, it might be that there have been a number of other books written on the topic and perhaps readers have had enough of renovating houses in Italy. In that case you need to be clear that your perspective on it is original. If you want to write your Italian renovation memoir, read recent publications on the same topic then perhaps look at your story again and see if there is something singular about yours that will make it a unique story.

- *Do I have the right to tell the world about my mad mother/my boyfriend's infidelity/my nasty neighbours?* This is the trickiest question of all and one on which many memoirs founder. The ethical issue of whether you have a right to tell the story can stop you in your tracks. This issue will be discussed further in Workshop fifteen: Difficulties of truth-telling, but to leap over at least the beginning hurdle, you need to ask yourself, 'How important is this story to me?' If it has been deeply significant in your life then, as a starting point, you have the right to tell it as part of your life. You can also try the Scarlett O'Hara trick: worry about that tomorrow.

- *I started, but work got in the way and now I just keep putting it off.* Most writers have jobs or other commitments and you might need to put your writing aside for a time, but don't let it drift away. It helps to put a time limit on putting it aside, rather than it being open-ended. Note the date you will get back to it in your diary so that your mind is preparing underneath its other jobs. On the pre-arranged date, allow yourself only a short session to plan what you will do in the next few weeks so that you are not daunted on the first day. It can be useful to give yourself a clear week—or more if you can afford it—to reconnect to your work.

- *I'm lost in a huge tangle and can't see where to go.* If you are in a muddle, it is time for a structural rethink. It could be that you have included unnecessary stories and need to prune. Read it, or ask someone else to read it, and see what the through-thread is, the structural spine. Or there could be an early flaw in the structure, often caused by avoiding the real issues. The solution may not be simple; it might mean throwing out material, never an easy task. Take a break of a few weeks before writing a paragraph or two clarifying what you were trying to do in the manuscript, then re-read it and see if you can spot where you left the rails. If you can't see the problem, again it can be useful to show it to someone else. A detached observer can often spot the gaping fault line on which you have been trying to build.

- *My family doesn't want me to write this book.* It's difficult enough to write, but with active discouragement it can feel too hard. Often discouragement comes from fear—perhaps that you will expose them. You could try enlisting support by reading extracts aloud so that they can see what you are up to. Or you could try the opposite—not mention your writing at all, so they don't feel threatened by it. Either way, remind yourself it is worth doing. If you 'Write what should not be forgotten', as Isabel Allende said, then you will be able to continue.

- *I'm running out of material—do I have enough for a whole book?* It's time to consider whether you have a short memoir, publishable in a magazine or collection, or a full-length book. Do you have too little material padded out, or too much material compressed? Sometimes, a subject you thought might be a book turns out to be more effective as a 5000-word memoir piece. Before you decide to stop, try brainstorming to see if there might be material that you have not considered because you have narrowed the focus too soon. Perhaps you need to let it expand with more research.

- *I've lost impetus and can't write.* The writing just won't go anywhere and you feel uninspired. It can be caused by over-planning—or anxiety about what people will think of you when they read what you have written. If overplanning is the problem, then you may need to throw the plan to the wind for a while and tack out in a different direction. Write something you had not thought of before. Try making a list, for example, of 'Things that I am never going to include in this story' then write a paragraph on each. It could open up a new direction. Sometimes all you need is to get other parts of your brain firing. Do something different. Take a class in Mongolian chanting, walk in the woods. If anxiety about others' opinions is the underlying problem, then the only solution I have found that works is to 'shut your eyes and pretend no one can see you'. Make a list of everyone you are anxious about, mentally lock them out of your writing room, then begin again.

- *Procrastination.* The most common issue for writers is the tendency to do everything but write. You tidy the book-shelf, look at social media, do some shopping—all of it an avoidance technique. That reluctance to face the work comes from anxiety about how difficult it will be—and fear that you won't be up to it. Some people advise willpower, to simply sit down and do it, but I think that first the fear has to be acknowledged. Look at why you keep shying away, notice the anxiety and sit with it for a while, feeling how large it is. Once you see it clearly, tell yourself you only need write for an hour today and stick to that hour. You can even reward yourself afterwards. Each time you notice yourself procrastinating, use the same sequence of observing the fear and then having a limited time to write. After a while you will notice your mind will have been retrained to a new, more disciplined practice.

For the days when you think your writing is terrible

- First of all, every writer, however many books he or she has written, has this feeling some days—it's part of the creative process.
- Accept that writing will feel impossible at times—that's not a sign to give up, but to just accept it, know that bad days happen and don't give yourself a hard time about it. Shrug and allow yourself a treat at the end of the writing day.
- Go for a long walk—many long walks—it's not wasting time, it's part of the process because it lulls the organising brain and lets the divergent thinking of creativity float to the surface.
- Remember that how you see your work depends on your mood. Perhaps you are tired or upset about something else. Read it again on another day and it may have improved a great deal!

- Forget about 'pushing through', and dance or play through instead—that is, don't write anything just because you think you should. Write what you feel like writing.
- Try to stay in the moment—put each thing you see down on the page, piece by piece, without worrying if it will work or not in the overall manuscript.
- Don't worry about being perfect the first time—everyone writes a fair amount of rubbish in their first draft. If it is rubbish, you can throw it out later.
- Show it to someone whose literary judgement you trust. It might be better than you think, or they might see the problem, which you can then fix.
- Read a writer you find inspiring—just a few pages works like a draught of fresh spring water.
- Replenish your storehouse of creativity by going to a play or film or art exhibition, or doing some painting, dancing or singing.
- Don't worry too much about original approaches—trust that your perspective is individual and the writing will follow.
- Writing is hard. To paraphrase George Bernard Shaw, 'writing wasn't meant to be easy', so sometimes—not too often—you might need to give yourself the day off. Remember Shaw continued, 'but take courage child—it can be glorious.'

Form a writing group

It can be difficult to persevere when you are writing alone. You may start to lose faith in your writing and in the value of your story. It is a good idea to find other people who are interested in nonfiction writing and form a workshop group. It is much easier to continue when you have like-minded people to encourage you. In life-writing workshop groups, especially, there is a rare warmth and generosity, which grows out of the sharing of stories.

A few tips about setting up a workshop group:

- Have a regular time to meet so people can arrange their life around it. Once a month is probably enough.
- Between four and ten members is a workable size. Always consult all the other members if you want to bring a new person along.
- Make sure that there is specific work to be done in each meeting—that some people will bring chapters to read and discuss, or that the group will do writing exercises.
- Designate a workshop organiser who will look after arrangements and who will keep the workshop on track. His or her job is to keep the others on the topic of writing—it is very easy for a workshop group to become a social gathering. The organiser needs to be rotated so that no one feels that one person is taking over.
- Set up some workshop guidelines. The three guidelines I use are: that the group respects the validity of each person's experience and does not query or undermine any person's interpretation of their own life; that the group respects the privacy of each person's story and does not repeat it outside the workshop if that is requested; that the group comments on the writing and not on the life and does not offer personal advice of any kind. This last is often difficult to do, but if a workshop is to be successful then each person must feel safe from personal comment or criticism.
- When you comment on each other's writing, make sure you acknowledge what is working well about the piece as well

as what needs improvement. Make your comments specific rather than general.

Read

Read other memoirs and creative nonfiction. It will inspire and remind you that you must keep going so that others can one day read your book. Don't be daunted by published books and especially don't compare them to your first draft—each one has no doubt been through many drafts. As a starting point, there's a reading list at the back of this book.

Reading

The Most Beautiful Walk in the World   John Baxter

Nobody has yet found a better way to travel slowly than to walk. It requires two legs; nothing more. Want to go faster? Don't bother walking—roll, slide or fly: don't walk. But once you are walking, it's not performance that counts but the intensity of the sky, the splendour of the landscape. Walking is not a sport.

Frédéric Gros

Every day, heading down rue de l'Odéon toward Café Danton on the corner of boulevard Saint-Germain or towards the markets on rue Baci, I pass them.

The walkers.

Not all are walking however. They'd *like* to be—but their stroll around Paris isn't working out as they had hoped.

Uncertain, they loiter at the foot of our street, at the corner of the boulevard Saint-Germain, one of the busiest on this side of the Seine. Couples, usually, they're dressed in the seasonal variation of what is almost a uniform—beige raincoat or jacket, cotton or corduroy pants, and sensible shoes. Huddling over a folded map or guidebook, they look up and around every few seconds, hopeful that the street signs and architecture will have transformed themselves into something more like Brooklyn or Brentwood or Birmingham.

Sometimes they appear in groups. We see a lot of these because our street, rue de l'Odéon, is to literature what Yankee Stadium is to baseball and Lord's is to cricket. At no. 12 Sylvia Beach ran Shakespeare and Company, the English-language bookshop that published James Joyce's *Ulysses*. Sylvia and her companion, Adrienne Monnier, lived in our building at no. 18. Joyce visited them there often. So did Scott and Zelda Fitzgerald, Gertrude Stein and Alice B. Toklas, and of course Ernest Hemingway.

Most days, when I step out of the building, a group stands on the opposite sidewalk while someone lectures them in any one of a dozen languages about the history of our street. They regard me with curiosity, even respect. But often I feel like a fraud. Instead of thinking lofty literary thoughts, I'm compiling my shopping list. *Eggs, onions, a baguette . . .*

After that, they set off again, a straggling column, following the guide's flag or, in bad weather, her umbrella. Few take their eyes off this object. They've learned that Paris for the pedestrian is both fascinating and deceptive. What if they did pause—to browse that basket of books outside *une librairie*, or take a closer look in the window of a boutique? The tour might turn a corner, disappearing from sight, casting them adrift in this baffling town. They would be forced to buttonhole a passing Parisian and stammer, '*Excusez-moi, monsieur, mais . . . parlez-vous Anglais?*'

Or worse, surrender to the mysteries of *le Métro*. A few lost souls are always hovering at the entrance to the Odéon station. Staring up at the green serpentine curlicues of Hector Guimard's cast-iron archway, they may read *Metropolitain,* but they *see* what Dante saw over the gate to hell: 'Abandon hope all ye who enter here.'

What most frustrates the visitor walking in Paris is the presence all around of others who share none of their hesitation. Confident, casual, the locals breeze past, as careless as birds in a tree. For them, the metro holds no terrors. They know exactly where to pause as a bus roars by on what appears to be the wrong side of the road. They make abrupt turns into alleys, at the foot of which one glimpses the most interesting-looking little market ...

How do they *know?*

Well, this is their habitat, their *quartier*, as familiar as their own living room. Because that's how Parisians regard the city— as an extension of their homes. The concept of public space doesn't exist here. People don't step out of their front door into their car, then drive across town to the office or some air-conditioned mall. No Parisian drives around Paris. A few cycle. Others take the metro or bus, but most walk. Paris belongs to its *piétons*—the pedestrians. One goes naturally *á pied*—on foot. And it's only on foot that you discover the richness and variety. As another out-of-town Paris lover, the writer Edmund White, says in his elegant little book *The Flâneur*, 'Paris is a world meant to be seen by the walker alone, for only the pace of strolling can take in all the rich (if muted) detail.'

John Baxter's travel book starts and ends in his own street in Paris. Baxter has written other books about Paris, but looking from the angle of a walker, he found he had more to see, more to say. This opening leads the reader into looking at Paris from this perspective. Read *The Most Beautiful Walk in the World* for an engaging exploration of Paris with well-researched literary and historical information, and for the way the author has structured it around the walks.

Writing exercises

1 Brainstorm association

This is a way of seeing if there is more to say on a particular topic. Write your subject in the centre of the page—it can be a word or a phrase, for example, 'Iraq 2003' or 'Michael and cancer' or 'Mountain climbing in Peru'. Then write the first association that comes to mind, then the association that comes to mind from that one and so on. You free-associate from the previous word, not back to the central word or phrase. When you have reached the edge of the paper or come to a stop, go back to the central word and start another line of association. Do this at least five times—up to ten. You will end up with a spider's web of interconnecting associations around your central idea or image. It will give you an idea of how rich—or not—your idea is—and it will give you a list of possible pieces to write. (Twenty minutes)

2 Midway ramble

If you are feeling tangled in the material or, on the other hand, blocked, try the ramble (Workshop one, exercise four) again. But this time, describe in outline what you have done so far, where you think it is going and where you hope it might go.

Talking to yourself on the page can be very helpful for sorting through tangles and blockages. (Twenty minutes)

3 Locking editors in the closet

This is for writers who feel paralysed or blocked by those who might disapprove of the memoir. You simply name all the people who might be upset, disapproving or in any way limiting to your writing and mentally lock them away in a cupboard in your mind, or send them to a tropical island if you wish—someplace where they are not going to see what you are writing. Next, start with the phrase *It is very difficult for me to write about*, then continue. It is interesting how naming the problem you are having will often lessen its hold over you, at least enough to get started. (Twenty minutes)

4 New beginnings

By the time you have written several chapters, your manuscript may have headed in a different direction. If so, read through your manuscript so far and see whether it could begin in a different place. Try writing a new beginning altogether. See whether a different beginning works better than the original. (As long as it takes)

12

WORKSHOP TEN

Madeleines and unicorns— Sensory detail

The only true voyage of discovery . . . would be not to visit strange lands but to possess other eyes, to behold the universe through the eyes of another, of a hundred others, to behold the hundred universes that each of them beholds, that each of them is.

MARCEL PROUST

To look through the eyes of another is an extraordinary privilege. It is the writer's job, in both fiction and nonfiction, to offer that privilege to others, to let them see what the world looks like to him or her. Proust lets us see what the world looks like to him by offering the detail of his experience, right down to the minutiae of dunking a cake in a cup of tea. This humble madeleine cake is celebrated in the literary world because it initiated a stream of memory, which, a million or so words later, became *In Search of Lost Time,* one of the twentieth century's most significant literary works. But it also reveals how the link between memory, the senses and fresh, original detail works, so let's look at it more closely:

> She [his mother] sent out for one of those short, plump little cakes called 'petites madeleines', which look as though they had been moulded in the fluted scallop of a pilgrim's shell. And soon, mechanically, weary after a dull day with the prospect of a depressing morrow, I raised to my lips a spoonful of tea in which I had soaked a morsel of the cake. No sooner had the warm liquid, and the crumbs with it, touched my palate than a shudder ran through my whole body, and I stopped, intent upon the extraordinary changes that were taking place. An exquisite pleasure had invaded my senses, but individual, detached, with no suggestions of its origin . . . I was conscious that it was connected with the taste of tea and cake, but that it infinitely transcended these savors, could not, indeed, be of the same nature as theirs. Whence did it come? What did it signify? How could I seize upon it and define it? . . .
>
> But when from a long-distant past nothing subsists, after the people are dead, after the things are broken and scattered, still, alone, more fragile, but with more vitality, more unsubstantial, more persistent, more faithful, *the smell and taste of things remain poised a long time, like souls, ready to remind us*, waiting and hoping for their moment, amid the ruins of all the rest; and bear unfaltering, in the tiny and almost impalpable drop of their essence, the vast structure of recollection . . .
>
> And just as the Japanese amuse themselves by filling a porcelain bowl with water and steeping in it little crumbs of paper which until then are without character or form,

but, the moment they become wet, stretch themselves and bend, take on colour and distinctive shape, become flowers or houses or people, permanent and recognisable, so in that moment all the flowers in our garden and in M. Swann's park, and the water-lilies on the Vivonne and the good folk of the village and their little dwellings and the parish church and *the whole of Combray and of its surroundings, taking their proper shapes and growing solid, sprang into being, town and gardens alike, from my cup of tea.* (My italics in each case)

The italicised words convey the essential point: that from a sensory stimulus, a whole and highly detailed world can 'spring into being'. The problem is that the mind will often go blank when asked to remember a general period of life; if I ask you about your schooldays, you will mostly likely say they were either good or bad, with no detail springing immediately to mind. For direct access to detailed memory, you need to find your 'madeleine cake'. In an interview in *Le Temps* in 1913, Proust said there were two kinds of memory: voluntary and involuntary. Voluntary memory is the deliberate daily recall of events of the immediate or faraway past. Involuntary memory, on the other hand, comes unbidden and more rarely and is the product of a sensory stimulus of some kind. Hot tea and madeleine cake. A smell or taste or other sense experience suddenly and powerfully brings the experience to mind as if it is being relived. Involuntary memory is now often referred to as Proustian memory. It presents in such vivid detail that you don't have to 'think' of the lively details—they are there in the memory. Involuntary memory is also more cohesive and more patterned. As Proust said, 'involuntary memory comes clothed in associations'. Both kinds of memory are necessary for the writer, but Proustian memory is especially important because of its sensory detail.

By its involuntary nature, Proustian memory is hard to come by, but we can prompt it with sensory input—see the first exercise in this chapter. The next step is using those Proustian memories in your writing—which is where the unicorn comes in.

The unicorn and sensory detail

The Lady and the Unicorn is a series of six tapestries displayed in the Museum of the Middle Ages in Paris. It shows a medieval lady and her maidservant surrounded by various items: a bowl of fruit, a carved chest, a harpsichord, berries, flowers, dogs, rabbits, monkeys, a lion and, of course, a unicorn. Each tapestry represents a sense, the sixth one being love.

The Lady and the Unicorn is one of my teachers because as well as being a beautiful work in its own right, it reminds me of what I need to do as a writer: it includes all the senses; it shows exquisite attention to detail; it recalls the actual world and the symbolic world with economy and clarity; it revels in colour and texture; it reveals the ordinary elements of life as extraordinary; it shimmers with what is unsayable. If you work with the same attention as those unknown tapestry makers, you can create from the strange silk, cotton, string and wool of words your own tapestry of marvels.

It begins with attention and observation. All good writing comes from paying attention to and observing yourself, your memories, others, your environment—you know this already. But it is so easy to let your attention become dulled, to become too busy to pay attention, to become immersed in paying bills, getting to the office, washing-up, arranging to go the dentist.

Writers must earn a living and do daily chores—probably not many of you have maidservants and unicorns—but do your ordinary activities with attention so that the mind is trained, ready to write, when you sit down. It is a quiet attention amongst the business of life that Buddhists call 'right attention' or 'mindfulness'. It means being properly 'awake', that is, being aware of what you are doing, seeing, feeling, thinking.

How do you wake yourself up? Here are a few possibilities.

- Find ten minutes each day to give 'right attention' to your immediate environment, to observe at least an aspect of your world with focused observation, with all your senses. Look at your own hand, listen to the sound of a car horn, smell the scent of a freshly opened book. Write what you observe in note form.

- Go back to a writer who has 'woken you up' in the past. Re-read passages that startle with their insights and observations. There is revelation in a garden well observed, an act of violence accurately witnessed. Remind yourself that you have the same capacity to observe your world.

- Seek out an inspiring work from another art form: a painting, a piece of music, a song, a poem, a film—even a tapestry. Immerse yourself in it; give yourself over to another form of expression. Find artists who 'tear the veil of habit' that normally drapes itself over life. It is one of the best ways to refresh a dull awareness; neurones will begin firing and forming new neural pathways in your brain.

- Do something you haven't done before. Learn a new skill— singing or dancing—or go to a new place, even a suburb of your own town will do. Feel challenged, uncomfortable.

- Walk somewhere familiar and imagine you are a giant or an ant, and see how strange and full of marvels the world is.

Sex and death and the six senses

The smell of a towel warmed by a fire, the sight of redwoods in a Californian valley, the feel of cold air on cheeks early in the morning in a London park—the world is first, and every day, apprehended by the senses. Almost immediately afterwards you have an emotional response to it, next you may conceptualise what you have experienced and finally even philosophise about it, but the fundamental texture of lived experience is the sight, touch, sound, smell and taste of the world. To convey what it is like to be in the world, a memoir writer needs to show at least something of that texture.

The more overwhelming the experience, the more difficult it can be to find the words to convey it. In intense experiences such as the meltdown of sex or the devastation of death, the brain typically reacts in a paradoxical mode—senses can be heightened even though the mind feels as if it is floating, or numb. Emotions are difficult to write anyway without becoming too abstract, and when the feelings are powerful, words can feel inadequate. It is easy for writing about death, loss and grief to become 'purple' or sentimental, easy for writing about sex and romantic love to become flowery, technical—or uncomfortably explicit. I think the earthy, sensory body—skin, sweat, belly—is more engaging than the scientific body—testicles, labia—or the symbolic body—caves, moist jungles. (We all have a different sensibility about this!) There are no simple answers, but by remaining as honest as possible with the simplicity of sensory details you have a chance of conveying some of the texture of lived experience.

There is also the importance of spareness, of economy. In writing sex, in particular, it can often be more effective to leave space for the reader to interpret. On the other hand, if your memoir is your sexual life, then the sensory detail will be necessary.

Words about food can actually make the mouth water; words about a threatening situation can make the heart beat faster; words about sex can create arousal. It strikes me as bordering on sorcery that a system of signs on the page can enter the mind and cause the body to react as if it had received sensory input. I remember, for example, how the vile odours evoked in Patrick Süskind's *Perfume* caused my body to recoil, sickened, as if I actually smelled the filthy streets of medieval Paris. Of course, *Perfume* is a novel, but as a truthful representation of life, non-fiction writing needs to pay the same attention to the sensory world—pleasant and unpleasant. Writing that connects deeply, that makes the reader feel as if he knows and understands, affects the body as well as the emotions and mind. While words shape our experience of being, they can also re-create it in the mind and body.

Writing for the senses is often taken to be seductive, pleasurable writing; the smell of coffee brewing in a sunny kitchen, creamy lilies glowing amongst dark green spears, the silky grace of a baby's cheek—and it is true that sensual writing can reawaken any of the delights our senses afford us. But it is also the dark, decaying and repulsive: the stench of urine in a dank alley, yellow pus oozing from a child's infected eye, the scream of a woman late at night in the red-light district, the ugly thud of a fist on flesh. This is the lived texture of life; this is what our senses tell us.

The life of the senses is also rhythmic—there is a pulse, a throb, a to-and-fro that is an intrinsic part of the natural and built world. The rush of waves up the sand and the tugging back, the breath drawn in and let out in a sigh, the thumping of the engine in the shearing shed, the lub-dub pump of the heart muscle—nothing is still. Even the stone is weathered rhythmically by rain and wind. This rhythm can be re-created in the internal rhythm of sentences and the pattern of sentences within paragraphs. Read aloud so that you become aware of the rhythm; notice that some sentences are short and jerky, poking a finger at the reader, some are languid and lazy, twirling the reader around a finger, some mimic the movement of speed, sharp and racy, or the dreaminess of a hot summer afternoon, slow and long. The rhythm of sentences is essential to the re-creation of the experience of life. Virginia Woolf stated that for her, rhythm was the first impulse—that if she was blocked it was because she could not find the right rhythm.

Here is a long, languid sentence from my memoir *Whatever the Gods Do.*

There was a man flying a kite near the lagoon and, having nothing better to do, I stopped to watch. When I came upon the kite it was already flying long horizontal infinity signs back and forth across the sky. I don't know whether this was a beginning or a bold change of pace halfway through, but then it flew straight up and looped around and back down its vertical path, then glided gently down almost to the lagoon surface before curving upwards and into a sensuous jazzy dance across the top of an imaginary vertical dance floor, rolling and slinking and flirting, joyous and tempting, then suddenly diving in a death-wish straight down to the sand, jerking out of it at the last moment and dancing lazily over the lagoon like a dragonfly skitting and buzzing on a summer's day, playing with light and air, then another long slow climb upwards, nosing this way and that, testing the limits of the upper air before performing long slow arabesques across the top of the sky. It went on and on, intricate and patterned, an airy ballet in the sky.

Notice the contrast in rhythm with the following relatively short, sharp sentences later in the same memoir.

> On the shelf over his bed there was a photograph of Dina, her dark eyes sparkling. I sat down on the bed and looked up at it. Theo ignored my gaze.
>
> 'Your mum,' I said.
>
> 'Yeah.'
>
> 'She was beautiful.'
>
> 'Yeah.'
>
> I looked at him but he was busy pulling the axle out of a plastic wheel. I looked down at the flowery boots. There was a white smudge on the toe where the flowers had rubbed off.
>
> 'These were your mum's.'
>
> Theo looked at the boots briefly and then went on with the axle operation.
>
> 'Thought they looked stupid,' he said.

Writing for the senses is not an invitation to excess. It is about creating a convincing world on the page, be it the detailed world of a Breughel painting or a spare haiku by Bashō. In either case there is the desire to convey your perceptions of the world. An ornate style might suit some writers; for others an economic, understated style is more effective. To a twenty-first century consciousness, too many details can feel heavy, overdone, or simply outdated. You probably don't want your memoir to sound as if it were written in the nineteenth century—unless, of course, you are consciously creating a postmodern reference to nineteenth-century literature.

Still, if you feel your writing is becoming too dry and over-analytical, or if you simply want to build the richness of sensory experience in your writing, try rebuilding the connection between the senses and words:

- Return to the 'original' memory where the details are fresh rather than analysed 'stored' memory. Look for 'madeleine cake' in your own life.
- Include all the senses, not just sight. Many writers over-rely on sight. Remember the smell, taste, feel and sound of your life.
- Remember colour and texture. Crimson, cream, cobalt; sooty, scratchy, hairy.
- Be accurate about the detail—was it azure or cobalt? Were the leaves serrated or smooth? It's not about overdoing the detail, just being precise.
- Use more sensual words, less abstract: 'She wore a cream silk blouse and black Chinese trousers' instead of 'She was dressed elegantly'. It helps the reader 'see' rather than merely constructing an idea without colour or form.
- Find the particular names of things rather than general terms—instead of 'A bird flew out of the bush', look more closely and write 'A thrush flew out of the japonica'.
- Remember not to overdo it. Too many adjectives and adverbs look like clutter. As the American stylists Strunk and White said, 'It is seldom necessary to say all.'
- On the other hand, if luscious excess is your preference, do it in style! Taking it to an extreme might be just what is needed. And excess can be used for humorous or ironic effect. Not all writers need to be restrained and elegant!
- Replace a word of Latin origin with an Anglo-Saxon one. If you think your writing may be overly academic, check the origins of some of your words. Anglo-Saxon words tend to feel more 'earthy' and direct, even for abstract concepts. Try 'truth' instead of 'veracity', 'happen' instead of 'eventuate'.

- Read some poetry. Find Dylan Thomas's *Under Milk Wood* and luxuriate in the original imagery and rhythmic delights. Read it aloud. Go back to your own writing with a mind and body buzzing with the richness of the sounds and rhythms of language.

And what about that 'sixth sense', love? Perhaps the tapestry makers were suggesting that love uses all the senses, rather than it being a sense of its own. Or is it that paying 'right attention' heightens love and compassion? This is, perhaps, venturing too far, making too great a claim for the practice of writing, but it could be that the more accurately you try to represent your experience of existing, the more your heart opens to the mystery of being in the world.

The desire to impress

Many years ago, a friend at art school who was gifted with an extraordinary natural drawing ability said she distrusted 'the lovely line' which she could make easily. I didn't know what she meant at the time, but I can see now she meant that such a line is only decorative, that it did not convey any truth. She simply had the ability to make it 'look good'. When you have a facility with writing, it can be easy to write 'the lovely line', to write to impress. The desire to write with beauty can easily be confused with the desire to impress. If you are really ruthless, you will take out every 'lovely line'. How do you tell which ones they are? Look for a certain smoothness, a proud flourish, the sleek swan gliding on the still waters of your mind.

Writing for the senses is not decoration, not a pretty painting you hang on the wall to match your carpet. If it is, throw it out. If it is padding to make the writing look or feel more substantial, throw it out. And if it is to make your writing sound more impressive or clever, throw it out. Writing for the senses is not about showing how elegant you look clothed in such fine words.

Writing for the senses is the flesh and muscle of your writing, as essential as your own flesh and muscle. Every word you write must be necessary. Each one must be there to help construct the illusion of a world on the page. If you are using the senses to create a character, keep it. If you are building mood or atmosphere, keep it. If you are furthering the narrative or exploring an idea, keep it.

Writing for the senses is to acknowledge and celebrate and expose the marvel—or the horror—of anything existing, of letting the ordinary white bowl on the table glow with its own reality. Writing for the senses is part of three-dimensional writing, writing which gives the illusion of lifelikeness and, at the same time, honours the mystery of existence.

To make a textured and lifelike 'tapestry', it is worth returning to the perennial advice, 'Show, don't tell.' From a writer's point of view, it doesn't really matter if the reality you are creating is a representation of an actual or imagined world, you still need the reader to inhabit it. See Workshop four for a refresher on showing and telling.

The Diving Bell and the Butterfly   Jean-Dominique Bauby

After every day's session on the vertical board, a stretcher-bearer wheels me from the rehabilitation room and parks me next to my bed, where I wait for the nurse's aides to swing me back between the sheets. And every day, since by now it is noon, the same stretcher-bearer wishes me a resolutely cheerful, 'Bon appetit!', his way of saying 'See you tomorrow'. And of course, to wish me a hearty appetite is about the same as saying 'Merry Christmas' on 15 August or 'Goodnight' in broad daylight. In the last eight months I have swallowed nothing save a few drops of lemon-flavoured water and one half-teaspoon of yoghurt which gurgled noisily in my windpipe. The feeding test—as they grandly called this banquet—was not a success. But no cause for alarm: I haven't starved. By means of a tube threaded into my stomach, two or three bags of brownish fluid provide my daily calorific needs. For pleasure, I have to turn to the vivid memory of tastes and smells, an inexhaustible reservoir of sensations. Once I was a master of recycling leftovers. Now I cultivate the art of simmering memories. You can sit down to table at any hour, with no fuss or ceremony. If it's a restaurant, no need to book. If I do the cooking, it's always a success. The bourguignon is tender, the boeuf en gelée translucent, the apricot pie possesses just the requisite tartness. Depending on my mood, I treat myself to a dozen snails, a plate of Alsatian sausage with sauerkraut, a bottle of late-vintage golden Gewurztraminer, or else I savour a simple soft-boiled egg with fingers of toast and lightly salted butter. What a banquet. The yolk flows warmly over my palate and down my throat. And indigestion is never a problem. Naturally I use the finest ingredients: the freshest vegetables, fish straight from the water, the most delicately marbled meat. Everything must be done just right. Just to make sure, a friend sent me the recipe for authentic home-made sausages, andouillettes de Troyes, with three different kinds of meat braided in strips. Moreover, I scrupulously observe the rhythm of the seasons. Just now I am cooling my tastebuds with melon and red fruit. I leave oysters and game for the autumn—should I feel like eating them, for I am becoming careful, even ascetic in matters of diet. At the outset of my protracted fast, deprivation sent me constantly to my imaginary larder. I was gluttonous. But today I could almost be content with a good old proletarian hard sausage trussed in netting and hanging permanently from the ceiling in some corner of my head. A knobbly Lyons rosette, for example, very dry and coarsely chopped. Every slice melts a little on your tongue before you start chewing it to extract all its flavour. The origin of my addiction to sausage goes back forty years. Although still at an age for sweets, I already preferred delicatessen meats, and my maternal grandfather's nurse noticed that when I visited the gloomy apartment on the boulevard Raspail I would ask her in a beguiling lisp for a sausage. Skilled at indulging the desires of children and the elderly, she eventually pulled of a double coup, by giving me sausage and marrying my grandfather just before he died. My joy at receiving such a gift was in direct proportion to the annoyance these unexpected nuptials caused my family. I have only the vaguest picture of my grandfather: supine and stern-faced in the gloom, resembling Victor Hugo's portrait on the old five-hundred-franc note in use at that time. I have a much clearer image of the sausage lying incongruously among my Dinky toys and children's books.

I fear I will never eat a better sausage.

Bauby evokes a quintessentially French memory of the sensual delight of food. In the direst circumstances, deprived of movement and even the ability to eat, he creates for himself—and for us—the pleasure of food. Read *The Diving Bell and the Butterfly* for its extraordinary awareness of the detail of life. It is worth knowing that Bauby, paralysed by a stroke, blinked this memoir letter by letter (each blink like the jerky movement of a butterfly, hence the title) to his assistant.

Writing exercises

1 Remembered senses

Write a list of sensory experiences—of smells, tastes, sounds, touches and sights. The list must be very precise: don't write *the smell of roses* but *the smell of the red rose just inside my grandmother's front gate,* not *the taste of popcorn* but *the taste of the warm popcorn I ate the first time I went to the cinema with James.* Then select one of the sense memories and, beginning with the sense experience in the first line, use it as a springboard, following the memory wherever it goes.

2 Hands

Call to mind hands you have noticed. They could be your grandmother's, your son's, your own hands. If you are not someone who especially notices hands then use something else—eyes, smiles. Focus on one memory and start writing, letting it flow where it will. This is not an exercise in description—description for its own sake can be boring—but simply a way to find the sensory key to an emotional connection and thereby access the original memories. (Ten minutes)

3 Rooms

Take a pencil and paper and draw in as much detail as you can a room in which you have spent time. It can be a childhood bedroom, a backpacker dormitory in Barcelona, your first studio in New York, a university lecture hall, a doctor's waiting room, a bathroom in Paris, a barn full of machinery—any kind of room. Include details such as the feather pattern on the carpet in your studio, then start writing. This is not an exercise in description but a way into the creative network of memory. If it proves fruitful, it is an exercise you can keep using over and over to generate new material. (Twenty minutes)

4 Music

Select music from a particular period of your life. Listen to the music and let the faces and feelings of the time come back. Jot down whatever comes up. Take one of the people or events you have noted and write about them. You can also use music in association with most of the other exercises. Music is a skilled gatherer of memories. (Fifteen minutes)

5 Senses and emotion

Select an incident where you experienced strong emotion. Convey the experience without naming it and without using abstract words—no grief, love, anger, pity, joy! Evoke the experience through the senses and through 'showing'— action, dialogue and scene. This is an exercise in disciplined writing—it doesn't mean you leave out abstract words forever after. It is a revelation, though, to see how much a good, hardworking concrete word can do. (Twenty minutes)

6 Poets know

Read a poem by a twentieth-century poet—a poem about a person, place, thing or emotion rather than an intellectual or political idea. Read it slowly. Pick the three words that are most evocative to you. Write three short pieces using each word as a springboard for your own memories. (Ten minutes each)

7 Cross-fertilising

Find a CD or site online which demonstrates the sound of various musical instruments. Listen to, for example, the sounds of the flute, piano, cello, triangle, oboe. For each one, try to write its colour, texture and taste. Are flute notes pale blue or lime green? Does the sound of an oboe 'feel' like velvet and 'taste' like warm chocolate? Simply write a list of associations that come to mind as you listen. (Twenty minutes)

13

WORKSHOP ELEVEN
Research

The investigator, in fact, operates in an uncomfortable zone between insider and outsider, and that tension is often what fuels and makes interesting the project.

ROBIN HEMLEY

The Mitchell Library in Sydney, with its grand bronze doors, white marble columns and vast ceiling, is a kind of temple to research. Like city libraries all over the world, it affirms that knowledge matters, that it is worth conserving records and diaries and documents so that we in the present can access ideas and experiences from the past. Of course, the internet is now the worldwide library in most homes, schools and workplaces, an instant access to facts, stories, firsthand accounts, documents and photographs. It's clear that we value recorded knowledge as much as we value knowledge acquired in daily life. We are surrounded by information and have easy access to it, which is both an advantage and a difficulty for the nonfiction writer.

168

It's worth exploring the value of research for us as writers. It can enrich memoir, including travel memoir, and the personal essay, and is often central to narrative nonfiction and biography.

Memoir relies mostly on memory, of course, but there are many occasions when you need research: to check the facts, to offer a broader historical or other context, to save your story from becoming self-indulgent or falling in on itself, to support or open out your ideas. Without research a memoir can be without a framework to give it meaning, or it can become one-sided, unreliable, or too narrowly or inwardly focused.

For narrative nonfiction and biography, however, research is central. The emphasis is less on personal memories and more on the story you have found and are assembling. Personal memory may be threaded through it, but your key material will need interviews, documents, library and internet research and visiting locations.

Research can be used to give context to memories, to enrich the material, to add factual evidence, and it can also be used as a structural device. Your search itself, the journeys to other cities or countries, the rifling through boxes of letters and cards, the phone calls and internet searches and interviews, can all become part of the story. In fact, your investigations, your quest, can become the story thread. In *The Mind of a Thief*, I set out to explore both a native title claim by the local Wiradjuri people and my own history in my home town. The reader comes with me on this quest as I visit the Mitchell Library, drive to the country many times, talk to Wiradjuri men and women, and try to piece together the story. It is not necessary to foreground the research, of course, but it can provide a clear narrative thread to allow your material to unfold in an engaging way.

One word of warning before you plunge into the vast world of research: being a researcher is like being a detective—you find a thread, you follow it along, you come to a full stop and have to jump sideways and follow another clue, until at last you uncover the piece of information you have being searching for. It is such a pleasure that it's easy to become hooked on research. But many writers arrive at class with vast amounts of research material and feel utterly overwhelmed by it, which is why I suggest that you write and research at the same time. Find what you need to get started, start writing, identify what you next need and do some research, keep writing, even leave a gap if the research is going to require too much time, keep writing and come back to gaps later. Of course, you might need quite a large body of research to even get started if you are writing a biography or a nonfiction work where the material is outside your experience, but even then, try to write up sections as you go.

Kinds of research

Primary sources

Letters, emails, postcards, photographs, jewellery, memorabilia, diaries, certificates, documents—these are the tangible treasures of most people's lives. They are kept in drawers or in cartons or suitcases under beds, the material handed down through families. They are also key resources of primary research, our evidence of having lived. The fact that we need to prove, even to ourselves—or perhaps first of all to ourselves—that we really exist is a central issue of philosophy, but here it is enough to say that keeping photos, mementos, letters and journals is probably not foolish and sentimental but the result of a basic human need to 'keep the evidence'.

Primary sources are also found through searches on the internet. One of my most exciting discoveries when I was researching *The Mind of a Thief* was the diaries of the missionaries who had tried to convert the Wiradjuri in the early nineteenth century. They could not have known that their private thoughts, their observations and their judgements would one day be available on the internet for the whole world to read!

More traditional sources of documents are: official records such as births, deaths and marriages, the Bureau of Statistics, electoral rolls, and court, church, school, shipping and government department records. Nearly every organisation you or your subject has ever dealt with will have a record, somewhere. For current material, don't forget social media sources and blogs. And although, strictly speaking, they are not primary sources, I would include newspapers and magazines, which can supply historical facts as well as social and cultural context.

Interviews

Gloria, a workshop student, interviewed her family as she searched for more information about her father, who had left when she was a child. She eventually discovered that he was Indigenous and that on his side of the family she had dozens of Aboriginal relatives whom she'd never met or even heard of. Her newly discovered Indigenous heritage deepened her life story and added a richness she could not have imagined.

Some suggestions for interviewing:

• Explain your purpose and make clear your intentions; reassure people that your aim is not to hurt or upset. Most are more likely to open up to you if they perceive you as non-judgemental and non-threatening.

- Decide on an electronic recording device or handwritten notes, depending on what your interviewee is more comfortable with. I find it useful to take notes as well as record, as it gives me a better idea of what I noticed as significant at the time. It is not always necessary to transcribe recorded interviews if you take succinct notes. You can use the recording to check.

- Have a relaxed setting and approach. Try to put your subject at ease. A loose, rambling conversation may produce more interesting information than a stiff question-and-answer style.

- Ask your interviewee to select a few photographs or other things (books, jewellery, ornaments) that have some significance as springboards for stories.

- Prepare fact-oriented questions for information, such as: Where were you born? What school did you go to?

- Prepare experience-oriented questions for stories, such as: What was your favourite toy/dress/pet? What did you do in the afternoons after school?

- Ask particular rather than general questions, because the mind goes blank when faced with broad questions. The more specific the questions, the better the stories will be.

- Listen and ask questions from the responses. Be prepared to leave your questions and follow the line the interviewee wants to explore.

- Listen for what is not said as well as what is said. Some silences say more than words. Be sensitive to what can be asked— sometimes it can be too painful to revisit certain parts of a life.

- Some people may find it easier to respond to your queries

if you write out your questions and ask them to write their answers. They have time to think about their responses and the chance to express them in their own words.

- Keep your records of interview even after you have used them—you never know when you might need to refer to them.

Part of primary research is collecting data from a vast array of interview sources under academic rules and discipline, so if that is required, it would be useful to enrol in a course on research methods at a university or writers' centre.

Secondary sources

A secondary source is information already assembled and interpreted by someone else, for example, newspapers, histories, novels and films. These are not necessarily any less valuable for a memoirist or nonfiction writer. Writers used to have to go to libraries or travel to find most of their source material, but now it's often a matter of sitting at our desks and using a search engine on the internet.

Remember that such sources are not necessarily historical, as is often assumed. Depending on your writing project you could include secondary research material from any area of knowledge—psychology, sociology, geology, biology, fashion, literature, popular culture, the list is endless. Such material can add depth and texture to your story. In *The Blue Plateau: A Landscape Memoir,* Mark Tredinnick includes information from geology, geography, botany, Indigenous anthropology and literature to give his natural history of the Blue Mountains region near Sydney many layers of richness.

Experiential research

Sometimes it is not enough to find all your information in a library or online, nor even enough to ask a few questions. Sometimes the writer needs to get involved. Visiting locations, being 'embedded' in a situation or re-enacting events are all useful forms of firsthand research.

Visiting locations gives your writing the advantage of fresh, firsthand observations, especially the details of place or of people. Other people's reports and photographs can never replace your writer's eye on the scene, or on the expressions flitting across your subject's face. The atmosphere of a place can yield significant clues and fill in a human response.

Being 'embedded' or 'immersed' in a situation is a long-term research choice where the writer becomes part of what he or she is writing about. This is a major commitment of time and of yourself and you need to feel ready for that kind of choice. To write *The Bookseller of Kabul*, Åsne Seierstad lived with the family in Kabul who were the subject of her book. She would not otherwise have had access to the details of daily life in Kabul that make her story so vivid, nor to the kinds of personal experiences that make the stories so compelling.

A re-enactment is another all-consuming form of research where the writer decides to re-enact a certain event or situation. A well-known example is Julie Powell's *Julie and Julia: 365 Days, 524 Recipes, 1 Tiny Apartment Kitchen,* in which Julie cooks her way through all the recipes in chef Julia Child's recipe book. A much earlier example of the genre is Thor Heyerdahl's *Kon-Tiki,* in which he builds a raft to cross the South Pacific in a re-tracing of what he believed was the path of migration from South America to Polynesia. In these cases, the research does not so much add to the book as compose the whole material of the book.

For more on this kind of immersion writing, see Workshop eighteen: Creative nonfiction.

How to include research material

Including research to either enrich your memoir and nonfiction or to provide the central subject matter is a delicate matter. It requires the sensitivity of a natural cook, who mixes the ingredients not by following a set recipe but by sensing what this particular dish requires. Too much inclusion of research can make the book 'recipe' too dry, not enough research and it might not be nourishing enough. Too many research details can also clog the narrative. Be ruthless in what you choose, how much you use, and where you use it. There are a number of different combinations you can try, according to the kind of research you have done.

- Putting letters or journal extracts directly into your story can make it more lively and lend immediacy to the times you are describing. The events are fresh and unexamined, not layered over with years of retelling or interpretation. Direct extracts are best used sparingly and edited to keep only the most effective descriptions and insights.
- Using letters, journals, photos and mementos as memory keys is also fruitful. Re-reading journals and gazing at old photos is a good way to open the door to lost memories. You may not put the material directly into your story, but it can be a starting point or you can paraphrase the information. Pull out the diary your father kept during the war, the poem you wrote when you were in hospital. If objects are not connected with memory but are evidence of other people's lives, ancestors or otherwise, you can use them as

a way of inferring aspects or character, or even to imaginatively re-create aspects of their lives.

- Objects can also be used as a structural device. In *The Hare with Amber Eyes,* Edmund de Waal uses his family's collection of small carved Japanese creatures both as a way of re-imagining his family's past and as a structural image that connects his family's story down through history and across the world. Perhaps there's an object, letter or document handed down through your family that can serve as a connecting motif.

- Interviews can be included either as direct question and answer, a method often used in magazines such as *Rolling Stone,* or indirect, reworded or summarised speech, for example, 'My father straightened and told me he didn't think I should be asking him about his life before he met Mum.' A mixture of direct quotes and reworded summaries also works well. In each case, it will make the material more engaging if you also set the scene and make observations as the interview unfolds. Body language, surroundings and reactions can all add as much information as the actual interview. Very short excerpts of an interview can be threaded through a larger story if it would slow the narrative too much to have a large section of interview. Moving from narrative telling to interview can be done through a transitional passage that sets the scene for the interview.

- Firsthand or 'on location' research is more easily woven in when the quest for information is the structural thread. For example, while looking for your grandfather's grave in Ireland, describe where you are, the places and people you meet and your reactions to them. If your writing project involves being immersed or embedded in a current situation, then the 'on location' research is obviously going to be central to your story and its texture. It's important not to let such atmospheric writing overbalance your story, or let the logistics of research—the travel plans and appointments—clog the writing. Include details and events not because they happened but because they matter to your story.

- Secondary material such as articles, essays, histories and reports can be used in the same way as primary documents, either as direct extracts or explained in your own words. It might be that you only need a taste of the actual language of your source, or perhaps you need only the gist of a chapter. In *The Mind of a Thief* I used direct extracts from missionaries' diaries because I wanted their early nineteenth-century minds present on the page, but I reworded the points in the *Native Title Act* because the legal language struck me as dry and impenetrable.

With all forms of research you need to be judicious, even ruthless, about what you include and what is left out. It is very easy to become attached to the research and want to keep it all, or be afraid of misinterpreting it and as a result overloading the story with researched evidence. It is important to get the facts right, but that doesn't mean you include every fact, only what is relevant to the story you want to tell. Often, a day of research can become one line in your book.

There are different ways to reference the research you have done and to acknowledge the sources you have used. Academic referencing requires footnotes and a full bibliography, but for memoir, narrative nonfiction and personal essay it's usually enough to mention the name of the source as you come to it, the person or book or article, and to include a list in your thanks or acknowledgements section. It's important to acknowledge the general reading you have done, even if it hasn't been directly quoted within the book, and to acknowledge the people who have given you information or helped you in other ways.

Remember: keep a record of every piece of research material as you find it. Write title, author, publication and date. Trying to rediscover research material can be a nightmare.

Reading

Ransacking Paris Patti Miller

The rue Simart was a kind of littoral, I suppose, a shore between privilege and disadvantage, often delineated by race instead of class. The raging boy was white, and so were most of the *clochards*, street beggars, but all the *sans papiers*, refugees without legal status, and many of the poor were Africans or Arabs from former French colonies: Mali, Senegal, Algeria, the Sudan. Algerians have been in Paris longer, a lot of them coming to escape the civil war in the 1960s and are more likely to have jobs and small businesses—*allez chez Arab* meant 'go to the corner shop'. When shonky apartment buildings burn down and lives are lost, most of the names of the dead are African. Most lived in wretched state housing towers, called HLM, in the *banlieu*, outer suburbs, but there is a large African quartier on the other side of boulevard Barbès. They are 'the people' now, the disadvantaged and the oppressed.

Montaigne, Stendhal, Rousseau, de Beauvoir all wrote about 'the people', Rousseau especially: 'An inextinguishable hatred grew in my heart against the oppression to which the unhappy people are subject and against their oppressors.' And Montaigne lived in a peasant household until he was weaned because his father wanted him to have sympathy for 'the people'. Stendhal, in an age of revolutions, defended the people but was honest, more than once, about his distaste: 'I loathe to have dealings with the hoi-polloi while at the same time under the name of *the people,* I long passionately for their happiness.'

Madame de Sévigné—I'm sorry to say because I did come to like her over coffee—wasn't sympathetic even in theory; she describes the punishment of the leader of a people's insurrection in Brittany where she came from:

> The day before yesterday, a ruffian who had called the tune and begun the thieving of the official stamped paper, was broken on the wheel; when he was dead he was quartered and his four quarters put on view at the four corners of the town . . . Sixty burghers have been arrested: tomorrow the hangings begin. This province is a fine example to the others, and particularly that they should respect their governors.

In case the details of seventeenth-century justice are not clear: 'broken on the wheel' means being tied to a large wagon wheel and then beaten with wooden or iron cudgels until your body is bashed through the spokes. 'Quartered' means the body is then cut into four. I am sure it did make them respect their governors.

It was several centuries later and I was from the other side of the world, standing on a balcony, God-like, watching. Like Annie Ernaux, I had come from 'the people', as much as that applies in Australia. Neither of my parents had any education past primary school; my father's parents were a farmer and a housemaid, my mother's a house painter and a barmaid, all hardworking and quiet people. My father owned a farm but it was a small patch of dirt to support a family of ten—eleven counting my grand-mother lying in the dark room with no windows to the outside. The house was shabby; boards rotted on the veranda, in one of the bedrooms white ants had destroyed the walls, and cement, which had made do as plaster, was falling off the walls in the kitchen. We had no heaters, no inside toilet—*The Land* news-paper for toilet paper in the cracked fibro lavvy outside—and no hot water unless it was heated in a kettle.

For most of my childhood I had no shower and no bath, inef-fectually washing in a small tin dish. In my first few weeks of high school in town, I was drinking at the water bubblers one lunch-time and realised the girl next to me was looking at my arms. I noticed for the first time that both my arms, from wrist to past the elbows, had several 'high-tide' layers of dirt on them, dirty, dirtier and dirtiest. I had not realised I was dirty until I saw myself through her astonished gaze. Stendhal was right, the people are dirty—'dirty, damp, blackish'—but I think I spent the following decades hiding evidence of my grimy body. I succeeded well enough; I'm not 'the people' anymore. I'm one of those who can talk about them, watch them, from a balcony in Paris.

In this extract from *Ransacking Paris* there is a combination of personal history, memories and researched material from various French memoirists. I have used direct quotes, phrases and a whole paragraph, as well as summarising ideas, woven throughout with my own memories. Read *Ransacking Paris* for the way it combines research with daily life, for its observations of a life in transition and for its exploration of identity.

Writing exercises

1 Objects and documents

Take an object or document of significance in your story and use it as an entry point for writing about the particular episode it relates to. (Ten minutes)

2 Research and rewrite

Do some internet or library research related to your memoir. It can be from any area—science, music, medicine, politics, history—and then combine it with writing you have already done by rewriting the material in your own words. (As long as it takes)

3 Research and extract

As above, do some research in any area related to the story you want to tell. Try placing a relevant extract from the research material and write a lead-in and lead-out of the extract material. (Twenty minutes)

4 Interview

Identify an area in your writing that could be enriched by interview. Conduct the interview and weave the material into your chapter using a mixture of direct quotes and summa-rising. Remember to include scene and character details if that enhances the material. (As long as it takes)

14

WORKSHOP TWELVE

The storyteller's seat—Narrating position

A straight oak looks bent in the water.
What matters is not merely that we see things, but how we see them.

MICHEL DE MONTAIGNE

Once upon a time, in a country far away ...The ritual words are spoken and the storyteller has our attention. The centre of any story, fiction or nonfiction, fairytale or not, is the storyteller. The storyteller, or narrator, weaves the spell, en-chants (catches in a chant) the reader. As you spell out your story, the listeners and readers are caught and held by your voice. The voice of the story-teller is the sound going back to the beginning of human time; it is the voice spinning the strange shapes of words over what has happened, pausing, rushing on, slowing down, throwing out a net to hold the moment. It creates both an emotional connection and a structural thread.

Oral storytellers usually recount a story about someone else. In memoir, however, the storyteller and the main character (protagonist) is the same person. It's a confronting situation; you are required to be in two places, or two roles at the same time, both narrator and principal protagonist. Which perspective do you use, narrator or protagonist? How do you comment on yourself? Where do you stand—on stage or off? Do you leap back and forth between the two? Do you reveal, as narrator, events and insights that you, as protagonist, do not yet know? Being narrator and central protagonist can obviously create a number of difficulties in relation to voice and narrative position.

Narrating position—more on voice

Voice, as we have learned in Workshop five, conveys your attitude, your relationship to the material. Readers gain their cues about how to relate and react to the material from the narrator. If, in conversation, the speaker keeps changing his attitude from anger to humour, to bitterness, to gaiety, it is difficult for the listener to know how to react. The same is true for the reader. As narrator, it doesn't mean that you never vary your voice, but there does need to be a recognisable 'attitude' or relationship to the content, so that the reader knows how to relate to it, how to react.

The consistency of your narrating voice can be affected by your relationship to the material and by performance anxiety, that is, your relationship to your audience. If you are unsure of how you feel about the person or episode you are writing about, or when you have repressed how you really feel, the voice can become evasive, self-conscious, inauthentic or just plain embarrassing to read. It happens because the protagonist is suddenly writing the material instead of the narrator.

In one my own memoirs, *Whatever the Gods Do*, I wrote several scenes about singing classes I had taken one summer. I was very unsure about singing and, during the lessons, I felt overwhelmed by a sense of inadequacy. In early drafts, that sense of inadequacy swamped me as I wrote the scenes, so that the writing voice became self-conscious. My dauntless editor pointed it out to me, saying that it was jarring and uncomfortable for the reader. She said it was as if I had suddenly started playing 'Roll Out the Barrel' in the middle of a Bach cantata. *I had let the feelings in the material, the feelings of the protagonist, overwhelm the narrator.* It was necessary to step back from the material, step back to the position of the narrator to tell the story.

If you feel your material is overwhelming and distorting your voice, consciously step back to the position of narrator. In every case, the first step in finding your relationship to the material is moving into the position of observer. This is an inner process, a kind of detachment, which all writers cultivate to varying degrees.

Narrating voice can also be affected by 'performance anxiety', which happens when you feel very conscious of your readers and their reactions. It can be a specific anxiety regarding particular topics that you believe could upset your family or friends, or a more general worry that the public may criticise your writing. All of these concerns about other people's judgements need to be bundled together, tied up tightly and locked in a drawer—at least while you write the first draft. A first draft needs to be written freely, without worrying what your readers will think. There will be opportunities in later drafts to address the possibly legitimate concerns of other people.

You, as storyteller, must feel free to tell your story in your own way.

Narrating persona

It's important to understand at this stage in your writing—and perhaps you already have—that the person writing the memoir is not the whole of you. It is a specific, word-oriented, story-telling aspect of you. Much as the first-person oral storyteller or actor constructs a performing 'self' who may be wittier, more hopeless, wiser or sillier than their normal selves, so the narrator in literary nonfiction generally—and especially in the sub-genre of the personal essay—'constructs' a narrating self. It is made of aspects of yourself, but taken out of the general mix and heightened to some extent. Still you, but a more delineated you.

Narrating position—distance

As narrator, you are in a relationship with your readers. They are listening to you, sympathising with you, being charmed by you, perhaps disagreeing with you. As in all relationships, there is the issue of 'space', that is, how close or distant you are to your reader. Some people like to stand very close, to reveal intimate details on first meeting, to lay bare their emotions. Others are reserved, keeping their emotions to themselves or describing them from an analytical distance. The same kind of sense of 'personal space' operates in the writer–reader relationship and it is you, the writer, who determines how close or distant it will be.

How close or distant, that is, how emotionally engaged or not a reader feels, is determined to a large extent by the writer's voice. If you write with a detached and distant voice your writing may feel cold, which means readers may not feel engaged by the material. On the other hand, if you write in a very intimate voice the reader may feel you are standing too close. Responses to closeness and distance are individual—it's not a matter of a 'correct' distance, but one that feels right for you.

The distance the writer takes from her material is exactly the distance the reader will feel.

Interestingly, a sense of closeness or distance is not a matter of *what* you reveal but *how* you reveal it—where you, as narrator, stand in relation to the experience, whether, in fact, you write from *inside* or *outside* the experience. Catherine Millet, in *The Sexual Life of Catherine M.*, reveals intimate details about her sexual practices but with such detachment that the reader never feels pushed up too close to the experience. Millet is outside the experience as she writes, watching herself, thus putting the reader in the position of voyeur rather than participant. Perhaps you do not want your readers to feel voyeuristic either, and in that case there is always discretion! If, however, you want to write about intimate material, it could be useful to step back and write it from a more detached perspective.

If you want to draw the reader closer rather than keep them back, write from inside your material, that is, as if you are reliving the experience as you write it. It requires a leap into 'original' memory and, depending on the nature of the memory, can be emotionally painful. It does however give the reader a powerful, up-close taste of the experience.

Being aware of closeness and distance as a narrator means you can consciously choose how close to your material you want to be. It also means you can move closer or further away as you wish. If your material is too overwhelming, mentally stepping 'outside' it and then writing from that detached perspective may give you the control you require. If you see that your writing is becoming too dry, too cold, then you can take the plunge into the experience, remember the lived feel of it and write it as if you were reliving it. You could even try writing it in the present tense to give a vivid sense of immediacy and closeness.

In the opening paragraph of Robert Dessaix's *What Days Are For*, the narrator brings us close-up inside his mind in the present tense:

> His face beams down at me like God's from a dome of bright light. Everything gleams. Every blond hair on his tanned forearms glistens as he fits my mask. It's a glossy, muscled forearm, used to hefting bodies. I've always been taken with forearms and this is a singularly lustrous, sinewy example. 'So tell me, Robert,' he says gently, somewhere high up there inside his dome of dazzling light—am I already dead? No, not yet, soon—'have you had a good day?'

Further on in the same book, the distance is more detached, even though the narration is still present tense.

> In theatre and art gallery foyers you suspect you're among kindred spirits. That's the thing. Here, you imagine, a spot of sympathetic darshan, as Prakash might put it, will not be out of the question—although nothing too focused, nothing too clear-eyed, as might happen around a dinner table or in a café. For infatuation to blossom, room must always be left for misapprehension and the play of semblances; the possibility of having made a ghastly mistake must always be thrillingly present.

Narrative distance is also influenced by whether one is writing as a child or adult. Sometimes, if the child's perspective is too intense and unreflective, it can become claustrophobic for the reader. A shift to the adult perspective in the same material will result in a sense of space. Re-read the extract *The Long Way Home* in Workshop five to experience the shift.

The sense of 'space' is, naturally, a very individual experience. If you characteristically write 'close-up', some readers may criticise you as too self-absorbed, others will love the intimacy. If you write in a more detached way, some readers may find you too cool, others will revel in the drier intellectual atmosphere. It is up to you as the narrator to find the distance that suits you and suits your material.

Narrating position—time

'Time of narration' is the point in time from which you are narrating events. It is most often the same as the actual time you are writing, that is, after the events: *I was standing at the kitchen door when my father stumbled in.* But the time of narration can also be constructed as being at the same time as events, in the present tense: *I'm standing at the kitchen table when my father stumbles in*—although the reader knows it's not happening to the writer as they write!

Using the appropriate tense is particularly important in handling time. It can become confusing if, for example, you write in the present tense about the past and then use the present tense for your contemporary 'time of writing' thoughts. It can make it difficult for the reader to discern which 'present' you are in. It is helpful to use the present tense only for the 'time of writing' to avoid confusion. Because this is an issue that creates problems in many first drafts, let me illustrate with an example.

Jane sent a memoir manuscript recounting her travels in Europe. She began her story at her current age, fifty years old, then shifted the narrative to the time she set out at the age of nineteen. So far it was clear that the narrator was writing from the present about her youthful adventures. But then the narrator began writing things that seemed naive for a fifty-year-old—she 'sounded' nineteen. The narration often slipped into the present tense, making the 'time of telling' more unclear. I suspected that she had transcribed journals written when she was nineteen (which turned out to be correct). The effect was confusion, as if listening to someone who speaks like a child one moment and as an adult the next, making it difficult to know how to relate. The solution was simple: to signal clearly which 'time of telling' was being used at any given time using a device such as journal dates—*Ibiza, 23 April 1985*—when she was narrating from her nineteen-year-old self, and straight-forward text when she was narrating from the present. Another solution would be to tell the past events in the past tense and use the present tense only for the 'time of writing'.

If you want to change narrating time, a device such as a journal entry or email format, or a layout device, for example, a double space between narrators, can be enough to signal the shift in 'time of narration'.

In narration, it is also important that it is clear whether you are writing about general time or a particular time. General time is when you write about what usually happened, indicated by phrases such *I'd usually go to the beach* or *I eat muesli or eggs for breakfast,* and is often characterised by a series of quick snapshot images. Particular time is when you write a particular event close-up in chronological time. Confusion arises for the reader when it's unclear whether they are following a precise event or a generalised sequence. Use both types of time, but if you mix the two, be clear when you step between them so that the reader can follow.

Constructing a time-of-narrating frame

When you are interweaving a number of different times, to avoid confusion, the 'time of narrating' needs to be clear. In *Whatever the Gods Do,* the memoir about my friend Dina, who died, there were a number of different times I wanted to write about: the years of friendship when all was well, the intensive period when Dina was ill, the period when her son stayed with me every weekend after she died, the summer he left, the subsequent year when I visited him and he came back to visit me. Making it more complicated, I included the episode of my father's death, which occurred after these events, as well as incidents from my childhood many years previously.

To manage all these times, it was necessary to have a clearly indicated 'time of narrating' from which I could easily move around the various sequences. I used a 'framing device', a sojourn at a beach house where I had spent several weeks sifting through the various elements of the story. The 'time of narrating' was constructed; that is, although I was only at the beach house for a few weeks, it reads as if I were there the whole time. I mentioned the beach house a number of times in the narrative so that the reader knew I was narrating all these events from the perspective of a particular time several years afterwards.

To move about through the various times and not lose the reader, it was also necessary to regularly use 'directive' or 'locating' phrases. These are phrases like *It was a summer that makes me think now of paths crossing* or *I have come to this beach-house here on the coastal lagoon* or *It was about a month after the haemorrhage* or *I have The Book open in front of me now.* Or *One day when I was a teenager.* All these phrases are at the beginning of paragraphs and immediately locate the reader in the 'time of narrating'.

A 'time of narrating' can be implied. It does not have to be constructed in the text as a particular time and place. Often it is clear that you are writing from 'now' and there is no confusion. As narrator, you hold all the story threads in your hand. Your perspective on the threads, where you narrate from, will have a key influence on the texture of your story.

Narrator as structural device

The narrator is also part of the structure. The reader listens to the narrator who leads them through the various events, stitching them together, making sense of them. A strong narrating persona can hold together many different story elements and can, some-times, be enough to hold a whole life story or memoir together. It can act like a thread, creating a sense of continuity. In *Angela's Ashes* by Frank McCourt, the narrator is the main structural device giving cohesion and meaning to the many short narra-tives within the book.

The narrator can tell stories and can also comment on them; he can address the reader directly and create the sense of being in a conversation. Using asides, such as 'you know', or 'by the way', as Dessaix does in *What Days Are For*, or asking ques-tions—'What will I do next?'—can let the reader feel they are part of the dialogue. This sense of a conversation creates a struc-tural thread the reader can happily follow.

Reading

Whatever the Gods Do   Patti Miller

The house I have come to has nothing to do with Theo or singing lessons. But it suits because it looks out on the lagoon and not on the crashing waves of the beach. Waves are too excitable, too obvious, for the currents I want to follow. The house has wide glass doors across the front of a single room and from them the gleam of still water is visible through the she-oaks that grow at the water's edge despite the saltiness of the lagoon. The lines of their shadows move a little as waterbirds and breezes briefly disturb the stillness. I go through the doors and onto the veranda and gaze down at the water. Fragments surface in my mind as I stand and listen to the unfamiliar waterbird sounds.

Dina stood on a stage, singing, with a band behind her. She had black hair, thick and curly, and wore a blue suede dress with appliquéd pink suede hands—one across one of her breasts and the other reaching down between her legs. She had made it herself; she was a skilled designer and made most of her own clothes. She had also made a jacket of pieces of silk and brocade, emerald and jade green, wrapped and tied in a most intricate way—like a kind of rock'n'roll kimono (she liked the Japanese aesthetic—the pure relationship between form and function, she said, but she couldn't help bending it to her own ends). She told me she liked imagining the design in her head and then figuring out how to make it work. She knew the look she wanted, the fabric and colour and shape, but said she never knew when she began how it was all going to fit together, or whether it was going to work at all. I never saw Dina wearing the suede dress, but she showed it to me the summer before she died. She was Theo's mother.

I didn't know her as a singer. That was before I met her. I think she was performing in the country rock band when she first met Kit, Theo's father, but by the time they married several years later she had stopped singing professionally and become a designer. I had heard her sing though, in her earthy, slightly mocking voice, as if she didn't take it seriously. She simply opened her mouth and sang as if it were nothing. When I heard her, there was always a pang of longing or hunger—as if I was missing the thing I most wanted, the thing that would fill the hole I suspect is just under the false bottom of my soul (well-made, nicely covered, no one would notice, it seems as if you are whole, no gaps anywhere). So I'd stand back and listen and, if it was a song I was meant to join in with, 'Happy Birthday' or 'Auld Lang Syne', I'd mouth the words.

'Happy birthday, dear Theo,' Dina had sung, head back, hair tied in a ponytail, wearing a white shirt and blue jeans, just like any other mother. This would have been the last time I heard her sing. She was thirty-seven, Theo was two.

This extract from *Whatever the Gods Do*, my second memoir, shows the 'frame' of the beach house and the shift into the story of Theo and Dina that I was writing there. Look at this memoir to see how a frame might work in holding together a number of different stories from different times as well as providing a structure for the narrator to reflect on past events.

Writing exercises

1 Journal

Write an episode from the past—it could be childhood, adolescence or only a few years ago. The next day, without re-reading the first piece, write the episode again but this time do it as if in a journal kept at the time of the events. Remember that in your journal you are younger, probably have a more limited vocabulary, have less perspective on events and are probably still emotional about them. Notice if there is a difference in the closeness or distance of the narrating voice. (Fifteen minutes each)

2 Outside/inside

Write a significant episode in your life as if writing an account for a social historian or other researcher who wants to know about this period in your life. Write it as honestly and with as much detail as you can but write from your stored intellectual memory of events. The next day, without re-reading the first piece, immerse yourself in the memory of that time and write it again, in the present tense, as if it were happening right now. Write it as if the memory was going to disappear forever and you needed to re-create it as exactly as possible on the page. (Thirty minutes each)

3 Juggling time

Write five or more different episodes that have happened at different times, but which are connected in terms of the narrative. Next day, create a 'time of writing' frame to connect the various times, directing the reader by using 'locating' phrases. The frame can be a place, or a time, or even another episode in which you embed the other events. (As long as it takes)

4 Conversation

Write a piece where you are teasing out elements of your story as if you are having a conversation with your reader. Include any of your usual conversation asides and links, even questions. See whether this narrating persona gives you a strong thread with which you can hold your stories together. (One hour)

15

WORKSHOP THIRTEEN

Beauty of form—More structure

If you have a vision of the form early on, or even perhaps
before you begin, be open to the idea that though it may seem
like the perfect one, it may be simply what gets you started.

JUDITH BARRINGTON

Structure becomes more of an issue the longer you write. By this stage, you might be in need of an expansion of ideas on structure, some tips on how to proceed—and perhaps even some trouble-shooting notes if problems have already arisen.

A beautiful structure

According to a classic Aristotelian philosophy of art, a beautiful structure requires unity, proportion, a connection between all parts, and meaning, but I find it useful to observe the structuring principles of nature. There is a beauty of form in the natural world that comes from adapting to the environment to survive. The pencil-like elegance of the poplar is a successful adaptation to the need to conserve water in dry Mediterranean climates, the graceful shape of the panther evolved according to the requirement to be fast and agile. The beauty of both comes from necessity. If, when you are considering the structure of your memoir, you think in terms of what is necessary, you cannot go far wrong. *Be as ruthless as nature when you are considering what needs to be included.*

Meaning

For a memoir or any work of art to be more than pleasingly organised elements, there needs to be a sense that it is going somewhere, that it has *meaning.*

All the same, meaning is not necessarily a starting point. Starting with the abstract idea of meaning or themes tends to result in an over-controlled structure—the reader can see the writer running about with the plans. (Of course, you may want to foreground the structure—more on this later.)

You write a book not so much because of what you know but because of what you don't know. You have passionate questions that you want to explore. If you know exactly where you are going and how to get there, the incentive of discovery is missing. You would be merely filling in what you already know. If the passionate questions required to write a book have been answered, it makes it hard to start and plodding to write.

On the other hand, if structure is left too long, the whole memoir can become unmanageable and end up shapeless or, at least, lumpy. A fundamentally flawed structure can be very difficult to undo and sometimes requires starting again.

Rather than trying to work out the whole structure beforehand, or wandering aimlessly along, feel your way in the dark for a while. Be sensitive to what is emerging in your writing. Your memoir might not be about what you first think it is. The creative process has its own agenda, which does not always correlate with the conscious mind's plans. The process of trying things out, of playing, can help reveal what is in the dark.

Feeling the way

This is not a step-by-step list of things to do but some ways to feel your way in the dark and play with possible structures. Try the ones that suit you.

- Instead of sitting and thinking, try writing down your vague thoughts and ideas—unsurprisingly, writers tend to think more effectively on the page! This kind of writing does not have to be well formed—it is simply talking to oneself on the page, wondering and wandering through possibilities. The very act of writing can crystallise what had felt amorphous and unusable.
- Jot notes on everything you think you want to include but without ordering or arranging them. If you start with ordering, it stops the flow. Be disorderly to start with.
- Re-read a memoir you have admired, this time noticing how it is structured. Where does the writer start? What follows? How does she/he connect sequences? What keeps you reading? How does it conclude? Takes notes.
- Stop planning and start writing. It is easy to become addicted to taking notes, working things out. If the planning becomes too detailed there is a danger the desire to write the memoir will be satisfied by the plan.

- Again, follow the heat. Write what first excites you, then what next excites you.

- After you have stepped into the flow of the writing, let it wander where it will for a while, but then step back and start observing where it is going. It may be time to do some planning—decide what the limits of your memoir are—what is part of it and what is not. Perhaps decide on a straightforward chronology—or not. Has it started in the best place? Is it clear or confusing? Do you need to shift sections so that it will make more sense?

- Step back at 20,000 or 30,000 words and look at pacing. Is it sometimes a bit slow, or too fast? Do you need to move sections so that things unfold more quickly, or more slowly?

- Play with chronology. Although it is often useful to write the sequence of events 'as they happened' so that readers find out in the same way that you did, it can be effective to shuffle events. Draw a time line so that you have a good idea of sequence, then perhaps try starting at the end. Or at a hinge—the point where events swung one way and not another.

- Explore patterns and ordering from elsewhere—the pattern of seasons, the patterns of rooms. You could, for example, move from room to room in a house, telling stories from each room, as a way of structuring a period.

- Consider using structuring images—common elements of life, such as beds, or tables, or hands, or smiles. It's not a matter of selecting an image and making everything fit but using an image which is already there in your writing.

- Consider the structure of other things you do, or other art forms you enjoy. If you make patchwork quilts, consider whether a patchwork structure might suit your memoir. If you enjoy the structure of music, the repetition of motifs might be worth trying.

- Think about foregrounding the structure—including your writing process—so that you take the reader with you 'behind the scenes' as you write.

- Think outside the chapter. Rather than trying to force all the scenes to conglomerate into a chapter, try them as small pieces that you can move about as if they were pieces of a mosaic or notes of music.

- If you have many different times or episodes to write about, try a 'frame'. It is a strong structural device for connecting pieces which otherwise might become 'bitsy'. You could try, for example, foregrounding the physical place where you are writing.

- Try writing a full-length memoir as a series of short pieces rather than as chapters. Construct each one as self-contained, each complementing the others but able to be read alone as well.

- Remember beauty. Beauty of form is created when structure and content are one—when the patterns of the structure echo the material and its meaning. For example, if you are writing about a fragmentary life then a formal structure of fragments may be necessary and beautiful. If you feel the story you want to tell is circular, then a circular structure—the ending echoing the beginning—may be best.

More on pacing

Pacing refers to how quickly or slowly the narrative unfolds. What this means for you as the narrator is that you need to be sensitive to how to emphasise and arrange the material. How long or short does a particular passage need to be? Where does it need to go in relation to other pieces? Should this passage go first or should I move it to the middle? Is the unfolding of the story too slow if this piece is included? Have important events been rushed over? Should that paragraph really be a chapter—or the other way around? Will the meaning be changed if I leave it out?

Every so often, read back over your material, not to edit, but to observe the pacing. Notice where it seems to trudge or bog down, notice where there are too many things happening quickly, one after the other. If too much is going on, you can insert a quieter, slower piece—a stroll in the garden.

Pacing is closely related to 'showing' and 'telling' which were discussed in Workshop four. If you 'tell' about events, the pacing tends to speed up as you can cover many events in just a few paragraphs. If you want to increase the pace, it may be worth condensing some scenes and telling them instead. 'Showing', which unfolds events in close-up, paradoxically tends to both slow down and speed up events. This is because 'showing' is life as it happens, moment by moment, therefore slowed down, but if the events are inherently dramatic—like a violent argument—then it feels speeded up as the reader is emotionally drawn into the rapid events.

What goes wrong and how to avoid it

A first draft is really an experiment with structure. You cannot know until you have tried it what will work or not. Still, there are a number of difficulties that might be avoided or lessened if you know about them beforehand.

A 'baggy' structure with too much irrelevant material

You need to discriminate between what you have included merely because it happened and what is included because it relates to your story and themes. Read through your draft, asking yourself with each episode: why is this scene, these events included? Does it contribute to what this manuscript is about or have I just put it in because it happened? Be ruthless about what is necessary. At this stage you need to be in charge of your material rather than it being in charge of you.

A disjointed structure resulting from mixing topics and narrative

Some memoirs try to combine a chronological narrative with topics—for example, part of the story of a marriage break-up is told and then there might be a chapter on the nature of depression. The two organising principles—narrative and topics—rarely work together. Choose one or the other. If you need to have both then use them in a rhythmic way—moving back and forth between the two and without repeating material in both strands.

A 'lumpy' structure where some events are given disproportionate space

This problem can result from the 'just because it happened' inclusion, but also because the events may be unresolved in the writer's life. It can lead to avoidance, the issue being unduly minimised or, on the other hand, obsessive overemphasis. The event/s probably need to be included, but given more or less space. Perhaps the argument with your mother needs to be mentioned, but not given five pages. At times, a particularly emotional and intense passage can unbalance a whole structure. You may need to expand it, and related passages, to put it in context—or you may need to leave it out altogether.

Parallel story strands that become tangled or mismatched threads

Two or three story strands weaving in and out of one another can be an effective device; for example, your trip to Greece could be interwoven with your childhood in a Greek–American community in New York. Problems arise when one strand is more powerful, more interesting than the other, or when there is repetition of ideas in each strand, or when the links between the two strands are arbitrary or forced. If you are weaving two or three strands, make sure that they are both significant, that you are not repeating in slightly different words the same issues, and that they relate to each other in organic ways.

A confusing or jumpy narrative structure

When you are close to a story it can often be difficult to see if you have all the elements you need—and in the right order—for the reader to follow. If you jump about too much without any discernible connection between pieces, the reader can become lost. Or if you pre-empt—that is, tell the reader too much, too soon—it can lessen the impact, for example, you let slip that you marry Sam, when the reader has been turning the pages to find out 'will she/won't she'. To avoid leaving out, pre-empting important events and a disconnected order, draw out a time line of events. For events in which the time sequence is crucial, it is a good idea to maintain simple chronology, at least in the first draft. If time sequence is less important or you want a sense of the layering of life rather than a temporal unfolding, then you will need to find ways—images, themes—to connect your pieces.

A structure that doesn't seem to be going anywhere

Underlying structure is the question 'Why?': why you are writing this, why we are reading it. Whether stated or unstated, the 'why' of any memoir is set up early and it runs throughout, keeping the reader in the story. If it is not there, or is not justified by the material that follows, then the reader loses the sense that the memoir is 'going somewhere' and stops reading.

It is time to step back from the writing, read it through in as detached a manner as possible—or ask someone whom you can trust with structure to read it—and try to see the underlying story and/or patterns. Decide what needs cutting, or adding, or shifting. Sometimes it might be a matter of a different beginning to allow all the other pieces to make sense. Sometimes it might be that the 'why' you have set up is not true—you may have thought it was about alcoholism but it was really about growing up in a home where the parents did not like one another. It is often the case that a writer has not seen what the material is really about in the first draft. It is the nature of the creative process—the slow emergence of truth.

Jerky changes in perspective and pacing in the structure

Parts of your memoir may be an overview or summarising of several years or of a place or person, other parts will be close-up of a particular time. This shift in perspective also affects the pacing and the reader's sense of closeness. If it is not done well, the move between the two perspectives can result in the reader feeling dislocated. There is also a danger of repetition of material when you overview, then show a close-up as well. Check to see whether both perspectives are necessary—it might be that one can be deleted, tightening the structure.

In the beginning and the end, structure is a way through for the reader. Whether you stick to the road or lead them a merry dance through the woods, the reader still needs to feel that *you* know where you are going and why. You do not need to know in the first draft—if you could see the entire shape of the journey before you started, there may be no need to write it—but by the time the memoir reaches the reader, there needs to be a sense that it is going somewhere, and that the narrator knows how to get there.

Structure can take time and patience. Underneath the efficient mind there is another darker, dimmer mind that cannot even tie a shoelace—but it does know how a story works. Not that it could tell you how, it cannot explain anything logically, it cannot argue a point, it cannot defend the case. It does try to make itself heard and seen in daily life but because we have neither the time nor the quietness to see the connections, it comes across as confused and incoherent.

This dark mind seems to be made of infinite multi-coloured patterns of physical and emotional memory, insights, sensations, even dreams, flamboyantly filed in its own intricate 'Indra's net' structure where everything is connected to everything else—not by logic, but by poetic association. It's at the point when the rational organising mind gives up that a writer—or anyone who demands the time and quietness—enters that dark mind. There one writes memoir, paints pictures, finds theorems, designs a new object, rediscovers childhood, realises one has been on the wrong track, sees how change can be made. Afterwards, of course, there are still bills and getting to work on time—but something new has found form.

Reading

Eat First, Talk Later

Beth Yahp

We eat our eggs and toast, then walk my landlady's dog slowly out to look at the sea off the Clovelly cliffs—azure—and we huddle side by side on the wintry rocks in warm sunshine and a cold wind, our back to the carpark. We watch the surf froth around the rocks, rise and fall in white-beared swoops around Wedding Cake Island. A troupe of new divers frog-walks their gear to Gordon's Bay. The dog scrambles over the rocks after some seagulls, stops short too close to the cliff edge, leaning into the wind. Ears blown back.

'Clo-daa-agh!' I yell.

Matt is dazed on painkillers, but prefers being out and about to lying at home. He'd rather be distracted than absorbed in his aches and pains. 'So what's your book about?' he repeats.

'I'm not sure yet,' I say. I'm not even sure it's a book. I look at Matt who is staring out to sea. The codeine is making him dreamy. I give it a go.

'It's about this,' I say. 'Tell me if you get bored. It's about a simple love story. It's set after the Second World War, in Kuala Lumpur. There's a boy on a bicycle. There's a girl on a horse. KL is a wreck, the Japanese have surrendered and the British are back, and the communist fighters are still—briefly—heroes, not yet chased back to the jungle. Not yet enemy number one. It's about the moment before this story turns, and heroes morphed into villains. It's a kind of second golden age, a blossoming between war and the Communist Emergency—when things are freer and the future seems bright.

'In Malaysia this period even has a name, even though it's mostly forgotten: the "Malayan Spring". The boy's Chinese, the girl's Eurasian, they live in different worlds. The wind lifts, and the boy hears the sound of horses' hooves pounding past. Yes, in Kuala Lumpur! Hard to imagine these days. The boy doesn't know what's hit him. His bicycle wobbles, and he turns. The sounds, the horses and their riders, are thundering towards him. The girl flashes past. He's caught in her slipstream, in a glimpse of long dark reddish hair.'

I pause. 'That's all,' I say.

'That's the whole book?' Matt murmurs.

'Well,' I say, 'there's another simple *anti*-love story . . . OK, it goes like this. Stop me if you're bored.' Matt nods, and I continue: 'There's a broken-hearted woman, just arrived in town, from a cold, faraway country. She's come back to her homeland, which she both loves and loathes. This place has never loved her. It's the mid 2000s. It's like an enchanted kingdom, stuck under a spell. There's a big-hearted man fighting dragons the old corrupt powers throw at him. He's wielding his sword, losing more than he's winning. He thinks he's some kind of saviour—he wants to save the world. The man's heart is big enough for everyone, his people, his country, his leader—once heir to the grand vizier, now locked up in a tower—his ideals, even her. His hopes and his words are huge. It's crowded there in his too-big heart, and then there's another woman, younger, a fighter. More impressionable. More hungry. More useful.'

I pause again. Matt is still staring out to sea. 'It could be a fairytale,' he says, 'with dragons and towers. All you'd need is three wishes and a wicked queen.' He looks at me sideways. 'Or it could be *Days of Our Lives.*'

I laugh. I say, 'Or maybe it isn't a love story at all. Maybe it's a story of recovery, a making-do story. Forget the fairytale. It isn't a romance and there are no heroes or villains. There's a messed-up woman, newly arrived in town, a different town, in a different country. She travels a lot, it seems she's spent her life moving from one place to another, she can't settle. Here, on the other side of the world, she meets a man, who would like to travel. That's what he likes about her. Not much happens in this story, there are no dragons, no man-eating witches, no need for wishes, and they hang out together and eat and talk, and do ordinary things. Life's good and safe here. The sun shines. They're in a lucky country, an island. Bad things can be kept out . . .'

'That one sounds a bit boring,' Matt smiles. He creaks up to his feet, wincing. He holds out his hand and I take it. He inclines his head towards the horizon. 'I think I prefer stories set over there,' he says as he pulls me up. I smile back.

Yahp lets her readers in on the possible ways she could structure her memoir by letting us overhear a conversation with one of the characters. She lets us know several possible storylines, all of which are engaging, despite her concerns about them. Read *Eat First, Talk Later* for its complex structure which interweaves personal stories, political themes and historical information.

Writing exercises

1 Scenes in a relationship

Write five separate scenes in a relationship, past or present, in chronological order. It can be a relationship with anyone—mother, sister, lover, friend. The scenes must be self-contained, not referring to any of the other scenes, and each one no more than a page. The time between scenes can be anything from during a day to over many years. Now rearrange them backwards, that is, begin with the one that happened last. Note how that affects the structure. Try writing five more scenes in the same relationship and fitting them in or around the sequence you already have. Shuffle them about until you have the most effective structure. (Twenty minutes each part)

2 Patchworking

This exercise is also useful for writers who know the territory they want to write about, for example, 'Travelling alone in South America', but do not have a clear idea of the story or thematic thread. Write a short list of particular memories of the time—running into an old schoolfriend in an Aztec ruin, getting lost in Buenos Aires, the sounds of the jungle, and start writing the pieces, one by one. Do not worry about the overall shape; simply make each piece as if you were making the pieces of a patchwork quilt. When you have written a few, start looking at how they might be placed together. (Fifteen minutes each part)

3 Series of beds

Call to mind beds in your life. Write a series of pieces, at least five hundred words each, using the memories in relation to at least five different beds. Consider a wide range: perhaps a childhood bed, a boarding school bed, a lover's bed, a great aunt's bed, a hospital bed, a deathbed, a bed in a tent. As you read back through them, see whether the idea of 'bed' holds them together. You can also do the same exercise with another piece of common furniture, such as a table. Tables are very productive of memories as they connect to so many things in life: food, family, friendship, romance, arguments, study, work. But don't start writing on any of those topics—go into memory via the specific table. You can use this exercise with any kind of furniture! Consider if you could use a certain object to structure a whole memoir. (Two hours each part)

4 Exploring images

Begin with the sentence 'I think this memoir is a ...' (insert image such as star, journey, treasure hunt, jigsaw puzzle, mountain, river) 'because ...' (continue on with teasing out the likeness). This is a way of exploring image-based structure rather than a conceptual or logical plan. The aim is not to produce a fine piece of writing but to play with the possibilities of structure. (Fifteen minutes)

5 Long and short of it

Write two related episodes you have decided you want to include in your memoir. It might be two scenes from your year in Kenya or two scenes with your disabled son, for example. Write one in half a page, the other in at least three pages. The next day, write the same two episodes, this time with the opposite lengths. Note the difference in impact, in weight, that the scenes have at different lengths and how it changes the relationship between the two pieces. (Two to three hours)

16

WORKSHOP FOURTEEN
The magic spell—More narrative

We tell ourselves stories in order to live.

JOAN DIDION

The spell of narrative saved Scheherazade's life. She was a beautiful young woman who lived with her father, the vizier. One day she was sent for by the king. She had to think quickly; the king was in the habit of calling for a virgin each evening and next morning having her killed so that he could be sure he would not be cuckolded. (The king clearly had his problems, but let's not go into his story.) Scheherazade's father told her the king liked stories so, that evening at the palace, she settled herself on the cushions and began to tell him a fabulous tale. She continued the story through the night and, in the morning, stopped before it was finished. The king of course had to keep her alive so that she would finish the story—he had to know what happened next. The next night she continued on with the story and began another, again stopping at dawn before it was complete. Once again the king had to know how things turned out and spared her life. In this way, night after night, for one thousand and one nights, she kept herself alive—and the king tantalised. Finally he married her so that she would keep telling him stories and they lived happily ever after.

The story of Scheherazade is, of course, the frame for *One Thousand and One Nights*, one of the world's most famous collections of folktales, but it is also an allegory of the irresistible attraction of narrative and its capacity to heal and to save both the teller and the hearer. It seems to me that this capacity comes from the fact that, within a narrative, the random fragments of life are connected to create a meaningful whole. If one has had an overwhelming experience, the mind either shuts it out or goes over it obsessively, trying to come to terms with it. Writing the narrative or story takes it out of the mind and onto the page where it can be connected to other elements of life. The fundamental nature of narrative is to make causal links between things, that is, to try to show that things happen for a reason, that they make sense. Narrative, then, by its very nature, is integrating. By making the links between events, story helps us understand our lives—as the American essayist, Joan Didion said, 'We tell ourselves stories in order to live'.

But narratives are also told of the joyful and remarkable events of life. They are told to celebrate, to acknowledge, to remember, to weave community, to persuade, to create beauty, to make meaning. I would go so far as to say that a meaningful narrative is necessary to human life. Without a story, it becomes impossible to act. Why get up in the morning if you do not have a convincing inner story that says it is a worthwhile thing to do?

Story or narrative is also, as Scheherazade knew, immensely attractive. A mediocre novel or film can hold attention because of the narrative alone. Few people can resist an 'addictive' narrative; it is one of the most powerful human structures. There is an expectation, perhaps formed in earliest childhood from the stories read to us, that all the elements introduced will unfold and connect and come to some kind of satisfying conclusion where our questions are answered.

None of this is to say that a good memoir needs a strong overall narrative. A meditation, a series of anecdotes, a wandering yarn, a thoughtful contemplation of issues, all these can work just as well. For the moment, however, let's extend the possibilities of narrative.

Plotting and narrative tension are both key elements of storytelling. Plot is the order and emphasis of your story; narrative tension is the curiosity or desire aroused by unanswered questions. For a refresher on plotting and narrative tension, turn back to Workshop seven.

Myths and fairytales

In all cultures there are folktales, fairytales, myths and legends handed down over thousands of years. These are the narratives that make sense of the elements of life, explaining the natural and human world. Referring to a story as mythic doesn't mean that it's not true, rather that it has a fundamental story shape that has lasted for many generations. In fact, it could be said they are the archetypes for all our stories. Because these story shapes have endured for so long, it may be worth looking at them more closely to see whether they might be useful for writing the narrative of a memoir.

Many researchers have explored the relationship between myths and folktales or fairytales and our own lives. Psychoanalyst Carl Jung explored the mythic patterns of his life in his autobiography, *Memories, Dreams, Reflections*, as well as discussing myth in other essays. The mythologist Joseph Campbell in *The Hero with a Thousand Faces* offers a vast knowledge of myths from all over the world and reveals how we live them in our everyday lives.

One of the key story structures is the Quest myth. It has a three-part structure: departure, initiation, return. Departure involves a sign that something is about to change and, often, a gift of some kind, a talisman from an elder or even an animal. Initiation usually involves a journey and struggle against difficulties or temptations, but also, often, another gift or at least assistance of some kind—a magic spell, perhaps. Return involves the resumption of what might look like the old life, but it is a life transformed, or at least renewed.

It easy to see how Quest myth structure might echo the pattern of many life experiences, from a sequence of events as terrible as the death of someone loved to events as light as a sojourn in Greece. If a Quest structure appears to fit your memoir, then you could use those divisions and shape as a way of organising your material. If you are interested in this idea, *The Gift of Stories* by Robert Atkinson explores mythic structures in detail.

Another classic story shape, especially for Western culture, is the Redemption myth. These are stories where all seems to be lost, mistakes have been made, life has become too hard, and then, usually by an act of courage or a trial of some sort—illness, the death of a loved one, an extreme event, a dangerous journey—the narrator saves or redeems themselves. *Wild* by Cheryl Strayed and *Missing Christopher* by Jayne Newling follow a Redemption myth structure.

Look also at other folktale structures. Remember folktales from your own childhood, recalling particularly those stories that either delighted or horrified you. It is remarkable how often the tale that makes an impression, either positive or negative, contains an important theme; the story symbolically echoes a key story in your own life. For example, one woman in writing class was horrified by the fable of 'The Man, the Boy and the Donkey' as a child. In this tale the man listens to conflicting advice about how to travel with the boy and the donkey, changing his actions with each new piece of advice. Eventually, as a direct result of trying to please everyone, the donkey falls off a bridge and drowns. It was clear to this woman that she had lived too much of her life trying to please others rather than working out for herself the best course of action. This insight helped her select which incidents to include and which to emphasise. It gave her the shape of her story.

Re-read folktales from your own and other cultural backgrounds and look at the shared or common narrative points, objects, landscapes and characters:

- Narrative points such as loss of a parent, introduction of an evil force, denial of rightful inheritance, banishment, a contest for love, a journey.
- Objects such as wands, caskets, shoes (glass slippers?), talismans and amulets, thorns, spinning wheels, swords, spears.
- Landscapes such as mountains, dark woods, swamps, paths, mazes, caves, towers, rivers.
- Characters such as witches, sorcerers, dragons, wolves, birds, tricksters, stepmothers.

Consider what each element might symbolise and see whether your memoir might contain the same elements. You can use these correspondences to select a folktale to use as a prologue for your story, or use elements such as objects or landscapes as chapter titles, or just keep the tale and its elements in mind as a shaping device without foregrounding it.

Plots of fiction and films

The plots of fiction can be helpful when you are planning the structure of your life story. Look, in your own life, for the stories that remind you of novels you have read. You may notice elements of a particular fictional plot in your story. Would your life make a good thriller? A detective story? Re-read one of these genres and make notes on how the narrative unfolds—what is revealed first, what happens next. You can use the plot structure to shape your own story.

Films are particularly useful in learning how to shape a narrative because film plots are usually tightly structured. Note how the scenes, one by one, add to the story elements and allow the characters to unfold through their actions. It's worth sitting down with a notebook to watch a film whose narrative you have enjoyed and jotting down the sequence of events, scene by scene, to see how the story is structured.

Note too the techniques of film structure, not just the narrative. You could try starting with a number of different scenes in different places or with different characters, which eventually link up, or a montage of moments to show the development of a relationship, or a tracking shot that follows a character through a whole sequence of events. Because readers are also film literate, you can use filmic techniques to experiment with a more adventurous structure.

Narrative of ideas

A narrative does not necessarily have to contain outward action or suspenseful events. Your outward life might have a smooth surface, with the exciting narrative taking place in your interior life. A narrative of ideas, the unfolding of insights and thoughts, can be as involving and compelling as action and adventure. Look at Annie Dillard's Pulitzer prize-winning *Pilgrim at Tinker Creek*, in which, on the surface, very little happens. There is no action, adventure or romance in the usual meaning of the words; there is no violent childhood or broken heart, no fabulous journey to an exotic place. Dillard makes observations of nature centred on an American creek—it is one of the most absorbing and beautiful memoirs I have read.

A narrative of ideas can be shaped by the other arts—you could use a series of songs or books, for example, as a way in to exploring a certain experience or idea. Ramona Koval's memoir *By the Book* uses a lifetime of reading to shape both the story of her life and of her thinking. You could use the structures of science or the trades to shape your stories; Virginia Lloyd in *The Young Widow's Book of Home Improvement* uses the renovation of a house as the structure for exploring grief. Perhaps a mathematician could use mathematical concepts as shaping ideas for her story; a geologist could use the names and qualities of different rocks to provide structuring themes. In fact, every area of human knowledge can provide structures for your memoir. Look to the interests you already have and you may find the structuring elements are already there.

A different background

If your identity has been formed by the fact that your background has not been mainstream, you could try using that as the central organising idea of your story. *Purple Threads* by Jeanine Leane looks at being Aboriginal in white Australia. Yvonne Louis, in *A Brush with Mondrian*, explores her Dutch heritage through searching for the provenance of a family painting.

Or it could be another aspect of your life that has created a sense of identity apart from the mainstream, such as your sexuality, or a particular character trait that sets you apart, or your occupation. Sian Prior in *Shy* uses her sense of crippling shyness to shape her memoir, while in *Call Me Sasha,* Geena Leigh looks at her work as a prostitute to shape the story of her life.

Short narratives

Consider whether a series of narratives suits your material better. If you cannot see an overall narrative then it is best not to force one. A series of short stories might be more effective. Each story could be complete on its own, while building up an overall picture of a life. Before you try this, read short memoir collections so that you have a sense of the memoir short story and essay form. Both Helen Garner's *Everywhere I Look* and Tim Winton's *The Boy Behind the Curtain* are structured as a series of self-contained autobiographical stories and personal essays without an overarching narrative. In both a kaleidoscopic picture of a life is created. T.A.G. Hungerford's *Stories from Suburban Road* is another collection of autobiographical short stories.

Or you could write a set of stories around a single image as the English chef Nigel Slater did in his memoir, *Toast*. It consists of many short narratives, some only half a page, each one centred around food. He relates stories from his childhood and young manhood, but it is not a continuous conventional narrative. It tells the story of his life in relation to food, and because food is a constant factor in life he is able to recount the major experiences in his life through this one image.

You could also use a series of short narratives that, overall, create a series of themes. In *Whatever the Gods Do* I used many short pieces, which gradually told the story of a friend who had died and my relationship with her baby son. As I wrote, it was rather like putting together a jigsaw puzzle with only a vague idea of what the picture might be! But piecing it together, I started to see the theme of transformation: the slow transformations of relationships, and the abrupt transformation of death.

A few tips on making narrative

Start by reminding yourself that you already know how to construct a narrative. It may be difficult to accept that you innately know how to do something as complex as construct a narrative out of the thousands of elements of your life, but it is something that all humans do every day. You sift and arrange the events that happen to you each day automatically—and you recount those events as a narrative to others. And then, each night as you sleep, your unconscious, your dream self, constructs more narratives, even if they are bizarre and unlikely.

All human beings tell stories. You could argue it is a cultural construction—and its various forms undoubtedly are constructed—but the urge to make a narrative out of what has happened appears to be innate.

It is important not to be overwhelmed by techniques, by instructions on how to do it. If you were writing a detective story or a thriller then yes, you would have to plot in a detailed way. But memoir structure is not so much a controlled intellectual process but one that happens under the surface. It is often a matter of feeling your way, piece by piece.

Some people are at ease with this process and it flows naturally; for others, here are a few tips. Some of the suggestions contradict each other; that's because everyone's approach is different. We don't all need the same advice. You will see what suits you.

- Sit quietly, letting events play over in your mind, and observe which order to tell events. You don't have to start at the beginning—you can start, for example, at a key turning point—but remember the reader needs to be able to move between times and events without confusion. Often, when you are first starting out, chronology is best.

- Remember the question. At or near the beginning, a narrative needs an unanswered question, or a series of unanswered questions. It is not an openly stated question but one that ought to form in the mind of the reader.

- If you are clear about the storyline, select only those elements of your life that contribute to the narrative. Don't include the visit to Brighton Pier if it does not contribute to the story.

- Let there be light—and shade. If you give everything the same emphasis, the narrative will become flat. Some incidents deserve to be written about at greater length and intensity than others.

- Include enough information—be aware the reader does not know what you know. Too many gaps and the reader will fall through.

- On the other hand, you don't need to spell everything out. Readers like to make a few leaps of their own. It can be very tedious to be told everything.

- Withhold. You don't have to spill the beans on the first page. Because you know what has happened, you may be tempted to tell everything up-front—but hold back. Sense the right moment for information to be revealed.

- Don't withhold too much. Holding back information can just feel manipulative and annoying. Teasers and cliffhangers are mostly corny.

- Keep narrative tension. Be aware of not pre-empting important narrative points. If you let slip that your son became a surgeon while you are writing the scene where he is lost in the mountains of Colorado, then the narrative tension is loosened.

- Remember pacing. Sometimes you might need to slow down the unfolding events—write more on each event rather than recounting the affair, divorce and remarriage in two pages. Or you might need to speed up, not spend quite so much time on the end of the affair.

- Remember the pleasure of a narrative of ideas. An inner journey or the story of an idea can be very engaging.

- Observe the narrative structure of a novel or film that you have enjoyed—re-read or rewatch it and note down how scenes follow one another, in what order and to what effect. Try emulating the pattern you observe.

- Note the plots of traditional narratives—fairy stories and folktales from your own or other cultures. These are fundamental story shapes and have formed many people's sense of how a narrative unfolds. Does your story echo a myth?

- Think of good narrative as like good sex: seduce your reader by tempting them into your story, arouse the desire to keep reading, satisfy the reader's need to find out. Try not to be too predictable, too slick or too fast—or too slow.

- Be truthful to the essential shape of the story, the story that has formed or is forming under the surface of your mind. Don't tempt or seduce if that does not fit the integrity of your story—it will only seem forced or artificial.

Trust that the story is already there. Renaissance artist Michelangelo said that when he approached his block of marble, he started by believing that the form of the sculpture was already in the stone. What he was actually trusting was that the shape was already in his mind, it was simply up to him to chip away the unnecessary thoughts that had collected around it. Trust that somewhere in your mind the story is known and set to work, writing down what is necessary and leaving out what is not.

Reading

Wild Cheryl Strayed

The trees were tall, but I was taller, standing above them on a steep mountain slope in northern California. Moments before, I'd removed my hiking boots and the left one had fallen into those trees, first catapulting into the air when my enormous backpack toppled onto it, then skittering across the gravelly trail and flying over the edge. It bounced off a rocky outcropping several feet beneath me before disappearing into the canopy below, impossible to retrieve. I let out a stunned gasp, though I'd been in the wilderness thirty-eight days and by then I'd come to know that anything could happen and that everything would. But that doesn't mean I wasn't shocked when it did.

My boot was gone. Actually gone.

I clutched its mate to my chest like a baby, though of course it was futile. What is one boot without the other boot? It is nothing. It is useless, an orphan forevermore, and I could take no mercy on it. It was a big lug of a thing, of genuine heft, a brown leather Raichle boot with a red lace and silver metal fasts. I lifted it high and threw it with all my might and watched it fall into the lush trees and out of my life.

I was alone. I was barefoot. I was twenty-six years old and an orphan too. *An actual stray*, a stranger had observed a couple of weeks before, when I'd told him my name and explained how very loose I was in the world. My father left my life when I was six. My mother died when I was twenty-two. In the wake of her death, my stepfather morphed from the person I considered my dad into a man I only occasionally recognized. My two siblings scattered in their grief, in spite of my efforts to hold us together, until I gave up and scattered as well.

In the years before I pitched my boot over the edge of that mountain, I'd been pitching myself over the edge too. I'd ranged and roamed and railed—from Minnesota to New York to Oregon and all across the West—until at last I found myself bootless, in the summer of 1995, not so much loose in the world as bound to it.

It was a world I'd never been to and had yet known was there all along, one I'd staggered to in sorrow and confusion and fear and hope. A world I thought would both make me into the woman I knew I could become and turn me back into the girl I'd once been. A world that measured two feet wide and 2,663 miles long.

A world called the Pacific Crest Trail.

I'd first heard of it only seven months before, when I was living in Minneapolis, sad and desperate and on the brink of divorcing a man I still loved. I'd been standing in line at an outdoor store waiting to purchase a foldable shovel when I picked up a book called *The Pacific Crest Trail, Volume 1: California* from a nearby shelf and read the back cover. The PCT, it said, was a continuous wilderness trail that went from the Mexican border in California to just beyond the Canadian border along the crest of nine mountain ranges—the Laguna, San Jacinto, San Bernardino, Liebre, Tehachapi, Sierra Nevada, Klamath and Cascades. That distance was a thousand miles as the crow flies, but the trail was more than double that. Traversing the entire length of the states of California, Oregon, and Washington, the PCT passes through national parks and wilderness areas as well as federal, tribal and privately held lands; through deserts and mountains and rain forests; across rivers and highways. I turned the book over and gazed at the front cover—a boulder-strewn lake surrounded by rocky crags against a blue sky—then placed it back on the shelf, paid for my shovel, and left.

But later I returned and bought the book. The Pacific Crest Trail wasn't a world to me then. It was an idea, vague and outlandish, full of promise and mystery. Something bloomed inside me as I traced its jagged line with my finger on a map . . .

I gazed at my bare and battered feet, with their smattering of remaining toenails. They were ghostly pale to the line a few inches above my ankles, where the wool socks I usually wore ended. My calves above them were muscled and golden and hairy, dusted with dirt and a constellation of bruises and scratches. I'd started walking in the Mojave Desert and I didn't plan to stop until I touched my hand to a bridge that crosses the Columbia River at the Oregon-Washington border with the grandiose name the Bridge of the Gods.

I looked north in its direction—the very thought of that bridge a beacon to me. I looked south, to where I'd been, to the wild land that had schooled and scorched me, and considered my options. There was only one, I knew. There was always only one.

To keep walking.

In this prologue, Cheryl Strayed sets up the key narrative elements: a young woman, alone and bereft, taking on the huge challenge of walking through the wilderness. She begins nearly halfway through the narrative at what could have been a make or break incident. In this short extract she let us know a little of the backstory, then in Chapter one takes us back into the past in detail. Overall it has the classic shape of a Redemption myth. Read *Wild* for its strong and well-paced narrative, its emotional power and its thoughtful observations.

Writing exercises

1 A day in the life

Select a recent day in your life, within the last couple of weeks, and simply recount what happened that day. Do not plan it; simply write what you can remember. See whether it has a narrative. If you can see narrative elements, start cutting away what is not necessary and perhaps writing in more detail what seems significant. It will give you practice in shaping a narrative in a shorter form. (Thirty minutes)

2 Scenes

Write ten separate short scenes from an event that unfolds over time, each one no more than half a page. Take a few days to do the exercise if you need to. Write the scenes in any order, just as you think of them, but note which one you wrote first, second and so on. Then sort them into what you think is the best order for the unfolding of the narrative. See how close that is to the order in which you wrote them. (Twenty minutes each piece)

3 Quest myth

Write an outline of your life in the form of a Quest myth with the following divisions: setting out, challenge/s, resolution. See if you can fill in details such as what called you on your quest, whether you had a talisman or guide to help you, whether you turned away from the quest at times, what the goal of your quest was. (Thirty minutes)

4 Once upon a time

Write the story of your life in two pages, beginning 'Once upon a time', using the third person and the vocabulary of a fairytale. If you come from a wealthy background, write, for example, 'The queen gave birth to a beautiful princess', or if you come from a poor background, 'The woodcutter and his wife had a handsome son'. If there were destructive people, use words like wicked witch or evil king; if someone helped you, use fairy godmother or wise woman. It is important that you use this style of language rather than contemporary realistic or psychological terminology because it helps you to see the mythic shape of your life. Write it briefly, no more than two pages. See if it has revealed the bones of the story you want to write. (One hour)

17

WORKSHOP FIFTEEN
Difficulties of truth-telling

'Beauty is truth, truth beauty,'—that is all
Ye know on earth, and all ye need to know.

JOHN KEATS

Truth, Keats said, is a beautiful thing: *Beauty is truth, truth beauty*. The words, so familiar, even commonplace, are thrilling every time they are considered. The idea that truth, by its nature, is beautiful and that beauty, by its nature, is truthful is an irresistible one for any writer or artist. It is poetic insight of the highest order, economical and encompassing at once. Perhaps it is *all ye know on earth, and all ye need to know*. But for the nonfiction writer, truth is rarely so beautifully poetic, especially in the beginning. It is complex, messy, confronting and fraught with dangers. It is very difficult to avoid upsetting at least one of your readers, if not a community of readers— whether they have read your work or not!

There are many reasons not to tell the truth:

- You are part of a family, a circle of friends, a professional community, a country. As another English poet, John Donne, said, 'No man is an island'; no woman either. All these groups have varying levels of tolerance for the truth and, without the rules being stated, you know what they are. You know not to tell your mother about your father's affair because it would break her heart. You know that stating a particular political viewpoint will alienate half your school community. You know not to tell the truth every time you open your mouth—you and everyone else. In daily life, people who are not sociopaths edit the things they say. It can be a difficult habit to break when you come to the page.

- Editing the self comes not just from obeying social rules but also from a desire not to inflict pain. If you write about the impact of knowing of your father's affair when you were a teenager but not telling your mother, what is that going to do to your mother now? What will your children feel if you write that you had never wanted to have children? The likelihood of hurting or upsetting family members is the most often cited reason for not telling the truth.

- Sometimes, it's the desire to avoid embarrassing someone, or simply a wish to not invade privacy. Do you have the right to reveal information given to you in confidence or even things you observed which may be now embarrassing to others? How far is too far?

- In the wider community—in your work, school, sport or church communities—there are practical reasons for not telling the truth. If people in your small mountain town knew you were gay, would they still attend your medical practice? If your colleagues knew you worked as a prostitute when you were at university, would they still treat you the same? It's not that you are hurting others but you may be affecting the way that others respond to you.

- There may also be legal and personal safety considerations putting pressure on the truth. One woman writing a memoir about a court case involving business malpractice was concerned the other party could sue her. Another woman who had been involved with a criminal was concerned her revelations might physically endanger her or her children. A man writing about child abuse in an Indigenous community was concerned it could cause inter-family violence.

- The pressure to be 'nice' also shapes the truth. Women especially feel the pressure to keep the peace, to make everyone feel comfortable. Virginia Woolf personified this pressure as 'the Angel in the House' who was 'so constituted that she never had a mind or a wish of her own, but preferred always to sympathise with the minds and wishes of others'. For many women writing a memoir, this can be the least conscious, but strongest, pressure against truth-telling.

How can the truth be told when there are so many valid reasons not to? And do you always need to tell the truth anyway? And what of the ethics of truth-telling?

The ethics of truth-telling

Telling the truth, as you see it, matters. It's the first thing I rely on when I read fiction or nonfiction—that the writer will communicate her truth. The writer as 'savage artist', a truth teller no matter what the consequences to anyone else, takes the issue further. Does the writer have the right to destroy others' lives, relationships, reputations in their search for truth? Should you have a 'moral free pass' (as Ceridwen Dovey wrote in 'The Pencil and the Damage Done') to do what suits you? I think it depends on a few non-literary considerations.

- Check your motives. I don't mean literary motivations, such as the structure needs it, but personal motives. All memoirists probably have non-literary motives for some of the things they write—to honour someone, to tear someone down, to give thanks. What is the reason for revealing this piece of dirty underwear? If the story and themes concern dirty underwear then by all means reveal it, but if the reason is to embarrass or inflict pain then its inclusion might be reconsidered. Truth matters, but as the American memoirist Annie Dillard said, 'Writing is an art, not a martial art.'

- If the truth you have to tell will hurt others, weigh up its importance. This includes its emotional importance to you and its narrative or thematic importance. Does your story need the revelation about Aunt Kate's much younger lover? Perhaps yes, if it shaped your own sense of sexuality; perhaps yes, if it affected the family dynamic.

- If you have decided the truth you want to write is important, consider how many people it will damage, and how much. Include yourself in this tally. This is not to say that you should avoid the truth if the numbers are too high and the disruption too great, but be aware of it. Each writer needs to weigh up for himself if he is ready for emotional storms that could damage relationships.

- Consider the unreliability of memory. Although memory is fascinating, complex and often the only truth we have, it is manifestly not a totally reliable witness. All of us are made of our memories—they are the fabric of ourselves and it feels like a betrayal of self to question memory. While a memory always has value, it is clear that not all memories are equally valid. At least allow room for other possibilities.

It may sound as if the truth is impossible but I mean only to acknowledge the difficulty. There is no point in dodging the taboos against the truth because they can prevent you from going forward with your writing. Facing them, you can continue. There are a few ways to tell the truth and survive.

Writing the truth

- The tone of voice you use will make a great deal of difference to how your truths are received. *It's not what she said, it's how she said it.* If your tone of voice is whining, accusing or bitter then most people will find your words unpalatable, no matter how true. It is a curious fact that bitterness and self-pity are universally unappealing: both imply that everything is someone else's fault. If your voice is clear and direct, then even unpleasant truths can be listened to. At the same time, if you still feel bitter or self-pitying it's not worth faking a relaxed tone of voice—it is rarely convincing. It might be best to try to work it out in the first draft.
- Say everything you want to say in the first draft—you can take it out later. If a particular episode is stopping you from writing *your mother drunk, smashing plates in the kitchen,* write it anyway, telling yourself this is only the first draft. If you want to scream and rant about something, even if you want to preach about something, do it in the first draft. It might mean that you gain insights you might otherwise not have

reached; it might also mean that you realise it does not look so bad written down.

- Remind yourself that writing is not about being 'nice'. The truth would never be told if everyone kept up a smooth and smiling front. Sometimes, the Angel in the House has to be locked in the wardrobe, at least during the first draft. Truth has more power than Nice. (Although 'nice' in its rarely used sense of 'most precise' can be very powerful.)

- Remember that 'the truth' is not just about painful or unpleasant events. It can be just as or even more difficult to be truthful about happiness because, very often, happiness is not well observed. Even though it was Tolstoy who said it, I don't agree that 'Happy families are all alike; every unhappy family is unhappy in its own way'. It is more that the details of happiness are not noted with the same attention as the details of pain. Try to write the details of happiness, of love and parental pride and delight, with attention to the particulars.

- Remind yourself how liberating it is when a writer has written the truth about something that is usually hidden or glossed over. In *Is This My Beautiful Life?* Jessica Rowe reveals her alienation and despair after the birth of her longed-for first child. Her honesty about her postnatal depression, when life on the surface looked perfect, has given inspiration to many women struggling with the same condition.

- Telling the truth, especially when it involves what has happened to other people in your life, can be a matter of finding your perspective, your relationship to the story. What happens to other people is not necessarily your business, but sometimes it is. Find out what matters to you about the story and you will find your perspective and how to tell it.

- Consider the saving grace of humour. Many difficult topics can be written about—and read—more easily if there is a humorous or ironic approach. It doesn't mean that you are flippant about serious topics, but even the heaviest subject can have a humorous aspect. In *Running with Scissors,* Augusten Burroughs writes about his mother's avid and destructive desire for fame with such humour that the reader can see the truth but does not have to feel judgemental:

'Okay, now I need your honest reaction. Did it feel powerful to you? Emotionally charged?'

I knew the only correct answer to this question was, 'Wow. That really does seem like something you'd read in *The New Yorker.*'

She laughed, pleased. 'Really? Do you really think so? *The New Yorker* is very selective. They don't publish just anyone.'

- Admitting to your readers that your memoir is simply your version of events can be disarming. There are nearly always contending versions of events in any life, the more so when there is conflict, and admitting to this reality means that at least family and friends have some room to move. Being absolute is often irritating. Uncertainty is often more appealing and more believable than adamant assertion.

- Talk to the people concerned if possible. It may not be possible—that may be part of the problem of writing about it—but sometimes, especially if people are given the chance to air their point of view, it can make it easier for you to write yours. One woman wrote about her nervous breakdown and the subsequent breakdown of her marriage. She showed it to her ex-husband first and afterwards he admitted that reading her manuscript was the first time he'd understood what she had been going through.

- Be aware of the difference between fact and truth. Any number of facts does not necessarily add up to truth; facts are true, but to contain truth they must convey some illumination, some insight. A welter of facts can obscure the truth, making it impossible for the reader to discern what matters amongst all the detail you have included.

- On the other hand, it is a good idea to check the facts, particularly information that is a matter of record. It can be embarrassing to get the facts wrong—I still squirm when I see the wrongly named church in Paris in one of my earlier books. More seriously, in some circumstances you could even be sued. Fact check your manuscript when you are finished.

- Consider changing identifying details. This is generally not the best course of action as the people who know you will still be able to identify characters and for the general reader it does not matter anyway, but if there is a risk of legal action, or of identifying someone who does not want to be identified for a good reason, then it might be worth changing details such as places, dates and names if these details are not crucial to the story. In *Whatever the Gods Do* I changed the names of everyone because the child I was writing about was, by then, a teenager, and I did not want him to be embarrassed at school. I did not change any of the details of events or actions, as these were the essential facts of the story.

- Write it 'as a novel' to avoid the difficulty of exposing truth. As I have said, this is generally not a good idea. The memoir and the novel each require an allegiance to different kinds of truth: one to the truth of what actually happened, the other to the integrity of its fictional structure.

Too much information

Trying to construct your perception of truth on the page can feel like walking a narrow line between 'too much information' and skimming the surface. Memoir, by its nature, can easily tip over into details that, rather than enlighten the reader, make them squirm. These can be details about bodily functions, including sex, but can also be what feels like invasive information about parents, lovers, friends. The reader feels that the memoirist has gone too far.

On the other hand, it can be just as easy to avoid the truth by omission, by simply leaving out whatever feels too difficult. The reader is left sensing the gaps and feeling cheated that she has not been trusted with the truth. How far is too far? How to walk that line between too much and too little?

For a start, maybe you want to make your reader squirm. That, I suppose, is a legitimate aim. If that is what you are interested in, why not push the boundaries of comfort? Some memoirists defy boundaries so that the reader can enjoy burping, urinating, scratching—all completely human activities. It is a matter of your intention, the effect that you want your memoir to have. If it is to impress upon the reader the banal physicality of life, for instance, or the absurd and comic nature of pretensions, then this is a necessary part of your material. Shock, breaking taboos, has its place in memoir. But the more shocking the material, the more crucial the voice you use to convey it. Personally, I enjoy a contrast between tone and material, such as the contrast between Krissy Kneen's insightful poetic writing and the startling sexual openness in her memoir *Affection*.

It is more problematic when 'going too far' is in emotional or psychological territory, especially when it involves other people's lives. Readers express their outrage that a writer has gone too far in exposing a mother's faults or a lover's inner thoughts. The Norwegian writer Karl Ove Knausgaard distressed his family and friends and many readers when he revealed endless intimate details of his family life in his clearly autobiographical novel *A Death in the Family*. Discussing the fraught edge between the writer's responsibility to the truth and her responsibility to friends and family, Ceridwen Dovey's essay 'The Pencil and the Damage Done' offers the perspective of psychoanalyst Adam Phillips: 'if the art legitimates cruelty, I think the art is not worth having'.

Outraging a sense of privacy can be more shocking than outraging a sense of propriety but, again, there are no hard-and-fast rules, for each person has a different sense of what is private. I can only suggest that in writing about others it's a good idea to follow your own sense of privacy, exposing what you would think needed to be exposed if it was about yourself.

A sense of privacy ought not, however, be used as an excuse for sweeping everything unpleasant under the carpet, nor as an excuse not to trust the reader with difficult material. There is nothing so unnourishing, or unbelievable, as a memoir which gives only the light and sugar of life. It is like eating fairy floss: pretty and fun to have at a carnival, but insubstantial and boring for a long-term diet. Sometimes you might have to push your sense of privacy—peek into the tent and see how the fairy floss is manufactured. Sometimes you have to give yourself a push into the taboo territory.

That's not to say that everything ought to be exposed in great detail. Going into too much detail can become self-indulgent (see Workshop sixteen). What is not said can be as powerful or more powerful than what is said. Sometimes, withholding the full horror lets it expand in the reader's mind rather than it being constrained by your words. In her memoir *Second Half First,*

Drusilla Modjeska says of her years with partner Jeremy and his son, who suffered from mental illness, 'There is a lot I cannot say about the years I spent with Jeremy. Or rather a lot I will not say.' This terse comment lets the reader feel the vast impact of mental illness on a relationship. Suggesting or implying more than you say can be very effective when you do not want to expose others to scrutiny but still want to tell the truth.

What if I don't want to be identified in my truth-telling?

It may seem contradictory that someone should want to write their life story but not want to be identified. But some people have very good reasons for wanting to conceal their identity. They may want to write about traumas or personal struggles but not at the cost of publicly hurting or embarrassing their family. Or the legal implications of discussing the material openly may be uncertain.

In either of these cases, you may decide to write under a pseudonym and change the names of others involved. You may also need to alter some other details, such as dates, place names, names of organisations and characteristics which could identify a particular person. It's important to decide which details matter—you need to be careful not to distort the essential truth of your story.

Could I be sued for truth-telling?

In brief, you can only be sued if the material is largely untrue and it damages the subject's reputation. That means you will need evidence that your allegations are true if it comes to legal threats. If you are at all concerned about the likelihood of a defamation suit or about the legality of discussing a court case, consult a lawyer. Even if you have concealed your identity, it is worth checking with a lawyer to make sure. The Australian Society of Authors, an organisation dedicated to protecting the rights of authors, has legal advisers who specialise in the law as it affects writers. Once you join the organisation, their advice is available for a nominal cost. Publishers will also check, or ask you to check, if any of your material appears defamatory.

Truth and glitter

A photograph can make the most banal of scenes look 'romantic'. The stilling of the flux of life and choosing the right light and framing give the illusion of completeness, the gloss of ordinary life made into art. It is just as easy to overpolish experience with words and make it so 'shiny' that it no longer bears much relationship to raw reality. Truth is a slippery creature and it can hide itself just as well in pleasing language as in avoidance or self-indulgence. The more experienced and skilled you become as a writer, the more temptation to give everything the frame and gloss of a photograph. 'I seal loose ends with cadenced prose and add glitter where I know things were quite lustreless,' comments the American writer André Aciman in his essay 'Lies, Sweet Lies'.

It is not to say that this is necessarily a bad thing; beauty is truth, after all. But perhaps beauty can be emptied of truth. Perhaps it can happen that when beauty is the aim, truth can be lost and beauty becomes over-elegant and formal. Sometimes what is required, as an earlier American writer

Henry Miller said, 'is a gob of spit in the face of Art'. There is a raw energy, a fierceness of experience, which can be lost when you focus entirely on the word. Then you may need to write with your heart and with your gut, pegging the bloody mess out on the page without concern for appearance. Write wildly, fiercely, unrestrainedly, disturbingly, passionately. Write without respect, write inappropriately, scream if you want to. Write with only the fierce discipline of the desire for truth to guide you.

In any case, it is always difficult to know the truth, especially about yourself. Each one of us has a preferred version of ourselves and even in our secret moments we can entertain that version quite satisfactorily. We can maintain it for years too; the Chilean writer Isabel Allende wrote a story, 'Tosca', about a woman who managed to maintain a self-illusion her whole life long. Such a feat is not uncommon. There are doubts about the adequacy of the self that we can cunningly hide even from our own conscious awareness. Perhaps all writers write to build a screen against that doubt. As Aciman says, 'We write about our life, not to see it as it was, but to see it as we wish others might see it, so we may borrow their gaze.'

Still, the truth, however it is conceived, seems to me to be something worth trying for. Despite the quicksands of 'too much information' and the glossy shine of the stylish line, there is a way through which is yours alone. There is the possibility of putting down on the page what I inadequately term 'a real relationship with what is'. Where does this possibility lie? It comes when you let go the desire to impress, the greatest pollutant of the truth. The desire to impress others with our cleverness, sensitiveness, awareness and insight begins by muddying and ends up supplanting the desire for truth. If you can write free of that desire then you have a good chance of writing clear, passionate truth. You will recognise it when you have, even if you have never seen it before. It will have a beauty that is unmistakeable.

Reading

Out of the Mist and Steam   Alan Duff

I can smell her. Long before she starts walking up from the kitchen. Stinking of beer. And anger has a smell its own. I can smell something else about her, to do with her inner being—if she has one—the person she is. I'm up in the top room with my brothers, I have two sisters in another room, nearest to where the fuss is coming from. We can smell her before she leaves the kitchen. The moment we hear the door open to the passageway, her voice tells us she's headed this way. Before that we could hear her yelling. Thumps of her assaulting Dad. And he's restrained her as usual when we want him to punch shit out of her, give her some of her own back for once. But he won't. He won't. Even at eight, seven, six, maybe younger, you know something bad is happening to you beyond just the immediacy of the event, the incident itself. Your life juices are leaking out, your soul container has been ruptured, you're spilling out and you can't stem the flow.

We're in the top room and we know she'll come. Sooner or later, she'll make her dramatic appearance. That foul apparition in her children's bedroom doorway, beer-fuming breath finding her young one's nostrils and standing our hair and every poised nerve on end.

'Kids . . .?' she always starts off pretending she's a mother. 'I'm sorry to wake you up. But I want you to know something,' she lies. If she was sorry, she wouldn't be waking us up. And anyway, we know, we already know this story, this same tale of woe. Heard it a hundred times. It's your father's fault. Never hers. And each time she tries to convince us that she, this beer-stenching, swaying apparition in our bedroom doorway, backlit by the passageway light, is innocent, and that he, the sober, rational, non-violent man imploring us to leave her alone, is the guilty party. How stupid does she think her children are?

'It's not me,' she says in that plaintive voice.

She's mother of four of us in the top room, and of two in the room closest the kitchen in this state house, with one more yet to be born. A thousand square foot state box painted creosote black. There is no other state house like it. It's as if Dad wants us to stand out even more than what Mum's notorious deeds have already done, yet we know Dad's not like that. Our father has a mind, he has reason. And that's what he's yelling at her.

'Be reasonable, for God's sake!' Again. And again. Why the hell does he bother imploring her like this? Be hard on her! Finish this nonsense once and for all. For your sake, for all your children's sakes. This can't go on. And on. And on and on, incident after incident. It can't. Your kids are drowning, Pat Duff. Your wife, the kids' mother, is holding their heads under water.

Down the passage she comes. Up in the expectant bedroom we are making our adjustments, readying for it yet never really able to. Turn right, Mum, not left, you drunken fool. Past the telephone—hold it. Who's she going to ring this time?

'Mary, that you?' Mary is Mum's sister. She knows. We can hear her without having to hear the voice, asking Mum what the hell she wants at this hour when she was asleep and so should her sister be.

'Sis, can you come around?' No, sis can't come around. 'Mary? Mary ...? Mereana, don't you hang up on me!' But Mary has. So now Mary's a bitch and she'll keep, she'll keep. We can hear the muttered dire promise. Mum will get her back. It's the best-kept promise of her life.

Alan Duff doesn't not pull any punches in his description of his mother. It is so searing that no doubt some readers will draw back, whereas others will feel that he has shown the terrible truth. He writes from the perspective of the child, often using the present tense, so the reader sees and feels the child's shame and distress. Read *Out of the Mist and Steam* for its fierce account of a violent childhood and for the redemption Duff experienced through books and writing. Interestingly, Duff wrote first the novel *Once Were Warriors*, where the fictional violent parent is the father. It's as if he had to write the story as fiction first before he could write the memoir.

Writing exercises

1 Secret writing

Write something you have done or thought that you prefer no one knew about. Write with the full knowledge that no one is ever going to see it. It is not going to be part of your memoir. Notice the freedom you feel knowing there will be no judgement of the incident, no evaluation of the writing. You can even destroy it when you are done. But before you do, read it through. See if there is anything in it worth salvaging. (Twenty minutes)

2 I'm not allowed to write about

Write an episode that you know someone close to you would not like you to write about. Again, remind yourself that no one need see this piece of writing. When you are finished, clarify whether you want to include the incident in a memoir, and why or why not. (Twenty minutes)

3 Breaking taboos

Write about a topic that makes you squirm. It can be anything from bodily functions to embarrassing flaws. Write it twice, once from a serious perspective, once from a humorous perspective. (Ten minutes each)

4 Happy days

Write about an experience that carries strong positive emotions—anything from parental pride to love to happiness. This might sound like an easy exercise, but generally it is even more difficult to write about happy times because, often, they are less well observed than unhappiness. Try to avoid generalities; note the details of the experience. (Twenty minutes)

18

WORKSHOP SIXTEEN
Avoiding self-indulgence

I ought to write my life . . . The idea appealed to me. Yes, but the terrible quantity of I's and Me's! That would be enough to put the most well-disposed reader's back up.

STENDHAL

When autobiography or memoir is mentioned, a shadow sometimes flits through the eyes of the listener. I know that shadow well—it's the suspicion that memoir and autobiography might be simply an excuse for self-indulgence, that memoirists are navel-gazers of the highest order, that they use the excuse of truth for pouring their self-absorption out onto the page. Why would anyone want to read it? What makes you think anyone is interested in your particular angst? You see the shadow, feel the accusation and wonder if it *is* all self-indulgence.

In her memoir, *Second Half First*, Drusilla Modjeska writes of her earlier distaste for the first person, the 'I' of memoir: 'During the decade of my fifties, I'd developed an abhorrence of the first person: I, I, I, I, the sledgehammer of the controlling policeman, or colonialist, or conductor, if you prefer a more artistic image.' And Ben Yagoda in his essay 'A Brief History of Memoir Bashing' explores the long history of attacks on memoir for self-indulgence, starting with German philosopher Schlegel who said in 1798: 'Pure autobiographies are written either by neurotics who are fascinated by their own ego, as in Rousseau's case; or by authors of a robust artistic or adventurous self-love, such as Benvenuto Cellini; or by born historians who regard themselves only as material for historic art; or by women who also coquette with posterity; or by pedantic minds who want to bring even the most minute things in order before they die and cannot let themselves leave the world without commentaries.'

It hasn't stopped since then. People often ask me, 'Isn't auto-biographical writing egotistical and self-indulgent?' I'm here to say it is most often the opposite—in fact, one of the most striking aspects of life-writing classes is that the struggle to make sense of being here in this world creates not self-absorption but a rare warmth, a bond. Writing and sharing one's story breaks down the feeling of a separate, superior self and builds a sense of a community of being in the world. Understanding our own experience connects us more deeply to others; offering it to others creates a community of understanding. Writing about the self is one of the most demanding journeys you can take. It requires honesty, ruthlessness and courage. At the same time, the pitfalls of self-indulgence are real.

What, exactly, is self-indulgence? Everyone has a different sensibility about it, but it can include:

- Being overly sentimental about loved ones.
- Becoming too narrowly self-focused, not questioning yourself.

- Being the hero of every situation.
- Dishonesty, intentional or otherwise, about yourself.
- Self-pity or complacency.
- Including too much unnecessary information on current passions, forgetting others might not be quite as interested.
- Including unrelated material just because you like it.
- Ignoring the power of language—letting the writing become clichéd, sentimental, soggy, dishonest.
- Forgetting the reader—falling in on one's topic so the writing is more talking to oneself than communicating.

Avoiding self-indulgence

- First face that original accusing question: 'Why would anyone want to read it?' It is not so difficult to find the answer. Simply ask yourself, 'Why do I want to write it?' If the answer is simply to empty the bucketful of rubbish you have inside you then very possibly your memoir is for yourself, not for a reader. If you feel there is something of value in the rubbish, make your first draft a bucket-emptying procedure then get to work on it, making something for your reader to use.
- Take one step back from yourself as protagonist to become the narrator, still close enough to feel it, but not so close that you are drowning in a swamp of self-absorption. The 'I' who is telling the story steps back from being the protagonist to being the narrator. Phillip Lopate in *To Show and to Tell* describes this process as turning the 'I', oneself, into a character. He maintains that 'this process of turning oneself into a character is not self-absorbed navel-gazing but rather a potential release from narcissism'. This process of stepping

back to a narrating 'I' most often requires the solution of time. If you are too close to the experience in time then it is often difficult to take the necessary step back. Wait a bit longer. But it is also an inner step back from the material, looking at it in a ruthless way as material rather than as your life. In one sense, writers are scavengers, picking through the bits and pieces and selecting what they want.

- Remember that your particular passions and obsessions might not be of interest to others. That doesn't mean you shouldn't write about them, indeed you must—personally, I love reading about what occupies others. What it does mean is stepping outside of your passions for a moment to see how they might look from the outside, and then see how best to communicate them to others.

- Remember that you are writing this for someone to read, whatever the topic. At the same time, you don't want to become self-conscious, second-guessing what others might be thinking, but rather reminding yourself you are communicating, not purging. It means being aware that you are not simply pouring yourself out; you are making a world on the page. Avoiding self-indulgence is not about avoiding certain subjects—you can write about anything you want, no topic is taboo—but it is about remembering that you are creating a work made out of words for a reader to inhabit.

- Create a wider world around the individual life. Include a broader and deeper context. This suggestion is expanded later in this chapter.

- Remember the transforming power of fresh, evocative language. Check through for clichés and stock expressions. Remind yourself that *my stomach was knotted in despair* might not be the most original way of conveying your feelings.

Reducing the 'terrible quantity of I's and Me's'

Even if you have avoided the swamp of self-indulgence, it can be horrifying to see the forest of 'I's'. A memoir is nearly always written from the first person and this personal perspective, this access to the inner life, is part of what makes it so appealing. But at times it can revolve too tightly around the 'I', creating a claustrophobic, in-pulling atmosphere. The reader feels as if they have been dragged into a vortex of self rather than taken on a journey of exploration.

It is possible to remove some of the forest of 'I's' by simply writing from an impersonal perspective. Instead of writing 'I' each time as you name your response to your environment, evoke the event, scene or the person in such a way that the reader can see your response. For example: *I loved the pear tree flowering outside my window* could be rewritten *There was an elegant pear tree with creamy blossoms outside my window.* The reader can be led to see with your eyes, respond with your sensibility, without 'I' directing everything.

It may not just be the overuse of 'I'. It could well be that, because you are concentrating on following a particular narrative, you have made a world that is too small, too centred on the self. It can leave no room for the reader to stand. You may need to create a wider world.

A wider world

The worlds of history, politics, psychology, science—all the worlds that make up your individual experience—can provide a context and a place for the reader to stand in relation to your life. Seeing your life in the context of a wider landscape is one of the most effective ways to avoid self-indulgence.

The areas you expand into will depend on your own interests and the scope of your memoir. Include a history of the Irish uprising of 1916 if your family was involved and your memoir explores your own commitment to causes. If you are writing a memoir about the women in your family, you could include the history and influence of feminism. If you are writing about the impact of an illness, include the science of the illness and its treatment. In *Pilgrim at Tinker Creek*, Annie Dillard includes considerable ecological knowledge as well as her own observations. A wider context, but one which is related to your specific memoir, will take the limelight away from you for a while and make it richer, more textured, more layered.

In *Whatever the Gods Do,* which partly told the story of a friend who suffered a cerebral haemorrhage and remained alive in a 'locked-in' state for over a year, I included material about the brain. Because her brain had been severely damaged by the haemorrhage it seemed necessary to include a scientific understanding of what had happened. As well, I've always been interested in the way we have so many ways of 'knowing' a situation, from the emotional story of a friend to the scientific story of a doctor. They each come from different angles, from different areas of knowledge, but they are all 'true', all necessary to the overall story of what has happened.

There can be the danger of adding layers that are not intrinsically related to the themes or narratives of the memoir. Very often I have seen manuscripts that include all sorts of extraneous history, science and current affairs and look as if the writer feels she don't have enough material and is plumping it out with researched information. For example, a detailed history of the battle between the Stuarts and McDonalds in Scotland might be interesting of itself, but it probably does not need to be in your story of a year on a sailing boat, even if you are of Scottish descent. It might be more relevant to find interesting material on oceanography or weather patterns.

If you take the advice of including a wide world too far you can end up writing a memoir minus yourself. In class, an older man wrote comprehensively about his boyhood as a migrant, including information about the migration scheme and precise detail about the dimensions of various rooms in the migrant hostel he lived in for several months, but there was little sense of how he felt in this new and alien environment. He was missing from his own memoir. It is much less threatening to write about the wider world and, taken too far, it can become a social history rather than a memoir. Remember, a reader of a memoir essentially wants to know what it is like to be you.

You need to be sensitive to the effect on the structure that additional material will have. An eclectic approach can work— you can include a wide range of outward-looking information, especially if you have a roving mind interested in all sorts of things—but you need to be aware of the effect on the shape of your memoir. Too much added material can swamp the personal story and dilute the narrator's voice.

If you are interested in including research material, think about how to weave it in to the rest of the text. Reweaving other texts and sources of information into your story to create a multilayered effect can be very appealing and can give a richer reading experience. On the other hand, too many extracts from other sources, too much undigested material, starts looking like you do not have confidence in your own material. See Workshop eleven: Research for more tips on writing and research.

Writing inner life

Much of the experience of life happens on an inner level. Thoughts, insights, meditations—these are all part of life but have little action or scenery. Trying to convey inner life can result in highly abstract, dense, self-centred writing, inaccessible to the reader. The damning judgement of self-indulgence is easily flung at memoirists trying to explore their inner lives.

To open out that inner world, think like a filmmaker. In films, characters rarely say everything they are thinking—unless it is a Woody Allen film—but their thoughts and feelings are revealed by the spaces they inhabit and by their responses to the world around them. Writing about the world around you is a way of revealing yourself without self-absorption. *You can know what someone is like by what impresses him or her.* This doesn't only mean that you know what people are like according to whether they are impressed by money, wisdom, power or literary talent. It also means you can see what people are like according to what they notice, by what *impresses itself* upon their consciousness. Each person sees the world in a different way, notices different things, according to individual personalities and interests. One will notice the space, light and colour of a room, another the clothes of the people in the room, another the mood of particular people, another the expensive furniture. Each observation tells us something about the observer. By writing the details of your room, house, street or neighbourhood, the reader can see something of the person you are—without you having to talk directly about yourself all the time.

It is possible to write our experience passionately but without self-indulgence by remembering that experience and words are not the same thing. Each shapes the other: we form words and words form us. As writers we align ourselves with words, trying to create simulacra of experience. A memoir is about you, that is obvious, but it is more accurately about an experience of being. According to the extent and shape of the memoir, it will include elements of your physical, social, political, historical, scientific and other environments as they influence and even determine your experience of being. The 'I' will be there, letting the reader see what it is like inside and outside the millimetres of skin separating us from each other.

Reading

When Horse Became Saw
Anthony Macris

She asked us about Alex's recent progress and scribbled notes on her pad. We emphasised our concern about his language, expressed our frustration with not getting services. She wasn't surprised, and listened intently to descriptions of our efforts to help Alex. She seemed impressed. Then there was a strange pause. It had a quality of unhurriedness that was character-istic of dealing with professionals, where time was either their money or the government's. The pause said, Today is your day. We can take all the time in the world.

I asked her why the windows were covered up. She said it was so that the children wouldn't get distracted when they did the test.

Another pause.

It was time to start. It was fine if we were in the room. In fact, she might ask Kathy to assist. The more comfortable

Alex was, the better picture we would get of his abilities. In the meantime, Alex had got down out of the pram and started galloping up and down. He pressed his plaster cast close to his chest to stabilise it. It was as if it had become part of him.

The test Alex was given was called the Griffiths Mental Developmental scales. For the next hour or so, I watched him constantly run away from the table when the doctor asked him to perform a number of tasks, and Kathy coax him back again. At regular intervals the doctor made entries in a workbook.

He did well in gross motor activities. He could run (oh, yes, he could run), kick a ball and jump off a step. He turned when the doctor rang a tinkling bell, but not when his name was called. He couldn't name any of the body parts on a doll. He took no interest in the picture book he was shown. He couldn't name a single toy the doctor spread out before him. In fact, he didn't understand a word she said.

She produced some blocks and proceeded to build a tower that Alex was to copy. Towers weren't Alex's strong suit: no surprise when, with a swipe of his hand, he brought it tumbling down. He did, however, pull the green cloth away from the doll hidden beneath and look at the figure lying there with some recognition, as clearly he was meant to. Some points there, no doubt.

On to geometry, or at least this was what was suggested by the simple circle, square and rectangle puzzles that made up the next subtest. Alex managed to put a couple of shapes in their slots, but that was about it.

The doctor paused a moment. The next subtest, she told us, was the last. It was to do with practical reasoning and relied heavily on language. If it was okay with us, she would prefer not to test him in this area, but exclude it altogether. It would only serve to drag his aggregate score down and give a distorted view of his capabilities.

The test was over. We sat in silence as the doctor finished entering information in her workbook, while Alex ran up and down the middle of the room for a couple of minutes as a reward for having done the assessment. Then Kathy settled him in his pram with a drink and biscuits.

The doctor finally spoke. It would take her a little time to process the test, she told us. She had to collate the scores, reflect on the data, and include the observational material from this and the first visit. It was clear to her, however, that Alex's developmental delay was of a significant extent, and she thought this was probably due to autism. In her view, it would get worse before it got better. He would most likely lose all his language, before it came back again. *If* it came back: we had to prepare ourselves for it not happening . . .

When she asked if we had any final questions, Kathy said, 'His words. We've been reading to him as much as possible to bring back his words.'

The doctor didn't say anything for a while. She'd already given her opinion. She then appeared to think better of her silence and told us it couldn't hurt; any such stimulation was bound to help.

We knew she was just being kind. We thanked her for her time and efforts and left.

We were completely calm as we made our way back to the station. We discussed the test. There was really only one question left: how bad was it? Weaving through the crowded street, we felt the test recede, and slowly filled ourselves again. We were no longer just the event, no longer hollow. But we were changed.

In this extract Anthony Macris writes about one of the most emotionally difficult scenes for a parent—finding out their child has a serious disability—but there is no trace of self-indulgence or sentimentality. He writes in a calm, observant, matter-of-fact style, letting the reader feel but not be swamped by the events. Read *When Horse Became Saw* for it fearless writing, its insights, and its powerful narrative—a testament to a father's love.

Writing exercises

1 Emptying the bucket

This exercise has two parts. Part one: write about an experience that carries strong negative emotion—anger, shame, grief. Write it without restraint, without thought of how to best express it, without thought of anyone reading it. Part two: a few days later, without re-reading the first one, write about the same experience, but this time write it as if the piece has been commissioned for an anthology on this emotion. You are aware of trying to communicate the experience to strangers. See which is the more powerful. (Twenty minutes for each part)

2 Avoiding indulgence

Write about someone who provokes strong emotions in you, positive or negative—love, pride, guilt, anger—but do not name the emotion anywhere in the piece. Begin with a particular physical mannerism. This is an exercise in avoiding self-indulgence and in disciplining your urge to spell everything out. You must observe and evoke a person without naming your emotions in relation to them. (Twenty minutes)

3 Forest of 'I'

Write about a scene from any time of your life, preferably a scene that involves your perceptions of your environment. If you are stuck for a scene, perhaps evoke the first place you lived when you left home—the apartment or house, the people, the experience. Leave it until the next day. Now try to write it again, this time cutting the number of I's in it by half by changing the perspective from which you are writing. For example, change *I watched the cars in the busy street below* to *The cars in the busy street below rushed by*. (Thirty minutes for each part)

4 Passions

Write about one of your current passions—a cause, an activity or an area of knowledge. Write about your experience of it as if the person who will read it knows nothing about this passion. What do you need to tell them to convey how absorbing, exciting, fascinating this passion is to you? (Fifteen minutes)

19

WORKSHOP SEVENTEEN

Borderlands—Memoir and fiction

As one goes along, one wonders: is the novelist in me taking over?

PATRICK WHITE

At a writers' festival in Australia several years ago, I was on a discussion panel titled 'The Memoir Writer's Responsibility to the Truth' with a woman who had written a book about the 'honour killing' of her friend. According to her memoir, they had grown up in Jordan and opened a hairdressing salon together as young women. Her friend had fallen in love with a boy her parents would not have approved of. Of course, they were found out, and even though their love had only been expressed in hand-holding and one or two brief kisses, she was 'honour killed' by her father and brothers. As I read the memoir, I felt anger at the distortion of the concept of honour, incomprehension at familial violence based on ideology, grief at the loss of a young life, admiration of the woman who had so courageously set down the story of herself and her friend.

The problem was, a few weeks after the festival it was discovered that none of the key elements of her story were true. The author had, in fact, grown up not in Jordan but in Chicago, and none of her friends had been 'honour killed'.

More recently, there have been other memoirists who have written lives of tragedy, abuse and addiction, only for it to be discovered—after the 'memoirs' had sold extremely well—that most of the experiences were invented.

There was, of course, outrage at the deception, each time followed by debate about the differences between memoir and fiction. These cases highlighted the reality that, despite post-modernist realisations of truth as a construction, there is an accepted relationship of trust between a memoirist and a reader, mirroring the trust between friends. We are, as a rule, not post-modernist in our interpretation of our personal conversations. If a friend tells us they were hit by their father as a child, we accept that is what happened. We may question the friend's interpretation of the event, but we do not question that it truly happened.

The French autobiographical theorist Philippe Lejeune calls this the 'autobiographical pact', that is, the agreement that the author on the book cover, the first-person narrator and the person whose life is being narrated are one and the same, and that therefore what is being narrated is a true account of that life. Even though Australian critic David McCooey remarks that 'everything which passes through memory is a fiction', the reader still expects that the memoirist is at least giving an account of what happened as they have it constructed in their memory.

In categorising her work as a memoir, the memoirist affirms, 'I am telling you something about myself, which you can believe actually occurred.' This assumption of truth is as fundamental to memoir as it is to friendship but, even so, there are many areas where even the most factual of memoirists might need to use the techniques of fiction. It is worth exploring the borderlands between the two and finding out what parts of the territory you feel able to inhabit. How far can you go in memoir and still feel you are telling the truth of your experience?

Fiction in memoir

Many successful memoirs have used what might be fairly judged as fictional techniques.

Invented dialogue

If someone makes a remark which is particularly tender—or particularly cutting, for that matter—you will probably remember the exact wording, but in the majority of cases most of us cannot remember exactly what we ourselves said yesterday, let alone what other people said many years ago. Yet to create the lived texture of life on the page you must use some dialogue. You will need to 'make up' what was said. Most people accept that the memoirist has remembered only the gist and is making up the actual dialogue, keeping in mind the characteristic way that each person spoke. In a sense you are using invention, but it is grounded in your memory.

Then there are conversations at which you were not present but which you know took place. In *One Life*, Kate Grenville's story of her mother's life, many conversations are created from her mother's life that she can only have deduced, not heard, nor, in most cases, even heard about. Does the reader feel deceived? It seems to me that most readers in this situation realise they are being told a good story; they know, too, that she could not have heard the conversation, so they accept a little artistic licence. The reader knows the intent is not to deceive but to illuminate. Grenville also lets the reader know that her mother left her diaries to her, which gives authenticity to her construction of her mother's thoughts and feelings.

Imagining lives from a few facts

It has become increasingly popular in family memoirs to imagine the lives of long gone or absent family members. Strictly speaking, this is not memoir at all—memoir is remembered, not imagined—but such imagining has become part of memoir in practice. In Alexandra Joel's *Rosetta*, the author imagines the life of her great-grandmother in fine detail; this is the realm of fiction but the book is subtitled 'A Scandalous True Story'. It is a legitimate literary device—it can give an emotional richness and a lived texture to the otherwise bare bones of family history— and the trust with the reader is not broken because Joel uses the technique of discussing her sources and methods, so the reader is happy to make the leap with her into imagining the daily details.

Imagined inner lives

Clearly, the memoirist has no direct access to the inner lives of family members and friends. She can deduce feelings and perceptions from what is said and done, but cannot with certainty know the mental and emotional life which produced them. Yet some memoirists create the inner reality of other characters in their lives either by evoking them directly or by some device such as a fictional diary. Drusilla Modjeska in *Poppy* invents the diary of her mother to give the reader access to her inner life. Kristina Olsson in *Boy, Lost* imagines the details and the inner life of her mother who had her firstborn son snatched from her arms when he was a baby and wasn't to see him again for another thirty-six years. She writes of her mother: 'Somewhere in her own weary brain, she knows he is echoing her, responding to her own fear, her own curdled mixture of terror and sorrow and the adrenalin it has taken to get her here.' And then in the next section writes: 'This is the story my mother never told, not to us, the children who would grow up around it the way skin grows over a scratch.' Olsson makes it clear that she doesn't know how her mother felt for sure, that she is using a fictional device, so that in the confidence of her admission the reader trusts that she is trying to convey the truth of her mother's experience. Read the extract from *Boy, Lost* in Workshop one to see how she achieves this.

Sequence of events altered, condensed or left out

Life is a messy business—many things happen at once, not all of them related to each other and not necessarily unfolding at the same rate. You may want to write about the break-up with your husband, which happened at the same time as you started taking violin lessons, and at the same time as your mother had a car accident and you were visiting her every day, and at the same time as your son had a run-in with a teacher at school. What happens if you change the order of certain events, or put a number of events together and write them as one, for example, condense five visits to your mother into one? It's important when faced with these kinds of decisions to examine why you are writing the memoir. Is it as a legal record of the time? Probably not. Is it a history for the future? Maybe. Is it to convey selected strands of the pattern of life at a particular time? Probably.

And then examine your motives: why are you leaving these events out? Is it because you would be embarrassed? Because you want to protect someone? Because you want change the way the reader perceives what happened? There are any number of reasons to alter events in some way, but for me the reason needs to be based on two criteria: first, does the alteration change the truth I want to convey, and second, does it affect the structure. If it clarifies the truth and if it creates a stronger, more effective structure, then go ahead. If you cut and condense some of the visits to your mother it may convey the difficulty of the experience more effectively and at the same time improve the structure by eliminating repetition.

Combined or left-out characters

Scenes and events in life often have too many characters, or too many for the writer to manage, at least. Perhaps I am speaking personally here—I come from a family of eight children so most events in my childhood involve a large cast! If I write about my family it can become too crowded on the page, too many names for the reader to keep track of. People, however, are much more problematic than events to 'combine', that is, make two or more characters into one. You can almost hear them objecting as you try to melt them into someone else. Certainly, I don't feel justified in eliminating or condensing any of my brothers and sisters! The crowded confusion of people is part of the truth of my childhood experience.

But memoirists occasionally feel the need to combine characters, especially peripheral ones, for reasons of economy and avoiding repetition—and sometimes to avoid identification. The television presenter, essayist and poet Clive James admits in the prologue of his *Unreliable Memoirs* to having put people he knew 'through the blender' so that they could not be recognised. In *Whatever the Gods Do* I combined elements of two choir teachers, not because I didn't value their individuality but because it would have been clumsy and repetitive to have both teachers in the narrative. It is still truthful to the experience of being in the choir—I made nothing up—but in life, one teacher left to get married and another one arrived. It didn't seem necessary to my story to include this information.

I have also left people out of memoirs, for a number of reasons. In one memoir, a person was omitted entirely because her presence represented another narrative strand that I decided was not mine to tell. It was also clear that her narrative, being emotionally powerful, would have overbalanced the feeling and structure of the narrative I was exploring.

Leaving people out is often a structural decision, but again it can be to protect oneself or others. For example, you might decide to leave out an affair you had because you want to protect that person's present marriage—an important character is thus left out of your memoir. But a memoirist is not necessarily recording the whole truth of a particular time or experience; as the writer, she is deciding what elements of experience she want to explore. If leaving out certain elements means leaving out people who were there at the time, then that is the memoirist's decision. Of course, it is important not to use this reasoning as an excuse to distort or misrepresent other people.

Keeping trust

Keeping the trust of your reader does not necessarily mean you do not ever invent anything, but, I believe, it does mean that you let the reader know in some way what is true and what is imagined. It doesn't apply to novels, of course, because the definition of truth we bring to reading depends on the genre. When we read a novel, we expect that perhaps the writer has drawn on some of their own experience but that the narrative and characters unfold according to the demands of the imagination. In nonfiction, we expect that the narrative and characters unfold according to the demands of life. As in life, readers of nonfiction need to know what is true and what is invented if they are to give emotional and intellectual credence to your words. There are a few ways you can signal to your reader how to weigh what you have written:

- *The prologue statement.* Mention in the prologue that you have 'put characters through a blender' or that you have invented scenes, that you have become a conjurer. Or the dedication hint, as Drusilla Modjeska did in *Poppy*: 'To my mother who died in 1984 and never kept a diary', the only direct revelation in the book that her mother's 'diaries' are fiction.

- *The Mary McCarthy option.* In *Memories of a Catholic Girlhood*, McCarthy wrote her stories as she liked to remember them. Then, tempering the desire to fictionalise for the sake of a good story with the need for honesty, she created inter-chapters that told the reader what she had inferred or invented. This technique needs to be lightly used as it could come across as pedantic!

- *Layout design.* Using a layout device such as a different font or indent can suggest that the section is to be read differently. Readers will soon work out whether it is a leap back in time, a different perspective, or an imagined sequence based on the facts. You can also use subheadings with a question mark to suggest that the section may be imagined.

- *Unreliable narrator option.* Suggest in the title or within the text that you, as narrator, may not be entirely reliable. You can suggest that your memory is faulty, that you have a propensity for exaggerating, that you don't have enough respect for the facts. Confessing your unreliability, paradoxically, makes you more trustworthy. At least we know to take what you say with a grain of salt.
- *Confess to imagining events.* Within the story, indicate that what you are about to write is invented. In *The Last One Who Remembers,* I wrote of a great-aunt who died before I was born: 'She must enter the told world via a third-hand memory if she is to exist past that brief moment in the breathing world. Surely no one could mind if I gave her breath and speech again. I have no solid materials to work with, only the watered silk and lace of invention.' Such a device is direct and easy to use and clearly signals how the passage is to be read.

Autobiographical fiction

On the other side of the border between memoir and fiction there are novels that are so close to the author's actual experience that they might just as reasonably be called memoir. The genre of autobiographical fiction, which sounds like a contradiction in terms, has been part of the literary tradition for some time. Marcel Proust's *In Search of Lost Time*, first published in 1913, is often called autobiographical fiction, as is James Joyce's *A Portrait of the Artist as a Young Man*. More recently, Karl Ove Knausgaard's *My Struggle* so closely followed his own life and his family's that it generated debate about whether he was exposing his family then wriggling out of responsibility by saying it was fiction. In Australia, Helen Garner's *The Quiet Room* was published as a novel, although the central character was named Helen and most of the events mirrored life.

Basing the work on what happened but thinking of it as a novel can give the writer the room to make narrative, structural and character changes without losing the energy of lived experience on the page. It does not mean that characters in the story who 'recognise' themselves will be pleased, especially if the character is portrayed in a way that makes then feel misrepresented. It is a complex area: call it memoir or nonfiction and you may be attacked for 'inventing' scenes; call it a novel and you may be accused of using the shield of fiction while you expose others. Perhaps the only real answer is to be as ruthlessly insightful and honest with the 'character' based on yourself as with 'characters' based on others.

Where you stand on the border between fiction and memoir depends on your own sensibility as a writer and as a person. If only the facts in the right order at the right time feels truthful, then that's the way for you to go. As a memoirist myself, I don't mind altering the sequence or deleting a few elements, especially for structural demands, but each time it is crucial that I examine my motives and make sure I am not deceiving myself, let alone my readers. It is important that I try to tell the truth of my own perceptions as accurately as possible. Truth may be a construct, but truthfulness is not. It takes long and hard work to hit the severe metal of truthful perception—the ego is a constant and wily deceiver—but you always know when you have finally found some truthfulness in yourself. There is a clear unalloyed ring to it.

Borderland ethics

The ethical issues of memoir are much more complicated when you approach the borderlands with fiction. If you are presenting actual living characters—or even someone who has died—but invent some of their inner lives, what responsibility do you have to reality? What if you have blended two or three characters, and the actual people are offended or distressed to see themselves demolished and re-assembled? It is easy to say, 'That section is fiction, I've merely embroidered the truth, anyone can see that,' but the fact remains that if the overall book is presented as a memoir, or even as an autobiographical novel, most readers will believe the whole story and not differentiate between what is true and what is not. The first person, the 'I', gives the authority of lived truth, even when we know it's fiction. People can be hurt, embarrassed, humiliated, perhaps even have their reputations ruined, by what you have written. What is the hungry writer's ethical response? We each have to answer this question, but for me the answer starts with asking myself, 'How would I feel if someone else wrote about me and invented details of my character or my life?' To be honest, the answer might not stop me from writing on the borderlands, but at least it would force me to take responsibility for what I was doing.

Reading

Rosetta   Alexandra Joel

Three

I did not start seeking my great-grandmother until I had become a mother myself, and known tragedy. My life was ruptured, ripped apart. I had a child who died. It was a cataclysm that broke all the natural laws of the universe. How could it be that I would not spend another precious moment with her, that I would never, ever see her navy eyes or feathery hair, the sweet bow of her mouth again. As impossible as the sun setting in the east or rising in the west, it was beyond my imagination.

I tried not to scan the faces of other little girls in parks, on trains, in cars, on streets. Knowing the quest was hopeless, I did my best to resist. Come nightfall, though, my resolve evaporated. In my dreams I searched for her. And I began to wonder, did Rosetta ever look for her child, too?

Much later, with the balm of my son and another daughter, my world settled. By then I was aware that my great-grandmother had lived a passionate, daring life. Yet all the while she hid her secret shame, the little girl she left behind.

I was torn. Despite my growing fascination with Rosetta, I wondered: could I come or even want to know a woman I half thought a kind of monster? Despite my struggle, I found Rosetta irresistible. I went in search of her.

It was in the garage of my brother, Michael, that I first saw the results of my father's labours; tangible evidence of Rosetta's life.

'Here it is,' Michael said, running a protective hand over a brown cardboard filing box and three thick spiral binders, one black, one red and one blue.

'I've photocopied the family tree, but don't take anything else away,' he instructed. 'It can't be lost.'

She was his great-grandmother, too. But I did take it. I took everything.

When I arrived home I turned the contents out onto the smooth plane of my dining-room table and spread out what there was: a variety of ageing documents that had been assembled in shiny plastic sleeves, photocopies from the pages of old newspapers, the recollections of several people who knew Rosetta first hand and a few short pieces of prose that Dad had written himself, typed up in pre-computer days on a machine that over-inked the e's and smudged the d's. Best of all was a folder of fading photographs and an intriguing bundle of hand-written letters, a number of them bearing crests and coronets. But would this trove be enough to re-create the woman I sought? I wasn't sure.

In the end, it didn't matter. Even with the gaps and omissions, Rosetta became so real to me that not only could I picture her, I felt a kind of insistence, as if she were demanding to be brought back to life.

I did wonder if embarking on this process of re-creation I might be guilty of committing a transgression. Though I made a promise to myself that I would not change any known facts, there was some anxiety. I asked myself if it would be wrong to lay claim to what Rosetta thought, felt or said, as if these things were grounded in the pure reality of truth. But then I reflected, even were a hundred people to provide a hundred memories of my great-grandmother, would any of them have really known the contents of her mind, her heart?

It was then that I became a conjurer, calling forth a phantom with the name of Rosetta.

Four

MELBOURNE, 1905

There is a sign on a first floor entrance of 238 Swanston Street that reads '*Zeno the Magnificent*'; it is picked out in shimmering silver and gold. Rosetta, though her thoughts are whirling and she is out of breath, notes as she passes that it is not a gaudy thing, but a rather beautiful hand-painted arrangement of swirls and lines. A moment later the door opens—she wonders afterwards how he knew she was there—and Rosetta steps inside.

She finds she is looking at the great Zeno himself but, with a hot wave of shock, she realises she has seen this man before.

This extract from *Rosetta* reveals how Joel sets up the quest she is on to re-create her great-grandmother, showing us her materials—photographs, documents—and then that she is going to 'conjure' Rosetta from these materials. The reader is happy to go with her into the borderlands between memoir, biography and fiction. Read *Rosetta* for its compelling story of a woman who deserts her husband and child to run away with a daring con man, Zeno, and become the toast of European society, as well as for its fascinating structure, which moves between research and imagination with confidence.

Writing exercises

1 Imaginary diary

Construct a diary of a three-month period in your life when you did not keep a diary. Entries can be as frequent or as irregular as you like, but remember, you can only know what you know on that day. (It is a useful device, too, for putting events in sequence when there has been a jumble of over-whelming experiences.) (One hour)

2 Conjuring

Re-create a day in the life of one of your ancestors about whom you have only a few facts. Do some research about the times first—what kind of clothes did people wear? How were houses furnished? What were the attitudes and beliefs of the time? What kinds of things might they have thought about? (Two to three hours)

3 Remembering conversation

Write a scene, including some conversation, that someone has told you about but at which you were not present. It could even be a scene from before you were born—something recounted to you. (Thirty minutes)

4 Combining events

Select an event which occurred a number of times in the period you want to write about, such as going to the same holiday spot as a child or visiting an ageing parent in hospital over a few months. Combine the several events into one event, as if the various experiences all happened in the same time sequence. (Thirty minutes)

20

WORKSHOP EIGHTEEN

Creative nonfiction

There is nothing you can't do with it [creative nonfiction]. No subject matter is forbidden, no structure is proscribed. You get to make up your own form every time.

ANNIE DILLARD

There is a vast realm of literature that exists alongside novels, plays and poetry but is not nearly as recognised—it hasn't even found itself a definite name. Biography, autobiography, memoir and personal essay are included in this realm, and are recognisable, but they are part of wider field, sometimes called *creative nonfiction*, sometimes *literary nonfiction*, sometimes *narrative nonfiction,* each one suggesting a sightly different emphasis, but named for what it is not, that is, it's not fiction. It's one of my favourite areas of literature and I often find myself exploring it in my own writing, but it's rather elusive when it comes to definitions.

The 'nonfiction' part of the title sounds simple enough. Traditionally, nonfiction refers to histories, journalism, biographies and theoretical or practical texts from every discipline— science, philosophy, politics, humanities—and is expected to be evidenced-based information written in a straightforward prose style. It is factual, truthful, it can be mapped to a real-world situation.

Creative nonfiction—as I will call it—is more complicated, being a hybrid literary form. In brief, creative nonfiction aims to tell a true story, but it recognises that there is a broad and blurred territory between facts, fact-based re-creation and invention; it is happy to use the techniques of fiction, such as re-creating scenes and vivid, poetic writing; it also borrows the techniques of memoir such as using a first-person narration and personal observation and memory. All the various aspects of writing explored in the other chapters apply equally to creative nonfiction, but here let's examine some particular issues.

The narrator in nonfiction

In creative nonfiction, the first-person narrator, the 'I' telling the story, can be present to varying degrees and will determine the perspective. If your nonfiction story is closely connected to your own life then you as narrator will be not just giving the reader the perspective from which to see the action but you will be involved in it as a protagonist, so observation and personal history will form a large part of your material. The 'narrating I' will also provide a strong structural thread.

In *Stasiland*, which looks at the secret police in East Germany under communist rule, Anna Funder is on the outside edge of the story and takes the narrating position of a journalist, connecting to her interviewees but not looking closely at whether the issues connect to her own life. *This House of Grief*, which recounts the trial of a man who has driven his three children into a dam where they drowned, is not personally connected to Helen Garner's own life but is connected through her interest in the moral and psychological issues. She is present in the story as an observer of the trial, effectively a one-woman Greek chorus commenting on, interpreting and questioning the action to create a perspective from which the reader can see and understand highly legalistic material. In *The Mind of a Thief*, the exploration of a native title claim in my home town was closely connected to my own life, so there is a large amount of personal memory as well as research—the 'narrating I' links the research, interviews and personal history. The narrator in each of these creative nonfictions is present to a greater or lesser degree.

Types of creative nonfiction

The types of creative nonfiction, subject matter and forms, are hugely varied. As Annie Dillard suggests, the wonderful thing about creative nonfiction is that you can write about any subject in any way, but broadly speaking there is story-based nonfiction—hence the variation *narrative* nonfiction—and idea-based nonfiction. Of course they cross over—you can explore ideas in a narrative, and an idea-based book can have a narrative structure—but *it is useful to think about and ask yourself whether you have a story to tell, or an idea to explore.*

Creative nonfiction encompasses true crime and true thrillers, nature writing, history, some types of biography, travel or sojourn memoir, and the personal essay.

True crime and true thrillers

As the names suggest, true crime and true thrillers are narratives that explore a crime or a mystery, usually via a court trial or first-hand research, particularly interviews, and documentary research. Both genres, which vary mainly in subject matter, are a development of investigative journalism. The subject matter in fact will often come from the media, so if you are searching for a story, look at both newspapers and social media for a story that catches your interest. Sensational or extreme stories often catch our attention first, but look out for quieter and more layered stories as well. Environmental, political and business conflicts can make interesting true thrillers. A story with ethical and or personal dilemmas will have more substance, so look for a story that you find engaging in terms of the issues. The story could come from your own life, which means it will also include a larger degree of memoir material. Whether the story is from your own life or not, be prepared to be emotionally drawn into what may be very difficult and confronting material and complicated relationships with your interview subjects, who may be sceptical about your motives.

Be prepared to do vast amounts of research, to check and recheck your facts, and to face the task of sifting through conflicting accounts to make sense of them. Your research could involve 'immersion' where you are living in the situation, such as an activist collective, or could involve re-enactment where you are trying to find answers by reliving an historical event.

It is crucial to find your narrating perspective and how much you, as narrator, will be in the story. Will you stand outside it, narrating, or will you examine the issues as they relate to your own life as well? Will you take a position, align yourself with protagonists and issues?

Structurally, true crime and true thrillers are firmly narrative driven, so creating a time line and plotting out the narrative points fairly early on are both useful. They depend on the artful giving and withholding of information, to build tension and suspense. Read Chapter seventeen for more information on narrative structure.

Read other true crime books, starting with Truman Capote's *In Cold Blood*, which was the first to use fictional techniques such as allowing the reader to enter the mind of a character and the re-creation of scenes in the service of nonfiction. Read Janet Malcolm's *Iphigenia in Forest Hills*, Helen Garner's *Joe Cinque's Consolation* and *This House of Grief* for where and how to place yourself as narrator, and John Safran's *Murder in Mississippi* for its idiosyncratic narrating persona.

Nature writing

Writing about nature has always been part of literature—there's poetry, of course, and nineteenth-century first-person accounts of living close to nature such as *Walden* by Thoreau—but with our natural environment under threat, it has become a topic with wider implications than ever before. Nature writing is part of many memoirs and travel stories, but it also is an expanding area in its own right, particularly the relationship between landscape, the self and our responsibilities to the environment.

Nature writing includes writing about our relationship to the natural environment—to landscapes and to wildlife—and activities such as climbing or walking. It is experience-based rather than research-based, but often includes research in geography, geology, botany or any of the natural sciences. Like the whole genre of creative nonfiction, it has the personal perspective of memoir and employs scenes and poetic imagery to engage the reader more deeply.

The key feature of nature writing is detailed observation, so it's important to take notes from your own personal experience. Keep a small notebook in your pocket to jot down precise observations and sensory impressions. If you are adding in research, make sure it's in your own voice so that the writing does not become overly academic. Look at the inclusion of a vast array of research in *The Bush* by Don Watson to see how he blends personal observation and science-based research or, for a more personal connection, *Position Doubtful* by Kim Mahood. You can also include memoir material, memories from childhood from other times and places, which give both context and emotional engagement for the reader.

The personal voice in nature writing is just as important as in other forms of nonfiction. Your narrating persona can be thoughtful and serious, as Rebecca Solnit is in *Wanderlust,* or as lighthearted and self-deprecatory as Simon Armitage in *Walking Home.* Nature writing is an ideal genre for reflecting on ideas, including reflecting on the self, which allows plenty of room for an engaging, conversational voice.

To avoid the risk of becoming static, you need to find the forward movement in your nature writing. It could be a story or an idea unfolding. Consider whether your nature writing should have a quest structure, such as *Wild* by Cheryl Strayed, or a series of short observations, such as *The Blue Jay's Dance* by Louise Erdich. Because contemplating nature appears to encourage thoughtfulness, nature writing crosses over easily into the personal essay, into idea-based writing. It can be shaped around an argument as in Tim Winton's *Island Home,* which makes a case for conservation of natural heritage, or around a celebration of place, as in Mark Tredinnick's *The Blue Plateau.*

You can shape your nature writing around a journey—such as Robert Macfarlane's *The Old Ways* where he observes nature as he walks around England—or around a sojourn, like *Pilgrim at Tinker Creek* by Annie Dillard, or around an emotional journey as in *H is for Hawk* by Helen Macdonald.

If you are passionate about nature then nature writing is rich and flexible territory for exploring your experiences and ideas.

History and politics

Histories and political events written as creative nonfiction have become increasingly popular, perhaps because films have accustomed audiences to re-creations of scenes and three-dimensional characters. In selecting an historical topic, make sure it is one that fascinates you as a reader. If you are going to spend a long time with an historical event, it needs to sustain your curiosity as a writer. You can select events of national significance, for example *Girt* by David Hunt humorously recounts the history of Australia, or local events—in *The Mind of a Thief* I investigated a native title claim in my hometown.

The first necessity of creative nonfiction is that all your historical facts are correct, that every date and place and event can be verified. As for biography, there is a higher demand for factual accuracy in historical creative nonfiction than in memoir. You don't need to footnote, but keep a record of where you found each fact, including websites, so that you can include them in your bibliography. Keep all notes and records of interviews in case you need them at a later stage. Remember that what is written gains authority.

Ask yourself whether you are retelling an old story from a fresh perspective, or debunking an old story and coming up with a new one, or telling a story that has never been told before. These questions will help determine the narrative shape. If you are using the accepted version of events, your perspective on it and your arrangement of the plot points will need to be original. It means you need to ask yourself why you are retelling an old story. If you are critiquing an old story, then the shape of your story will be persuasive; you will be unpicking old versions and suggesting a new way to look at material. If you are telling a previously untold story, it will be up to you to create the story from the material you uncover. Be prepared to change the story as you research and discover more material.

Consider where you will stand as narrator. If the material is not personal to your life then you can stand to one side as Anna Funder did in *Stasiland*, but still be involved as the investigator or detective. In *The Mind of a Thief*, because it explores the history of Indigenous and European settlers, the story is intimately connected to my life as the daughter of a long line of European settlers. It means that I am in the story as a protagonist as well as the narrator; it is as much memoir as it is history writing. Inga Clendinnen's *Tiger's Eye* is more memoir than history, and she places the individual in relation to history when she says 'how much there is of ourselves in the stories we tell about the past'. This is the key to good creative nonfiction history—where are you in your stories of the past?

Biography

Traditional biography is a well-established genre. It was originally considered part of history with a focus on a figure of historical importance, and began to emerge as a distinct genre in the eighteenth century with the publication of James Boswell's *The Life of Samuel Johnson*. The subject is normally a person who is or was well known in public life—a politician, sportsperson, actor, writer; it is research-based, using letters, diaries, newspaper reports, interviews; it includes only information that can be verified; and it claims a degree of objectivity. Here, though, in considering biography as part of creative nonfiction, I mean a contemporary development of biography that is more related to both memoir and to fiction.

In biography as creative nonfiction, the subject can be an individual personally known to the author, often a family member, who is not necessarily a public figure. It includes the use of the fictional technique of writing scenes in the subject's life, that is, imagined scenes which the writer deduces or supposes might have taken place but where the dialogue and actions cannot be verified. Biography as creative nonfiction can include the inner life of the subject, that is, thoughts and feelings that the narrator can only deduce or imagine; it is narrated from a subjective point of view; and it can include the personal experiences of the narrator, that is, include memoir as well as biography.

If you want to write creative nonfiction biography then your subject, as for traditional biography, needs to be complex and interesting enough to sustain a full-length exploration. Because your subject may not have a public profile, you will need to consider what it is about them that makes them of wider interest. In *One Life,* Kate Grenville wrote about her mother as an example of a twentieth-century woman seizing opportunities for herself at a time when women's lives were narrowly circumscribed. As she remarks in the prologue, 'My mother wasn't the sort of person biographies are usually written about . . . The point of her story was that it was part of a bigger one.' Ask yourself what it is about this person's life that either makes them emblematic or distinctive or inherently fascinating.

Even if the person is or was known to you, there may still be research you need to do. Letters, emails, photographs, personal documents and interviews can all help to give your personal account more substance. Biography has a commitment to the facts, and factual statements of dates and locations and public events, even in creative nonfiction, do need to be verifiable. You will need to decide whether to use extracts or to summarise or rewrite materials. In *One Life*, Grenville has used her mother's journals to imagine scenes from her life and re-create events using the same techniques as fiction.

You will need to decide how much you, as narrator, will be present—or not—in the biography. Are you simply telling their story from your subjective position, or are you also involved? This can be more complicated when your subject is both a family member and a public figure, because it can be difficult to claim the right to be in the story. It's not just that you as a family have seen a different character from the public's perception but that you can feel your life does not matter.

David Leser's *To Begin to Know: Walking in the Shadows of My Father* explores his relationship to his father, a legendary magazine publisher, and we see the evolution of his story from biography towards memoir. It becomes the narrator's story as much as his father's, the journey as much about self-knowledge and claiming the validity of his own life as about knowledge of his biographical subject. Gabrielle Carey's *Moving Among Strangers* also falls between biography and memoir as she unravels her family's connection to a public figure, Australian writer Randolph Stow. She explores the facts and issues of Stow's life as well as her family's life, connecting the themes of his writing, such as human mortality, to her own experiences. Janet Malcolm in *The Silent Woman: Sylvia Plath and Ted Hughes* writes from a journalist's perspective, not involved with her subject, but her insightful and incisive eye makes her presence as the observer and narrator strongly felt. If you are writing about a public figure, you will need to find a balance between your subject and your place as narrator and participant.

Some biographers, such as David Marr, author of *Patrick White: A Life*, believe the narrator ought to stay out of the text altogether, so as not pull focus from the subject. As he says in his essay, 'The Art of Biography': 'I'm on the side of the invisible biographer. I don't give a damn about their happy thoughts as they tread in the footsteps of their subjects . . . I'm not interested in their research triumphs. I want the life, not the homework.' But then he says, writing rules are made to be broken. Marr agrees with the English biographer Frances Spalding, who said: 'It [biography] is a hybrid and fluid genre, always spilling out of neat packages and persistently reshaping its enquiry as the questions that interest each generation change.'

When using re-created scenes, consider whether you will write from your biographical subject's point of view or not, that is, include your subject's inner thoughts and feelings. For many biographers, this may be a step too far into fiction, but it's worth looking at some creative nonfiction biographies which have done just that. In *Rosetta*, Alexandra Joel imagines scenes from her great-grandmother's life, using a few original letters, photographs and research into the period. She intersects the scenes with her own research and questions so that the reader knows what she has imagined and how. In *Boy, Lost*, Kristina Olsson uses directing phrases such as 'In my head, it happens like this', to let the reader inside her mother's mind and heart as she tells the story of the baby, the firstborn son, stolen from her mother's arms. Each of these biographies is partly fiction in that the writer cannot have known their subjects' inner lives, but creative nonfiction is large enough to allow such techniques. If you let the reader know, either in a prologue or dedication or directive phrases, how you have imagined your biographical subject's inner life, then most readers will go with you.

Read biographies, both traditional and creative nonfiction, and decide which approach suits you and your subject. Read biographies in the area that interests you—politics, arts, sports—to learn how to approach research and how to structure material. Read the creative nonfiction biographies mentioned above to see how memoir and fiction might shape your biographical writing.

While ethics is important in all life writing, it becomes more crucial when you are writing biography. In this situation it is someone else's life you are offering up for public scrutiny and comment, and however commanding your biographical subject is, you as the writer have the power of the written word, which carries an authority that can overrule everything else. The issue is heightened when your subject is no longer alive; without right of reply, your account may stand as the accepted truth of that person's life. Many writers believe that they have the right to use whatever material they require in whatever way serves their art, and to some extent I agree, but I also believe writers are not exempt from moral responsibility. It doesn't mean you should shy away from the truth—truth as you perceive it is always at the centre of all life writing—just that each person needs to examine his or her motivations and be aware of a responsibility to others.

Creative nonfiction is an exciting and expanding field of literature. Travel and sojourn memoir (Workshop nineteen) and the personal essay (Workshop twenty) are also part of the territory.

Reading

Joe Cinque's Consolation   Helen Garner

I understand now that I went to Canberra because the breakdown of my marriage had left me humiliated and angry. I wanted to look at women who were accused of murder. I wanted to gaze at them and hear their voices, to see the shape of their bodies and how they moved and gestured, to watch the expressions on their faces. I needed to find out if anything made them different from me: whether I could trust myself to keep the lid on the vengeful, punitive force that was in me, as it is in everyone—the wildness that one keeps in its cage, releasing it only in dreams and fantasy.

That day, though, as I went straight home, called the airline and packed a bag, I was still thinking of myself as the writer at a loose end who had stumbled on something interesting. I thought I would be able to slip quietly into court with my notebook for a shield. I could watch and listen for a while, satisfy my curiosity, and wander out again at will, unscathed and free of obligation. But I was about to learn a hard lesson. A story lies in wait for a writer. It flashes out silent signals.

Without knowing what she is doing, the writer receives the message, drops everything and turns to follow.

When I got to the ACT Supreme Court on 6 April 1999, Anu Singh's defence was already in progress. It took me a moment to get my bearings. The courtroom was so palely timbered and greenly curtained, so shallow and wide and muffled by carpet, that it could have been a suburban loungeroom.

Two women were stationed side by side on padded chrome chairs. One was a tall, blonde, scraggly-haired security guard. The other was Anu Singh. Her hair, dark and reddish-tinted and very long, was pulled back and firmly bound into a thick club that bulged on the nape of her neck. She was wearing street clothes: a long skirt and a dark-blue jacket laced criss-cross in the small of her back. Her bare feet were slipped into high wedge-heeled sandals. She sat very still, very erect, with her right leg crossed over her left. Beside her slouching escort she looked dainty, almost prim. A sliver of profile was all I could see of her face.

The witness on the stand could only be her father. Heavy-shouldered, with a close-clipped beard, Dr Singh leaned back in the chair with his hands folded over his belly. He was a man of substance, unfazed by the formality of his surroundings; but the version of his daughter's life that the barrister was drawing from him, as I slid into the back row of the gallery, was a sorry one.

Anu, he was saying, had been barely a year old when the family migrated from the Punjab and settled in Newcastle. She was a clever little girl, but very clingy. She slept in her parents' bedroom until she was four or five. Puberty hit early—by thirteen she was 'fully developed'.

As a teenager she became a real headache, slacking off on schoolwork, wearing revealing clothes, refusing to help her mother, always sneaking out to see boys. Then, from year eleven, the dieting started. Somehow she stayed near the top of her class, and in year ten she was dux. Her HSC score was high, but not first rank. In 1991 she went to Canberra to study economics and law at the Australian National University.

She coped poorly away from home, he thought—always on the phone to her mother—until in late 1993 she took up with a fellow student, Simon Walsh. Dr Singh was annoyed with her for becoming a vegetarian and overdoing the aerobics classes, but for a while she seemed to become more stable.

In 1995, the doctor went on, the Singh family left Newcastle and moved to a middle-class suburb of Sydney. That year Anu came home from uni at the September break in an odd state. She wouldn't go out or dress up, but sat about in casual clothes, crying for no apparent reason. Whenever her father saw her, she was coming out of the shower. She paced the floor all night.

In *Joe Cinque's Consolation*, a true crime story, Garner covers the trial of a young woman who is accused of murdering her boyfriend. She attends the trial each day and interviews both the accused and the victim's parents, becoming particularly close to the victim's mother and father. In this extract we see Garner with her characteristic honesty, positioning herself in relation to the trial. Read *Joe Cinque's Consolation* for its powerful story-telling, its brilliant use of first-hand research and its searingly honest narrating perspective.

Writing exercises

1 Finding a subject

Select an item that attracts your interest from a newspaper or magazine. Make a plan of how you would find out more: who you would interview? Where would you research? Then write a page about why the material has caught your interest, starting with an anecdote from your own life. (Two hours)

2 What is on your mind?

Over a week, keep notes about what you have been thinking about. What keeps coming to mind? Political issues? Children? Work? At the end of the week, select one to research in a wider context over the following week. If it holds your interest, continue. (As long as it takes)

3 Nature

Take an environmental issue that interests you, do some online research on the topic, then, beginning with a story from your own childhood, connect it to the issue you have researched. This of course can be used for any other area of interest, historical, political or psychological. (Two or three hours)

4 Ethics

Take an ethical issue that is related to your own life, for example, responsibility to ageing parents. Find and interview people involved in the area, then combine it with your own memories and your own thinking on the issue. If it feels like it has substance, continue. (As long as it takes)

21

WORKSHOP NINETEEN

Wish you were here—Travel memoir

*One thinks one is going to make a journey, yet soon it's the
journey that makes or unmakes you.*

NICOLAS BOUVIER

Dear Hope,

*The coconut palms are swaying in the tropical breeze and in front
of me the aqua sea looks like a dreamscape beneath the blue sky.
The resort is set amongst hibiscus and frangipani—and every
evening the friendly island people sing and dance for us. (In other
words, I have the best life because I am here and this card is
intended to make you envious. I am not going to mention the
infected coral-scrape on my knee, or the motor-mouth woman in
the next room who keeps bailing me up to go shopping with her,
or the fact that Max looks so fat and white in his bathers that I do
not want to sit with him at the pool.)*

Wish you were here,

Verity

The postcard used to be the most common, and possibly the most dishonest, form of travel writing. Now it is a social media post or blog instead of a postcard, but the glossy effect is the same. Perhaps that's being too hard on all the innocent travellers who simply want to stay in touch, but when I write travel posts I'm conscious of editing out all but the best experiences.

It is easy to make the same mistake when you come to more extended travel writing. So it is useful to remember that travel or sojourn writing is essentially a branch of memoir writing, with all the same requirements of truth, clarity and evocative writing. Travel writing explores sights, people and experiences, just as memoir does, the defining difference being that the location is 'elsewhere' and that it is characteristically more outward looking than memoir. It is a wide genre and can include analysis of history, culture and politics, as in Patrick Leigh Fermor's *A Time of Gifts*; it can emphasise characters and events, as in John Berendt's *Midnight in the Garden of Good and Evil*; it can be a literary meditation on a city, such as Edmund White's *The Flâneur*; or a crossover with philosophy, such as Alain de Botton's *The Art of Travel* or *A Philosophy of Walking* by Frédéric Gros.

It is one of the most popular forms of memoir and it has its own pleasures and pitfalls, which deserve to be explored more closely. It is also worth looking at where travel writing came from, so first, a very brief idiosyncratic history to give some idea of the depth and richness of travellers' tales.

Background

Travel writing appears to have existed in various forms in ancient Roman, Greek, Arabic and Asian cultures. The Arab writer and geographer Ibn Hawqal wrote about his tenth-century travels in *The Face of the Earth*, and Marco Polo wrote *The Travels of Marco Polo* in the thirteenth century after his long journeys in the Orient. The Italian poet Petrarch gave an account of his ascent of Mt Ventoux in 1336, one of the first pieces of literature expressing pleasure in travel for the sake of it. Richard Hakluyt's *Voyages to the New World* (1589), on the discovery of the Americas, is also considered an early example of travel writing.

But travel writing didn't really develop a mass market until the nineteenth century when, in Europe, there was a surge of interest in exotic lands. One of the most famous travellers was the English adventurer Richard Burton, who wrote numerous books about his journeys, including *Personal Narrative of a Pilgrimage to Al Medina and Mecca*. A more gentle adventurer was Robert Louis Stevenson who wrote *Travels with a Donkey in Cevennes*, the beginning of a long line of writing about the south of France. Robert Byron's *The Road to Oxiana* also belongs in this category of learned and literary travel writing. Women were well represented by French travellers Flora Tristan (*Peregrinations of a Pariah*) and Alexandra David-Néel (*My Journey to Lhasa*), and English traveller Marie C. Stopes (*A Journal from Japan*).

The twentieth and twenty-first centuries have seen an explosion of travel writing as travel has come within the means of most Westerners and many Asians. Some of the well-known names are Paul Theroux, Jan Morris, Bruce Chatwin, William Dalrymple, Eric Newby, Bill Bryson, Rebecca Solnit and Martha Gellhorn. Writers from countries colonised by Europe in the nineteenth century have also begun 'writing back', for example, Suketu Mehta's *Maximum City: Bombay Lost and Found*.

A current form of travel writing, the blog, is an online account of travels at the time of travelling. A blog is an extended form of the postcard in that it is a contemporary report on travel experiences, but usually more honest—and certainly with more room to expand than postcards. It is also often accompanied by images.

This is the merest sketch of the history of travel writing. If you are interested in reading more travel writers, look online—the Wikipedia list of travel books is a good general starting point. If you want to write about your travels, acquaint yourself with the best travel and sojourn writing.

Where to go

As with any journey, the direction or aim of travel writing is the first consideration—what is the territory you want to explore? There are a number of main strands to travel memoir:

- *Adventure memoir:* Recounting exciting and/or romantic tales, such as Eric Newby's *A Short Walk in the Hindu Kush* or Sarah Turnbull's *Almost French*. The narrative of what happens is often more important than the traveller himself. It is usually narrative driven—that is, the reader wants to find out what happens next. There is a personal perspective, but the voice can be impersonal. This requires an adventurous spirit to try different and possibly dangerous travel experiences as well as the skill to create a strong narrative.
- *Character-based writing:* Sketching or exploring individual people and, sometimes, animals, as in Karen Blixen's *Out of Africa*. The personal voice and perspective is central, but again, the self is not. The structure is often picaresque—that is, no overall narrative but a series of events connected by the narrator. An interesting cast of characters is the key element, well observed and enriched by interview and research.

- *Personal journey memoir:* Chronicling self-discovery as much as discovery of another culture or place, for example, Robyn Davidson's *Tracks*. There is a personal voice and perspective with the self at the centre of the narrative. It does not mean the writer is always writing about the self, but it does mean the journey is given purpose by the desire for self-knowledge. There can be exploration of ideas, particularly spiritual ideas, cultures, individuals, geographical and historical place, but the central theme is the inner quest. Also worth noting are many of David Sedaris's essays, which also qualify as travel memoir and explore the self in a humorous way.

- *Sojourn writing:* Traversing a period of time spent in one, often exotic, location, such as *Under the Tuscan Sun* by Frances Mayes. Again, there is mostly a personal voice, but the self can either be the centre of the narrative or the observer. It is similar to the 'character' memoir in that individuals can be important, but, often, a process, such as restoring a farmhouse or setting up a café, provides a central narrative. An inner psychological or spiritual process can also provide the heart of the narrative. It is based on observation rather than research and is subjective in its perspective.

- *Ideas writing:* Exploring history, culture, geography and politics in the context of travel, such as W.G. Sebald's *Rings of Saturn* or Lucinda Holdforth's *True Pleasures*. Although there can be a personal voice, the self is to one side. This type of travel memoir focuses on offering and exploring information. It demands research as well as acute personal observation. You can focus on any area that interests you, from gypsy culture in Europe to the history of Bolivia. If you have a particular area of interest and knowledge already then a journey can make an appealing vehicle to explore your passion.

- *Walking writing:* Walking memoir could fit into any and all of the above categories, but there has been such a blossoming of travel memoir specifically about walking that it is worth singling out. It can be a narrative-driven redemptive tale such as *Wild* by Cheryl Strayed, an intellectual discussion of walking itself as in Rebecca Solnit's *Wanderlust,* or nearer to nature-writing such as Robert Macfarlane's *The Old Ways,* as well as the many books about walking the Camino pilgrim route, usually structured around a journey of self-knowledge.

This is not to say that your travel memoir needs to fit neatly into one of the above categories. It could turn out to be a mix of all of the above. The categories are a way for you to start thinking about the travel memoir you want to write.

The suitcase

You need to think about the size and type of your 'suitcase', that is, how long the traveller's tale should be, and how it can be structured. Is it a travel article, a blog, a book? The form of your travel chronicles will be determined by how much material you have, and by your purpose.

Most travel writing published in newspapers and magazines aims to promote a destination or activity and is journalism rather than travel memoir. It conveys information on sights, services and accommodation. However, if it has a personal voice and includes personal stories, as some travel articles do, it could be considered short travel memoir. If you have engaging personal stories about a trip you have taken, a short travel memoir for a newspaper may suit. Check the length of travel articles in magazines and newspapers before you submit.

If you want to explore your travels as you go then writing a blog might suit. Travel blogs are written contemporaneously, and therefore have a freshness of style, and a looseness of structure. It is important to have an original eye on the world, an engaging voice and, of course, interesting experiences. A thematic approach can be useful—for example, shaping the blog around food, or literary travels, or following in the tracks of an earlier famous traveller. There are thousands of travel blogs, so finding a readership outside family and friends will be your main challenge.

The structure of a travel memoir is normally chronological, dictated by the journey itself unfolding in time. You can use the format of a diary, journal or letters to keep an orderly chronology, or you can use seasons, places or incidents as your chronological markers. Chronology is easy to use and is an effective first step in managing your material, but you need to be wary of repetition. Your readers do not need to know about every time you see a glorious view over the Alps, or every time you stop at a curious wayside inn. And you can arrive at a place without having taken the plane or boat or train to get there, unless, that is, the story happened on the plane or boat or train. In other words, to create the structure, be ruthless about your journey—tell us what we need to know rather than a record of everything you did.

You can successfully write a travel memoir that is not chronological but organised, for example, around ideas such as V.S. Naipaul's exploration of the Islamic diaspora, *Beyond Belief*, or based structurally around a theme, such as Ailsa Piper's *Sinning Across Spain*. Such memoirs are the frame for exploring concerns which are not necessarily to do with travel, or at least not to do with the physical act of travel. They are vehicles for inner journeys of ideas or emotions.

Poetic and metaphoric images can be used as a way of structuring your travel writing. In *Ransacking Paris*, I used the image of bees as a connecting thread, linking experiences and ideas in a symbolic way.

If you want to write a book-length travel memoir, first ask yourself: do you have enough material? Do your three weeks in Nigeria warrant a book? Be ruthless—your adventures may work well at five thousand words but become very thin at book length. The desire to record one's travels is no free pass to the reader's attention.

WHAT TO PACK

When you set off to write travel memoir, bring all the same awareness, clarity and economy that you bring to any memoir. Leave woolly perceptions, overworn phrases and shapeless generalisations in the wardrobe. Whether you are writing an article, a blog or a book, here are a few hints for a well-packed travel-writing suitcase.

Travel-writing 'suitcase' packing list

- *A sharp perceptive eye for what is original, fresh, illuminating.* Don't repeat descriptions of well-known sights. In this age of the image, everyone has seen a representation of everything already. Jean Baudrillard, a French philosopher, called it 'the precession of the simulacra', that is, we are familiar with the image of the Eiffel Tower long before we see the actual tower. There is therefore no point in saying it is remarkably tall and elegant—everyone knows that. With your sharp eyes wide open, see instead the elderly Italian woman in high heels tottering up the steel steps of the tower, trying to keep up with her grandchildren.

- *A sharp perceptive eye for what is ordinary amongst the extraordinary.* It is often people going about the ordinary business of life which most sheds light on an 'exotic' place. What is exotic for you is ordinary for the people who live there. Try to see the marvel—Angkor Wat, or Mt Rushmore—as part of your daily life and it will lose its gloss of 'difference' and you will be able to clearly see and evoke it without gushing clichés.

- *A selective judgement about what you include.* Don't write about every place you stayed, every meal you ate, every sight you visited, every peasant you met at the local market. You are not making a record or even a history of a journey or a place, you are re-creating the experience—or, better still, you are creating a new experience based on your travels. You are taking the reader on a journey, inviting them to stay with you on your sojourn, but more than that, you are exploring the territory that interests everyone: the relationship between a person and his or her world.

- *Your own unique perception of people, events, places.* Bring your own interests and knowledge to your travel writing. You are a distinctive person with your own personality, education and interests—look at the world through your own particular frame and reveal something new about it. Paris may always be Paris, but if you have a literary knowledge you will see a different Paris to someone who has an architectural or engineering or sociological knowledge. Each city, each place, is made anew by the people who experience it.

- *Your own unique voice.* The voice of the narrator is just as important in travel memoir as in any other memoir—perhaps even more so, because the reader is alone in a foreign place with only you for company. You, as narrator, are travelling companion and guide and we, the readers, want you to entertain, instruct, illuminate and keep us safe. You can make us laugh or cry, or amaze, startle or horrify us, but don't whinge, accuse or be dull.

- *A feeling for the meaning of your travels and sojourns.* It doesn't mean you need to know this from the beginning—why head off on a possibly perilous journey if you already know the answers?—but by the time you have redrafted, there needs to be some sense of either an unfolding narrative or underlying meanings emerging. There doesn't have to be a cataclysmic climax or world-shattering insights but a sense that this is more than just a record of what you did one year. You have opened up a new territory somewhere in yourself and your world, and also in your reader.

- *Knowledge of local history and culture.* This will prevent you from writing extraordinarily foolish things. George Sand is not a Frenchman but a Frenchwoman, the pointed hoods worn in a parade in the Spanish town you visited do not indicate the wearers are members of the Ku Klux Klan but religious penitents. And apart from preventing faux pas, the more you know about a place, the richer your travel writing will be. Do your research.

- *Sensitivity to religious and cultural difference.* Offence can be minimised if you are respectful. It is not that you must agree that everything about a culture is wonderful, but knowledge of why people carry out various practices and rituals can make your writing more interesting, less patronising, less judgemental.

- *An awareness of unintentional racism.* Everything about a people different from your own can become charming, sunny, innocent, but racial clichés, however benign, are always patronising. Perhaps all Balinese can dance, but it is a cultural, not a racial, characteristic. The same goes for generalised national characteristics—they are neither useful nor true. Not all Frenchwomen are chic, not all Americans are gregarious, not all English are reserved.

- *A sensual awareness of place.* Notice new smells, sounds, textures and tastes as well as sights. A new place is a new experience for the senses as well as for the mind, and even when your writing is focused on cultural, historical or political concerns, it will be more powerful if the senses are also engaged. Ground your observations in the senses—in the smell of cumin, the colour of emerald silk saris, the sight of cow dung on the heel of a businessman's shoe.

- *Original words and phrases.* Pack only the freshest expressions. They must not be tired, obvious and overused (no *gorgeous Alpine sunsets*) and not excessively elaborate (no *roseate blush on ebony skins of Mali maidens*)—unless you are satirising hyperbolic style, that is. Take every type of cliché out of the suitcase and put them back in the wardrobe. You will not need *beckoned at every turn*, nor *tropical paradise* or *fabled ruined city.* Better still, take them out and put them in the bin—you won't ever need them.

- *Take out generalised adjectives.* Leave behind amazing, awesome, brilliant, fabulous, magical, wonderful, extraordinary—and every other word not doing its fair share of the work.

- *Take out long static descriptions of locations or people.* That is, remove descriptions in which nothing happens. Even if you are writing about a still pond, observe the dancing movement of dragonflies, the croaking of frogs, the shivering of the morning wind on the surface of the water. Be wary of overlong, overindulgent descriptions of anything.

- *In a side 'suitcase' include journals, notes, letters, postcards, emails, social media posts, blogs.* Read them with critical eyes—they were probably most often written to reassure family and friends, and yourself, that you were indeed having a good time—and so are probably full of generalisations and hyperbole. They can, however, serve to locate places and people that might have blurred in memory. Most often it is not a good idea to use writing directly from these sources because even if it is precise and evocative, the narrating voice is probably different to the one you use now. Use the material, but rewrite it.

- *Pack novels and memoirs by other good writers on the same topics.* The point of this is not to make you feel it has all been done already but so that you can be inspired to go further. We all at times require a draught of some consciousness-enhancing words from an inspiring writer to help us take that extra step off the ground and into flight.

The travel or sojourn memoir is often thought of as more glamorous than everyday memoir. It includes exotic locations and all the attractions of life outside the ordinary: the kinds of places and experiences people dream about at their desks or kitchen sinks. But it still requires discipline and clarity and attention to detail. Essentially, what is interesting is your perception of, and relation to, the environment. Alain de Botton said in *The Art of Travel* that 'I had inadvertently brought myself with me to the island'. We all do that—and that is what makes travel memoir interesting. The island remains more or less the same; each perception of it is different.

Reading

The Way of the World
Nicolas Bouvier

In the seventeenth century, Isfahan, with six hundred thousand inhabitants, was the capital of an empire and one of the most crowded cities in the world. Today it has no more than two hundred thousand. It has become provincial, it has shrunk, and the vast, graceful Safavid monuments float above it like clothes that have become too big. It is also run down and crumbling away, because Shah Abbas was in a hurry to impress and didn't take the time to build soundly. It is precisely because of this very human vulnerability to time, which is their only imperfection, that these buildings seem so accessible and moving. 'To defy time': I am quite sure that, since the Achaemenians, no Iranian architect has succumbed to that inane ambition.

The Royal Mosque, for example: not a storm passes without its losing a heap of irreplaceable earthenware tiles—a few dozen out of more than a million—but the whole thing is so vast it would take a fifty-year storm before the loss was noticed. Nevertheless, they fall in the slightest wind; from a great distance they bounce down and then break into dust without you hearing more than a faint sound of falling leaves. They are a famous blue—I am back to blue. This time it is combined with a little turquoise, yellow and black which makes it vibrate and gives it that power of levitation which we usually associate with sanctity. The enormous cupola, covered in blue, lifts into the sky like a captive balloon. Beneath the dome and in front of the palaces forming the maidan, the Isfahanis go to and fro, out of scale, affable but not particularly trustworthy, with that air common to inhabitants of towns that are works of art: they seem to be the jury in a competition which the foreigner, no matter what he does, will never understand.

That said, Isfahan was exactly the marvel we'd been promised. It alone was worth the trip.

Last night we went for a walk by the river. Is it really a river? Even where the waters are highest they get lost in the sand, scarcely sixty miles out of town. It had almost dried up, forming a wide delta of sluggish, luminous rivulets. Old men in turbans crossed it on donkeys in a cloud of flies. For two hours we followed a hot and dusty path bordered by croaking frogs. In the gaps between willow and eucalyptus, we could already make out the whiteness of the desert and the mauve Zagros Mountains; their jagged outline reminded us of Provence, and there was exactly that warm, dangerous intimacy with nature that one finds sometimes on summer nights near Arles or Avignon. But it was Provence without wine, boastfulness or women's voices; in short with none of the obstacles or uproar that usually separates us from death. I had no sooner said this to myself than I began to sense it everywhere: death in the glances we exchanged, in a herd of buffalo, in the lighted rooms open to the river, in the tall spirals of mosquitoes. It came at me, full tilt. And what about this trip? A mess . . . a failure. You travelled, you were free, you were heading from India . . . what then? I could repeat 'Isfahan' to myself as much as I liked; Isfahan meant nothing. This impalpable town, this river which didn't flow anywhere—these were not the right things to provide an anchoring sense of reality. Everything spoke of dissolution, refusal and absence. At the bend of the riverbank, the uneasiness became so strong that I had to turn back. Thierry's heart was also in his boots; he shared my feelings although I hadn't said a word to him. We returned at a run.

It's odd how the world suddenly goes bad, turns rotten. Perhaps it was the lack of sleep? Or the effect of the vaccinations we'd renewed the previous night? Or the Djinns who, it is said, attack at night if you walk beside water without mentioning the name of Allah? No, I believe that there are landscapes that are out to get you, and that you must leave them immediately otherwise the consequences are incalculable. There are not many of them, but they certainly exist: five or six on this earth for each of us.

In this extract from *The Way of the World,* Nicolas Bouvier combines first-hand observations, researched knowledge and personal experience to give the reader a sense of Isfahan in Iran, where he lived for a short while on his journey across the Middle East in the 1950s. He includes small details, such as the willows and eucalypts, then moves to his interpretation of his surroundings, for example 'a warm dangerous intimacy with nature'. Read *The Way of the World* for its compelling and original evocation of a journey from Europe to Asia, its fine observations and its fresh awareness of a world that changed him.

Writing exercises

1 Memento

Take a memento from a journey—a souvenir—and use it as a springboard to write of a travel experience. Do not plan what you are going to write about, simply look at the memento for a couple of minutes then begin. (Fifteen minutes)

2 Backgrounds

Take a photograph from a particular place and look at something in the photograph other than the main subject. See what else is in the photo—the young mother on rollerskates in the corner of your picture of the Seine River, for example. Use the 'background' detail as a way in to writing about that day or that place. (Twenty minutes)

3 Research

Do some online or library research on the countries or cities you want to write about. The research can be historical, political, cultural or any other area that interests you. Try weaving the research into the story of your travels there, rewriting the information in your own words. (As long as it takes)

4 Senses

Write, in note form, five different sensory impressions of a place you have travelled to, one impression for each sense: sight, sound, taste, smell and touch. Beginning with one of the senses, evoke the place using all the senses. Remember that static writing is generally less interesting than writing where something is happening. (Twenty minutes)

5 Playing with structure

Write five distinct short pieces, half a page each, about a journey you have taken or a place you have stayed, each piece about a different aspect of the same journey or sojourn. Each one must be close-up, that is, showing an event or place or person, and self-contained, not consciously linked to or referring to the other pieces. When you have finished, read through them and arrange them in relation to each other. See which order best re-creates your experience. Do you need to write more pieces?

See whether you can build up a longer piece, say, five thousand words, using this method. (Twenty minutes each piece)

6 Truthful travel

Next time you are away from home, try writing a completely truthful social media post or blog or postcard. (Fifteen minutes)

22

WORKSHOP TWENTY

Random provocations—
The personal essay

*I live in the World rather as a Spectator of Mankind,
than as one of the species . . .*

JOSEPH ADDISON

At university I was one of those atypical students who actually liked writing essays. I enjoyed the teasing out of an idea, the propounding of a theory, the pulling together of various threads.

You will notice, however, that I have left out 'research'. I was not so keen on research. The texts had always been borrowed from the library already by more organised and diligent students than I, and when I did find something I invariably failed to record the footnoting details and had to spend hours refinding the references before the essay could be handed in. Now, when there is endless availability of research sources on the internet,

I love the detective thrill of the search, but I am often waylaid by fascinating sidelines and lose sight of the facts.

The truth is, I lack an unwavering respect for verifiable information. Fortunately for all concerned, I recognised this flaw in my character early on—indeed, before leaving high school. Although I achieved decent marks in the sciences, it was clear that that I did not have a sufficient respect for data to make a good scientist. In fact, I would have been one of those reprehensible scientists who invent data to support the wonderful theory she had concocted.

It's not that I don't like facts per se. Fascinating facts are a delight, but my overruling passion is the mad leap from the fact into the 'grand idea'. (Mine may not be so grand, more small meditations on odd fragments of middling ideas, but you know what I mean.) I like to circle around the idea, stretch it out, wriggle it about, snap it back, tease it out again and give it a good shake. That is why the endlessly elastic form of the personal essay is perfect—with only a fact or two in my possession, I can stretch and wriggle and circle to my heart's content.

The personal essay is related to the academic essay in that it explores ideas, but an academic essay requires that you have research and facts at your command. A personal essayist does not command anything; she wanders with great attention across the topic, regarding everything with wonder. The personal essayist has something to say but is not quite sure what. She is like a messenger who doesn't know what the message is, whom it is from, or where it is going. But she feels if she wanders around with it long enough, stares at it often enough, she will decipher what it is saying and where it needs to be delivered.

The personal essayist also ignores the academic essayist's rule on objectivity. In academic essays you are required to be objective and impersonal, that is, to leave yourself out of the situation. A personal essayist is the opposite: she looks at everything from her own subjective point of view and will even tell stories about herself.

You may say that the personal essay is an excuse for every kind of intellectual laziness and self-indulgence and maybe it is, but it is very charming at the same time. And it has the added advantage, in my eyes, of being closely related to memoir. If the personal essay is the academic essay's disreputable cousin, then it is also memoir's intellectually playful sibling and the child of uncomfortable truth, an expression of the urge to note as honestly as possible the gap between the dream we have of ourselves and what we actually are.

Genealogy

It sounds oxymoronic to say so but it is both dull and dangerous to name 'important people' in any field. Dull because a list of names—without room for explanation or narrative—must necessarily be unexciting, and dangerous because of the ire of those who know how many names have been left off the list. Still, I must take the risk because a list also gives the necessary thread of 'somewhere to start' for the would-be essayist, an introduction to the complex extended family of the personal essay.

Essai was the name given by the sixteenth-century French writer Michel de Montaigne to his own style of writing—short explorations of himself in relation to his world. He took the word from the French *essayer*, meaning 'to try' or 'to attempt'. He was attempting to know himself and thereby know humankind, believing that 'Every man has within himself the entire human condition'.

Although he was the first writer to devote himself to it in post-Renaissance Europe, Montaigne did not invent the personal essay. At the beginning of the first millennium, early Romans Seneca and Plutarch were writing essays; in the tenth century in Japan, Sei Shōnagon wrote her famous *The Pillow Book*. Around the same time in China, Ou-Yang Hsiu 'let his brush write what it would'. In the early fourteenth century, Kenkō, also Japanese, wrote *Tsurezuregusa*, the original title of which comes from the expression 'with nothing better to do'.

The English personal essay had a famous flowering in the eighteenth and nineteenth centuries with such names as Addison, Steele, Johnson, Lamb, Swift, Hazlitt and Robert Louis Stevenson. The tradition was kept up in the early twentieth century by English and American writers G.K. Chesterton, Max Beerbohm, Virginia Woolf, George Orwell, Walter Benjamin, Henry Thoreau, E.B. White and James Thurber. Since then, the form has been kept alive by, amongst others, Joan Didion, Annie Dillard, Susan Sontag, Phillip Lopate, Robert Dessaix, Helen Garner, David Sedaris and Janet Malcolm (although Malcolm is perhaps more of a journalist than an essayist). To read extracts from some of these writers' works and much more, try Phillip Lopate's indispensable collection *The Art of the Personal Essay*.

Your material

The personal essay is the literary form for the writer with an attic mind—everything is stored there, trash and treasure, and in no particular order. Your topic can be anything you find in that attic, often the smaller and less regarded the better. Walter Benjamin wrote about the different ways one acquires books, a delight to anyone who is a compulsive acquirer of books, but not of world-shaking importance. I once wrote an essay on how to select a book to take with one when travelling in foreign lands, again a topic of no great import. But in writing about the small, the daily, the ignored, the essayist is making a democratic claim for the wonder and complexity of all of life.

Wander into the attic or labyrinth of your mind and notice what is there. Not your large concerns about violence and peace, poverty and injustice, but the smaller, daily observations: the eternal battle between the tidy and the messy; the embarrassment people feel when they trip in public; the pleasures of obscure knowledge; the irritation of eternal cheeriness; the way people purse their mouths when they look in mirrors. In the hands of a personal essayist, these humble topics become an exploration of aspects of the human condition. G.K. Chesterton wrote about the foolishness a man feels when he is chasing his hat and it becomes a light but sharp meditation on the general absurdity of much of life.

The personal essay is very ecologically sound because it is a way of using everything you know, of recycling every little scrap, of not letting anything go to waste. That difficult book by a French writer you once read, that item you noted in the newspaper, your knowledge of odd history facts, that childhood memory, the remark your son once made—they all connect to your subject.

You can use knowledge gleaned from your formal education as well. If you know about the making of copper, or the theories of Jung, or the history of European painting, or philosophy, then let your knowledge find its place. This is not to show how erudite you are but is part of the eclectic nature of the essay: the essayist is never too proud to think that other people have not said it better than him. Even our hero, Montaigne, wrote,

'For I make others say what I cannot say so well, now through the weakness of my language, now through the weakness of my understanding.' The trick is in creating the atmosphere of easy access to learning which will allow you to use such quotes or extracts without appearing pretentious.

Thus, in finding a topic, what matters is that it has lain in the attic for a while. It must have gathered to itself various connections and associations. Perhaps it seems like a new thought—you have suddenly noticed the etiquette of pointing out scraps of food on someone's face when out at restaurants, for example—but once you notice the new thought, you become aware that it has numerous associations. This for me is the test of a good topic: if once you start tugging it a whole jumble of things come falling out after it, landing on your head and falling down to the floor, then it is a good topic.

The narrator

Once you are standing there stunned, or perhaps knocked down to the floor in a foolish position by the material you have uncovered, you can hardly look or sound earnest or dignified about the matter. Carrying off this situation requires attitude. Personal essay is all about attitude.

To find his attitude, the essayist cultivates aspects of himself—often a flaw, a waywardness, a clumsiness—and makes it an identifying part of his writing persona, a heightened version of his own personality and character. The American essayist David Sedaris cultivates a narrating persona who is generally anxious and hopeless at managing the practical and emotional details of life, giving him endless opportunities to elaborate a persona who is always getting it wrong. On the other hand,

Joan Didion (*Slouching Towards Bethlehem*) and Janet Malcolm (*Forty-One False Starts*), both contemporary American essayists, are serious and thoughtful narrators, each with a piercing gaze on their worlds. Didion places her own experience in relation to her observations, but without foregrounding her own life and without sentimentality. The reader mostly sees Malcolm through her perspective on her topics. Both have a sense of authority and a sharp humour in their narrating voices.

The voice of the personal essayist is often conversational, playful, confiding, amused. It can be serious but not plodding, nor complacent. If you are, by nature, self-satisfied and very sure about everything then you possibly will not be a good essayist. As Montaigne suggested, an essayist is trying something, he is not sure of anything—the sixteenth-century Frenchman even went so far as to say only fools are certain. You can reveal your ignorance, your folly, your faults, not with a self-pitying desire for forgiveness but with a humorous shrug—this is the way we all are. This questioning, intimate voice can be gently humorous, acerbic, world-weary, mock-bossy, or as tender as Virginia Woolf writing about a moth fluttering to death against a window, but not earnest or pontificating. Nor is self-righteousness permitted, except to the ironic essayist who can do whatever he chooses.

The personal essayist can be as intimate and as subjective as she likes. An open frankness about topics not normally mentioned can be very winning as the reader recognises her own thoughts, the curious pleasure of the stripping away of illusion, of seeing oneself in someone else's mirror. You can even be frank to the point of shock—so long as it doesn't destroy the reader's trust in you. Be as cheeky, humorous and ironic as you like. You can also be as contrary as you like—a personal essayist thrives on contrariness. Phillip Lopate wrote an essay called 'Against Joie de Vivre' and managed to charmingly win the reader over to what looks, at first, like a curmudgeonly world view.

Conversational language is part of the charm. The essayists will say 'that's all very well' and 'of course, you know'—and the reader feels part of the conversation. This is the pleasure and the danger of the essay. It is pleasant for the reader to feel confided in, often flattering to feel herself the recipient of considered thoughts, but there is the danger of the egotistical 'I'.

The secret is to realise, in whatever you say as an essayist, that you are speaking not just for yourself. An essayist uses 'I', but in a sense she is really saying 'we'. In fact, the 'I' is also sometimes modulated to 'we' or 'you', or, for the more polite and correct essayists, 'one'. This is a way of including the reader more closely, of acknowledging the reader as part of the conversation. A mixture of pronouns can work, but be careful not to be too random about who is speaking and who is listening.

At the same time, you have the chance to hold the floor, to be as witty and quick as you like and have no one interrupt you. It's not a matter of 'trying hard' to be clever—it's all about sitting back in the armchair or on the canvas chair on the balcony and relaxing with your idea. The narrator of a personal essay is the perfect host, letting everything happen without seeming to do anything. He appears to be an idler, a wanderer, an onlooker; no one realises he has instigated the whole affair. He doesn't rush about rearranging the furniture or organising anybody or making big speeches. He wanders quietly looking at things in the living room or out in the street or office or forest, and then idly begins to turn these things over in his mind.

The essayist agrees with R.L. Stevenson, who said, 'Extreme busyness ... is a symptom of deficient vitality ... They [who cannot be idle] have no curiosity; they cannot give themselves to random provocations.'

Underneath the idleness, however, there is always the struggle for truthfulness. Paradoxically, the narrating persona removes the mask, as Montaigne said the essayist must. Personal essayists are against falseness, flattery, prudery, priggishness—any kind of dishonesty about the self. The American essayist E.B. White wrote, 'There is one thing the essayist cannot do, though—he cannot indulge himself in deceit or in concealment, for he will be found out in no time.' The essayist makes himself vulnerable and his best protection is truthfulness.

Holding it together

If the narrating voice of the idler—sorry, essayist—is that of an intriguing, challenging, amusing onlooker, it also provides the thread that holds the whole essay together. The essay is bound by the charm of the narrator, the 'I'. The voice of the 'I', combined with topic and characteristic approach, creates the essayist's 'persona', the strongest single element of an essay's structure.

Throughout the various 'random provocations', the strong persona holds the reader's attention, maintains a consistent perspective, wins the reader back if the challenges have been a little difficult. The persona needs to be flexible enough to move from gossip to wisdom and back again without jarring. The persona can address the reader, ask questions, challenge—in fact, be an engaging and interesting friend.

While an engaging persona is a necessity, it is not necessarily all. It is not a guarantee that you won't end up with a ramble only marginally more interesting than Uncle Stan's mishmash of tales that went all afternoon last weekend. An essayist may use the same techniques as Uncle Stan—circling, digressing, meandering—but uses them consciously, always reaching towards some overall purpose. While an essayist might seem at times to be wandering off the point, she is actually elaborating, refining, teasing out.

The art of elaboration is a delicate one. It is not to be mistaken for mere embroidery, although I must say I have nothing against a little well-done embroidery—it can be very pretty. Elaboration does not add pretty details but unfolds, untangles and dismantles what is already there. The personal essayist likes to pull out the tangle bit by bit, following various threads, finding origins and possible implications. This can involve examples, lists, quotes, historical reference, anecdote, personal history. It can be done step by step but the essayist generally digresses and circles, moving from childhood memory to yesterday's reading, to a quote from Freud, bit by bit unfolding the whole curious piece of cloth.

While I am being metaphorical, it might also help to think of the structuring of an essay as a kaleidoscope. A kaleidoscope breaks up the usual scene into many tiny pieces but, because of its inner geometry, puts the bits together in a new and rhythmic way. The essayist puts the bits of her world together in a new way so that the familiar is refreshed.

Or, again, think of the essay as a long wander across town—or across the country—with no particular timetable. There's no urgency, just your senses and mind wide awake. Collect what you see as you wander and hold it together with the shape and idea of the journey itself.

The essayist also tells tales, and I do mean *tells*. Here is where you can ignore the maxim 'Show, don't tell', for the essayist tells everything they know, have seen, have heard other people say. As an essayist, you are a scavenger of anecdote, family tales, memories, all told in your own way to serve the purposes of your essay.

Play, free-associate—these are your formal practices when you write a personal essay. I nearly said 'sit down to write', but I invariably find that I begin personal essays when out walking. There is something about the easy movement of walking and the changing scenery that creates a model of the personal essay. It is not a static form, nor even a pre-existing form; it is found in movement, in play. Start writing because an idea or observation interests you then follow any connections or associations as they arise.

The essayist, in terms of the structure she finds, the idea she pursues, needs to be a trusting creature. It is not a definite form, like a sonnet, nor even as recognisable as a short story, so you need to believe that you can head off into uncharted territory with no precise destination and still get there. I usually start by jotting down some of the main landmarks, with no real idea of where I will end up, but somehow, I always do know when I've got to wherever it was I was going. There is always an 'epiphany'—as James Joyce called it, the 'aha' moment—this is where I meant to get to all the time.

How long one can permit oneself to wander is a question that needs to be faced. Personally, I find it easy enough to decide— I stop when I am done, when I have got to my destination. It is much easier than deciding when a short story or a memoir or a novel is done. There is an inevitability about the end of an essay which is easier to recognise. In some sense, before starting I have an idea whether this will be a short wander, perhaps 1000 to 1500 words, or a long wander, 5000 to 10,000 words. Of course, there are book-length wanders as well, but these are generally made up of a number of shorter journeys.

While there may be a number of small revelations throughout the essay, its full meaning is not usually revealed until the conclusion—probably because the essayist herself did not know the answer until she got there. This is the delight of the essay; you really are trying something out, you do not know where you are going to get to. If you already know there is nothing to try, no *essai*. You are working not with a pre-existing shape, not with a whole monolithic form, but with a form that can endlessly break into smaller pieces and re-form, like pieces of mercury fallen on a table. And Mercury, after all, was the messenger of the gods.

Reading

'The Love List' from *(and so forth)*   Robert Dessaix

There can be few readers who at some point in their lives have not had the following fantasy: miraculously you are granted twelve months, preferably on Patmos or some outer island in the Tonga group, to catch up on your reading—you have no other obligation to either yourself or the rest of the world. With quickened thoughtfulness, and a good dictionary on the deck-chair beside you, you immerse yourself at long last in ... (and here the fantasies become intensely private): Virgil's *Aeneid*, perhaps, or Gibbon (a common choice, as is the Bible), *War and Peace*, *Ulysses*, *A Hundred Years of Solitude*, *Crime and Punishment* ... or you might just want to establish once and for all why everyone keeps mentioning Wittgenstein all of a sudden, yet no one appears to have read him.

At the end of the year you return to your job and your loved ones *earthed* at last. Indeed, you are now civilised in the very best sense. You know about *The Iliad*, relativity, Cortés and

315

Napoleon; you know what Coalport is, and the names of Picasso's mistresses; you can conjure up a Holbein or two next time his name comes up; you've got three Drabbles under your belt for lighter moments in any conversation; you know Hungarian isn't an Indo-European language; what it was Pericles actually said in his famous oration ... Now at last you get *on* with things instead of just muddling through ... Everything now fits in—Persephone, Pushkin, Michelangelo, the Modern Moment, DNA, Derrida, the T'ang Dynasty, surplus value, Monet and Manet ... except that it doesn't. And never will. And it doesn't matter a scrap.

One of the reasons biographies are so popular at the moment, I suspect, is that they function so brilliantly as quickie self-improvement courses. Spend a weekend with *Darwin*, for example, and by Sunday evening you've brushed up on the history of religion and science, nineteenth-century English social history, and, almost in passing, the details of one of the most momentous shifts in human thought since the world began. An hour or two of *Baudelaire* every night before you drift off and in a week or ten days you've plumbed poetry, Symbolism, Decadence and French history, and you've sprouted probing tentacles in the direction of Verlaine, Rimbaud and Mallarmé whose names do keep cropping up in sensitive circles as if they should mean something to us. Biographies give us a wonderful sense of control; they clean up the mess, and so authoritatively, too.

Now, while the fantasy of a year off to catch up on our basic reading is, for most of us, never likely to come true, the fact that so many of us entertain it should prompt us to ask why it tempts us in the first place. Is a tamer version of the fantasy in fact not out of the question and a good idea? Should we be arming ourselves with one of the several available Good Reading Guides and following its branching geometry through to knowledge and pleasure? Should we have a Plan? Should we be jotting titles and authors down in a notebook somewhere? Can, in fact, our thirst ever be slaked? Can our wobbly grasp on what has come before ever be tightened? Instead of devouring the latest Kerry Greenwood or Margaret Atwood the next time it rains all Sunday afternoon, perhaps we'd be doing ourselves a service if we brushed up on the Gospel according to St Matthew (although John is more in vogue at the moment, because he starts with the Word), got Jung straightened out or at least dipped into *Madame Bovary*—so seminal after all.

Take this afternoon as an example and take Nietzsche. It's almost impossible to get through a day without someone mentioning Nietzsche. (Or Kant, for that matter, but that's going too far altogether.) The Second World War, racism, multiculturalism, Superman comics, George Bernard Shaw, Zarathustra, Zoroaster—it doesn't seem to matter what the topic of conversation is, Nietzsche is dragged into it. Now I have never read Nietzsche, although I have him upstairs. If I had the will, I could go upstairs and get him and spend the next few hours actually reading him. What I'd much rather do—in fact what I'm aching to do and soon will do—is plunge back into Alan Hollinghurst's tantalisingly erotic, non-post-modern, deliciously readable novel *The Folding Star*. Reading it is like working your way through a beautifully wrapped box of fine Belgian chocolates. In terms of a plan for self-improvement it's virtually useless; in terms of delectable literary company for the afternoon, it's just the ticket.

The beginning of 'The Love List' in Robert Dessaix's collection of personal essays gives a taste of his engaging witty voice and his wide yet lightly held knowledge of literature. His personal experience, opinions and attitudes are used to support his argument that we should follow our loves rather than our duty when we read. Read (*and so forth*), for its wide-ranging topics, its warm and charming voice, and its easy command of the personal essay form.

Writing exercises

1 A week's worth of thoughts

Write a list of the things you would think about in a week. Your list needs to be democratic and non-judgemental—that is, include things you may consider shallow as well as your intellectual or aesthetic thoughts. Include anything from choosing which shoes to wear to the article you read on post-modern architecture. Pull one out from the list and see if starts pulling other associations out with it. Jot down whatever you think of in relation to it. Write a paragraph for each association. (One hour)

2 Another week's worth

Write a list of the things you might think about in a week. As above, your list needs to include anything and everything—do not screen for suitability. This time, write about as many of the topics as you can, using as your central idea 'the things I think about in a week.' *Essayez*—try it out, see where it goes. Perhaps it will yield a new insight into life, perhaps not. (Thirty minutes)

3 Pillow book

Write a list of 'hateful things', as Sei Shōnagon did in *The Pillow Book*—things that annoy you in any particular situation. It could be a list of things that irritate you at parties, or in lifts, or the hairdressers. Write a paragraph on each and see if they join up to become an essay on the minor difficulties of being human. (Thirty minutes)

4 Mirror

Look at yourself in a metaphorical mirror. Notice something characteristic in the way that you think or go about things. It could be anything from the way you love idiosyncratic or useless information to the way you always tidy the apartment when your mother is coming to visit although you are a grown woman yourself. See if you can use this observation as a way of exploring an aspect of yourself and others. Jot down associations such as other people you have observed with the same trait, scientific research on the trait, literary connections, news items—anything in the attic of your mind. Try out the various associations and see where it leads you. (One hour)

23

Where to now?—Publishing

If my design had been to seek the favour of the world I would
have decked myself out better and presented myself in
a studied gait.

MICHEL DE MONTAIGNE

There is nothing quite like the mixture of emotions you experience when you have finished a manuscript. There is a sense of pride in your achievement, joy and wonder at what you have done, and an unexpected feeling of loss because it is over. When you have been writing from your own life, the feelings are even more complex. It's as if the retelling of your life has become as real and important as what is happening to you now.

Once the manuscript is complete, what then? It's rather like a birth—the difficult work of labour is over, but now there are lots of details to attend to for the future. If it is your first draft then you will almost certainly need to redraft and edit—there are some suggestions on the editing process in Workshop eight. You might also want to get input from an experienced manuscript editor who can give you unbiased advice before you rewrite.

Most writers will want to see their manuscript published in some form. This might mean commercial publication with an established publishing house, or self-publication, either printed or as an ebook.

Commercial publication

Nearly all books in bookshops are commercially published. An established publisher has paid the author for the right to turn the manuscript into a book. Usually the author is paid an *advance* before the book comes out, and once the advance has been earned through sales the publisher pays the author *royalties*, which are a percentage of sales, normally no more than fifteen per cent of the retail price of the book. The publisher pays for the editing, proofreading, internal and cover design, printing, distribution to bookshops and marketing, and organises publicity. Obviously, the publisher will only publish your manuscript if she believes it will sell enough copies to cover the cost and earn a profit.

If you feel your life story or nonfiction topic has something to offer the wider community, consider sending the manuscript to a commercial publisher. First look at your manuscript from an outsider's point of view. Is there enough to interest someone who doesn't know you? The publisher is looking for a manuscript which is well written and is also exciting, insightful, moving, funny or original in some way. A story dealing with an area of wider interest such as Aboriginality, migration, adoption, a social or health issue, an unusual occupation or journey, or a sensational story may also catch the publisher's interest.

To find out which publisher to send your work to, go to a bookshop and note which publishers take on the kind of book you have written, research websites of publishing houses online, and acquire a publishing guide—see the useful contacts in the back of this book. See whether the publishing house you are interested in takes unsolicited manuscripts; those who don't will often have one day of the week when you can send in unsolicited pitches. Check online for these opportunities.

You can also try finding a literary agent first. If the agent likes your work and thinks she can sell it, she will present your manuscript to the publisher for you. The advantage of having an agent is that they know who would be the best publisher for your particular manuscript, it will be looked at more promptly and the agent may be able to negotiate you a better deal. The agent will take a percentage of your advance and royalties for the work she has done. Ring or email agents first before sending your manuscript.

A word of warning: of the thousands of manuscripts arriving on publishers' desks each year, only a small number can be published. Don't be too disappointed if you cannot find a publisher. It may be no reflection on your story's value: perhaps the publisher has recently published another similar story or feels it would not sell enough copies to justify the cost.

Presentation of your manuscript to agents and publishers

Check the website of each publisher and their requirements, including what genres they publish, but here are some general guidelines:

- Write a brief—no more than one-page—outline of the story and themes. Don't tell the agent or publisher your book is wonderful—they will work that out for themselves.

- Type the manuscript, double-spaced. Publishers will let you know whether they want an electronic copy or a printed one.
- Make sure the pages are numbered and identified.
- Double check that the manuscript, outline and covering letter are free of spelling errors.
- If you send a printed copy, it should not be bound but held together in a folder or with a bulldog clip. Always keep a back-up or printed copy.
- Email or post the outline and first two or three chapters. Covering letters must be brief. If the publishers or agents are interested, they will ask for more.
- Agents and publishers will let you know how long it will take. Be patient.

Self-publication

If you have not been able to find a commercial publisher, or if you would prefer to direct the whole publication process yourself, then you could opt to self-publish. Self-publication means the author pays for the editing, proofing, book and cover design, printing and distribution, and organises publicity and marketing themselves. This work can be done by an individual with a desktop publishing program, or by a publishing house that specialises in self-publication.

These publishers offer a range of services, generally editing, book design, printing and binding for a fee per book. Some offer publicity on their website as well. You can decide how many copies you want to be printed, although there's sure to be a minimum print-run requirement. The fee is less if you can do part of the production yourself, such as book design. Whether you are doing the design yourself or not, don't forget photographs, drawings and newspaper extracts, which can all add character and interest to your finished book.

There are also many online publishers who will publish your manuscript as an ebook and will also sell your book online. It is much less expensive to create an ebook as there are no printing costs. A few writers have been successful with ebook publications, but the reality is that it is very difficult to stand out amongst the hundreds of thousands of other books on the same site. Again, see the useful contacts list if you want to find out more about self-publication.

Three things to remember

The only real way to learn to write is to write. From my experience of reading and writing, there are three things to keep in mind—all the rest can be used or put aside as necessary:

- Write with attentive awareness: whether you are writing from life or imagination, faithful observation will give truth and beauty of style.
- Write because it matters to you: this will give truth and beauty of voice.
- Write with a sense that you are making something: this will give beauty and truth of form.

Near the beginning of this book there was a question: *What is it like for anyone to be in the world?* It seems to me that this is the essence of what we do as writers. Whether we are writing our own life or a researched subject, fiction or nonfiction, we are trying to explore and communicate what it is like to be here in the world. It is individual and it is what we share with everyone else. What *is* it like for you to be in the world?

Reading list

This is by no means a comprehensive or even a bare essentials reading list; it consists of books and other sources mentioned in *Writing True Stories*.

Memoirs, personal essays and creative nonfiction

Armitage, Simon, *Walking Home*, Faber & Faber, London, 2012

Baker, Russell, *Growing Up*, Congdon Weed, New York, 1982

Bauby, Jean-Dominique, *The Diving Bell and the Butterfly*, Fourth Estate, London, 1997

Baxter, John, *The Most Beautiful Walk in the World*, Harper Perennial, New York, 2011

Berendt, John, *Midnight in the Garden of Good and Evil*, Random House, New York, 1994

Blixen, Karen, *Out of Africa*, Penguin, London, 1954

Bouvier, Nicolas, *The Way of the World*, Eland Publishing, London, 2007

Burroughs, Augusten, *Running with Scissors*, Hodder Headline, Sydney, 2003

Burton, Richard, *Personal Narrative of a Pilgrimage to Al Medina and Mecca*, MacMillan, London, 1972

Byron, Robert, *The Road to Oxiana*, Penguin, London, 1992

Capote, Truman, *In Cold Blood*, Vintage, New York, 1994

Carey, Gabrielle, *Moving Among Strangers*, UQP, Brisbane, 2013

Clendinnen, Inga, *Tiger's Eye*, Text Publishing, Melbourne, 2003

Dalrymple, William, *The White Mughals*, Viking Penguin, London, 2004

David-Néel, Alexandra, *My Journey to Lhasa*, Harper Perennial, New York, 2005

READING LIST

Davidson, Robyn, *Tracks*, Granada, London, 1982

De Botton, Alain, *The Art of Travel*, Hamish Hamilton, London, 2002

Dessaix, Robert, *A Mother's Disgrace*, Angus & Robertson, Sydney, 1994

—— (*and so forth*), Pan Macmillan, Sydney, 1998

—— *What Days Are For*, Knopf Australia, Sydney 2014

Didion, Joan, *Slouching Towards Bethlehem*, Farrar, Straus & Giroux, New York, 1968

—— *The Year of Magical Thinking*, Fourth Estate, London, 2005

Dillard, Annie, *Pilgrim at Tinker Creek*, Harper & Row, New York, 1974

Douglass, Frederick, *My Bondage and My Freedom*, Penguin Classics, London, 2003

Duff, Alan, *Out of the Mist and Steam*, Tandem Press, Auckland, 1999

Durrell, Gerald, *My Family and Other Animals*, Penguin, London, 2004

Erdich, Louise, *The Blue Jay's Dance*, Harper Perennial, New York, 1995

Fermor, Patrick Leigh, *A Time of Gifts*, John Murray, London, 2004

Funder, Anna, *Stasiland*, Granta, London, 2011

Garner, Helen, *Joe Cinque's Consolation*, Picador, Sydney, 2004

—— *This House of Grief*, Text Publishing, Melbourne, 2014

—— *Everywhere I Look*, Text Publishing, Melbourne, 2016

Ginibi, Ruby Langford, *Don't Take Your Love to Town*, Penguin, Melbourne, 1988

Grant, Stan, *Talking to My Country*, Harper Collins, Sydney, 2016

Grenville, Kate, *One Life*, Text Publishing, Melbourne, 2015

Gros, Frédéric, *A Philosophy of Walking*, Verso, London, 2014

Hakluyt, Richard, *Voyages to the New World*, MacMillan, London, 1972

Heiss, Anita, *Am I Black Enough for You?*, Random House, Sydney, 2012

Heyerdhal, Thor, *Kon-Tiki*, Simon & Schuster, New York, 2013

Holdforth, Lucinda, *True Pleasures*, Vintage, Sydney, 2004

Hungerford, T.A.G., *Stories from Suburban Road*, Fremantle Arts Centre Press, Perth, 1991

Hunt, David, *Girt*, Black Books, Melbourne, 2013

James, Clive, *Unreliable Memoirs*, Pan Macmillan, London, 1984

Joel, Alexandra, *Rosetta*, Vintage, Sydney, 2016

Jung, Carl, *Memories, Dreams, Reflections*, Random House, London, 1979

Kneen, Krissy, *Affection*, Text Publishing, Melbourne, 2009

Koval, Ramona, *By the Book*, Text Publishing, Melbourne, 2012

Leane, Jeanine, *Purple Threads*, UQP, Brisbane, 2011

READING LIST

Leigh, Geena, *Call Me Sasha*, Allen & Unwin, Sydney, 2013

Leser, David, *To Begin to Know*, Allen & Unwin, Sydney, 2014

Lloyd, Virginia, *The Young Widow's Book of Home Improvement*, UQP, Brisbane, 2008

Lopate, Phillip (ed.), *The Art of the Personal Essay*, Doubleday, New York, 1995

Louis, Yvonne, *A Brush with Mondrian*, Murdoch Books, Sydney, 2010

McCourt, Frank, *Angela's Ashes*, Harper Collins, London, 1996

Macdonald, Helen, *H is for Hawk*, Jonathan Cape, London, 2014

Macfarlane, Robert, *The Old Ways*, Hamish Hamilton, London, 2012

Macris, Anthony, *When Horse Became Saw*, Viking, Sydney, 2011

Mahood, Kim, *Position Doubtful*, Scribe, Melbourne, 2016

Malcolm Janet, *Iphigenia in Forest Hills*, Yale University Press, New Haven, 2011

—— *The Silent Woman*, Knopf, New York, 1994

—— *Forty-One False Starts*, Farrar, Straus & Giroux, New York, 2014

Marr, David, *Patrick White: A Life*, Random House, Sydney, 1991

Mayes, Frances, *Under The Tuscan Sun*, Chronicle Books, New York, 1996

Mehta, Suketu, *Maximum City: Bombay Lost and Found*, Vintage, London, 2005

Millet, Catherine, *The Sexual Life of Catherine M*, Serpent's Tail, London, 2002

Miller, Patti, *The Last One Who Remembers*, Allen & Unwin, Sydney, 1997

—— *Whatever The Gods Do*, Vintage, Sydney, 2003

—— *The Mind of a Thief*, UQP, Brisbane, 2013

—— *Ransacking Paris*, UQP, Brisbane, 2015

Modjeska, Drusilla, *Poppy*, McPhee Gribble, Melbourne, 1990

Montaigne, Michel de, *The Essays*, M.A. Screech (ed.), Penguin Classics, London, 2004

Morgan, Sally, *My Place*, Fremantle Arts Centre Press, Perth, 1987

Nabokov, Vladimir, *Speak Memory*, Knopf Doubleday, New York, 2011

Naipaul, V.S., *Beyond Belief*, Picador, London, 2010

Newby, Eric, *A Short Walk in the Hindu Kush*, HarperCollins, London, 2010

Newling, Jayne, *Missing Christopher*, Allen & Unwin, Sydney, 2014

Olsson, Kristina, *Boy, Lost*, UQP, Brisbane, 2013

Pearson, Bob, *A Penny on Fridays*, Lexington Avenue Press, Copacabana, 2003

Pieper, Liam, *The Feel-Good Hit of the Year*, Hamish Hamilton, Melbourne, 2014

Piper, Ailsa, *Sinning Across Spain*, Victory Books, Melbourne, 2012

Polo, Marco, *Travels of Marco Polo*, Jonathon Cape, London, 1928

Powell, Julie, *Julie and Julia: 365 Days, 524 Recipes, 1 Tiny Apartment*, Little Brown & Company, Boston, 2005

Sacks, Oliver, *The Man Who Mistook His Wife for a Hat*, Summit Books, New York, 1985

Safran, John, *Murder in Mississippi*, Hamish Hamilton, Melbourne, 2013

Seierstad, Åsne, *The Bookseller of Kabul*, Virago, London, 2002

Shayler, Kate, *The Long Way Home*, Random House, Sydney, 1999

Slater, Nigel, *Toast*, Fourth Estate, London, 2003

Solnit, Rebecca, *Wanderlust*, Granta Books, London, 2015

Stevenson, Robert Louis, *Travels with a Donkey in Cevennes*, Chatto & Windus, London, 1987

Stopes, Marie C., *A Journal from Japan*, Blackie, London, 1910

Strayed, Cheryl, *Wild*, Atlantic Books, London, 2012

Thoreau, Henry, *Walden, or, Life in the Woods*, Library of America, Boone, 1989

Tredinnick, Mark, *The Blue Plateau*, UQP, Brisbane, 2009

Tristan, Flora, *Memoirs and Peregrinations of a Pariah*, Virago Beacon Travellers, London, 1987

Turnbull, Sarah, *Almost French*, Bantam, Sydney, 2002

Waal, Edmund de, *The Hare with Amber Eyes*, Vintage, London, 2011

Ward, Biff, *In My Mother's Hands*, Allen & Unwin, Sydney, 2014

Watson, Don, *The Bush*, Hamish Hamilton, Melbourne, 2014

White, Edmund, *The Flâneur*, Bloomsbury, London, 2001

Winton, Tim, *Island Home*, Penguin Random House, Melbourne, 2015

—— *The Boy Behind the Curtain*, Hamish Hamilton, Melbourne, 2016

Yahp, Beth, *Eat First, Talk Later*, Penguin Random House, Sydney, 2015

Novels and short stories

Allende, Isabel, 'Tosca', in *The Stories of Eva Luna*, Penguin, London, 1991

Haddawy, Husain (ed.), *The Arabian Nights*, Everyman's Library, London, 1992

Knausgaard, Karl Ove, *A Death in The Family* (*My Struggle*, Book 1), Vintage, London, 2014

Marshall, Alan, 'Tell Us About the Turkey, Jo', in *The Complete Stories of Alan Marshall*, Allen & Unwin, Sydney, 2012

Proust, Marcel, *In Search of Lost Time*, Penguin Classics, London, 2003

Süskind, Patrick, *Perfume*, Penguin, London, 1986

Useful writing books

Hemley, Robin, *A Field Guide for Memoir, Journalism and Travel Immersion Writing*, The University of Georgia Press, Athens, Georgia, 2012

Lopate, Phillip, *To Show and to Tell*, Free Press, New York, 2013

Metzger, Deena, *Writing for Your Life*, Harper, San Francisco, 1992

Rubie, Peter, *The Elements of Narrative Non-fiction*, Quill Driver Books, Fresno, 2009

Strunk, William Jr. & White, E.B., *The Elements of Style*, Longman, Massachusetts, 2000

Articles, essays, and further reading

Aciman, André, 'Lies Sweet Lies', *The Sydney Morning Herald*, 9 September 2000

Atkinson, Robert, *The Gift of Stories*, Bergin & Garvey, Westport, 1995

Campbell, Joseph, *The Hero with a Thousand Faces*, Pantheon, New York, 2008

Dovey, Ceridwen, 'The Pencil and the Damage Done', *The Monthly*, November 2014

Josephs, Sue, *Behind the Text*, Hybrid Publishers, Melbourne, 2016

Kenkō, 'Essays in Idleness' (*Tsurezuregusa*), in Lopate, Phillip (ed.), *The Art of the Personal Essay*, Doubleday, New York, 1995

Lejeune, Philippe, 'The Autobiographical Pact', *Theory and History of Literature*, vol. 52, University of Minnesota Press, Minneapolis, 1989

Lopate, Phillip, 'Against Joie de Vivre', in Lopate, Phillip (ed.), *The Art of the Personal Essay*, Doubleday, New York, 1995

Marr, David, 'The Art of Biography', *The Monthly*, December 2016

Shklovsky, Viktor, 'Art as Technique', in Rivkin, Julie, and Ryan, Michael (eds), *Literary Theory: An Anthology*, Blackwell Publishing, Oxford, 1998

Shōnagon, Sei, 'The Pillow Book', in Lopate, Phillip (ed.), *The Art of the Personal Essay*, Doubleday, New York, 1995

Trungpa, Chögyam, *The Myth of Freedom*, Shambala Press, Boston, 1975

Woolf, Virginia, 'Professions for Women', in *The Death of the Moth and Other Essays*, Harcourt Brace, San Diego, 1974

Yagoda, Ben, 'A Brief History of Memoir Bashing', *Slate*, 30 March 2007

Poetry

Keats, John, 'Ode on a Grecian Urn', *Selected Poetry*, Oxford University Press, Oxford, 2008

Thomas, Dylan, *Under Milk Wood*, J.M. Dent & Sons, London, 1975

Useful contacts

Writing workshops, manuscript assessment, correspondence courses and editing

The author of *Writing True Stories* may be contacted through:
www.lifestories.com.au
pmiller@lifestories.com.au

Information and support for writers

Australian Society of Authors:
www.asauthors.org
Tel.: 02 9318 0877

Writers' centres

Australia has a network of writers' centres in each of the state capitals and some regional centres, offering classes, discussion groups, some residential writing programs and information:
www.asauthors.org/writers-centres

Publisher and agent listings

Australia: *The Australian Writer's Marketplace*, Queensland Writers Centre, Brisbane, (updated every two years), or online at www.awmonline. com.au

UK: www.publishersglobal.com/directory/united-kingdom/publishers-in-united-kingdom

USA: www.publishersglobal.com/directory/united-states/publishers-in-united-states

Self-publishing

There are numerous resources online for both traditional paper books and ebooks. A few possibilities:

Advice: www.cnet.com/au/news/self-publishing-a-book-25-things-you-need-to-know

Ebooks: Amazon Kindle, kdp.amazon.com/help?topicId=A37Z49E2DDQPP3

Paperbacks: Impact Press, www.impactpress.com.au

Copyright questions: Australian Copyright Council (tel.: 02 9318 1788), www.copyright.org.au

Legal queries: Arts Law Centre of Australia (tel.: 02 9356 2566 or 1800 221 457), www.artslaw.com.au

Family history

Family history research: Society of Australian Genealogists (tel.: 02 9247 3953), www.sag.org.au

Acknowledgements

The author and publishers are grateful to the following for permission to reproduce copyright material:

Allen & Unwin, Sydney, for extract from *In My Mother's Hands* by Biff Ward © 2014.

Atlantic Books, London, for extract from *Wild* by Cheryl Strayed © 2012.

Eland Publishing, London, for extract from *The Way of the World* by Nicolas Bouvier © 2007. Reprinted by permission of Eland Publishing Ltd. Text © Editions La Découverte, Paris, France, 1963, 1985. Translation © Robyn Marsack, 1992.

Fourth Estate HarperCollins, London, for extract from *The Diving Bell and the Butterfly* by Jean-Dominique Bauby © 1997. © Éditions Robert Laffont for ebook rights.

Harper Perennial, New York, for extract from pp. 1–4 of *The Most Beautiful Walk in the World* by John Baxter. Copyright © 2011 by John Baxter. Reprinted by permission of HarperCollins Publishers.

Pan Macmillan Australia Pty Ltd for extract from *Joe Cinque's Consolation* by Helen Garner © 2004, reprinted by permission of Pan Macmillan Australia Pty Ltd.

Pan Macmillan, Sydney, for extract from *(and so forth)* by Robert Dessaix © 1998.

Penguin Random House, Sydney, for extracts from *The Long Way Home* by Kate Shayler © 1999, *Eat First, Talk Later* by Beth Yahp © 2015, *Rosetta* by Alexandra Joel © 2016, *When Horse Became Saw* by Anthony Macris © 2011, *The Feel-Good Hit of the Year* by Liam Pieper © 2014.

ACKNOWLEDGEMENTS

Penguin Random House, UK, for extracts from *The Old Ways* by Robert Macfarlane © 2012 (Hamish Hamilton, 2012) and *In Search of Lost Time* by Marcel Proust, translated by C.K. Scott Moncrieff © 1922.

Tandem Press, Auckland, for extract from *Out of the Mist and Steam* by Alan Duff © 1999.

UQP, Brisbane, for extracts from *Boy, Lost* by Kristina Olsson © 2013, *Purple Threads* by Jeanine Leane © 2011, *The Mind of a Thief* by Patti Miller © 2012 and *Ransacking Paris* by Patti Miller © 2015.

I also want to thank my agent Clare Forster, and the team at Allen & Unwin: Angela Handley, Annette Barlow, Siobhán Cantrill, Romina Panetta, Simone Ford and Emma O'Brien.

I am also grateful to the former students whose writing exercises appear in the workshop chapters: Judith Bunn, Mahima Price (deceased), Bob Pearson, Anni Webster, Susan Wilson, Lucienne Fontannez, Samantha Selinger-Morris, Steve Castely and Tanya Lake. But I also want to thank all the people who have attended the Life Stories writing workshops; most of what I know about life writing I have learned from them.

Index

INDEX

337

INDEX

INDEX

INDEX